Glencoe

United States Government

Democracy In Action

Reading Essentials and Study Guide

Student Workbook

McGraw Hill Glencoe

TO THE STUDENT

The *Reading Essentials and Study Guide* is designed to help you use recognized reading strategies to improve your reading-for-information skills. For each section of the textbook, you are alerted to key terms, asked to draw from prior knowledge, organize your thoughts with a graphic organizer, and then follow a process to read and understand the text. The *Reading Essentials and Study Guide* was prepared to help you get more from the textbook by reading with a purpose.

The *McGraw·Hill* Companies

 Glencoe

Send all inquiries to:
Glencoe/McGraw-Hill
8787 Orion Place
Columbus, OH 43240-4027

ISBN: 978-0-07-891360-0
MHID: 0-07-891360-8

Printed in the United States of America.

2 3 4 5 6 7 8 9 10 079 14 13 12 11 10 09

CONTENTS

v

STUDY GUIDE  Chapter 1, Section 1

For use with textbook pages 5–11.

PRINCIPLES OF GOVERNMENT

CONTENT VOCABULARY

state A political community that occupies a definite territory and has an organized government with the power to make and enforce laws without approval from any higher authority *(page 5)*

sovereignty The supreme and absolute authority within territorial boundaries *(page 6)*

nation A group of people who share the same race, language, customs, traditions, and, sometimes, religion *(page 6)*

nation-state A country in which the territory of both the nation and the state coincide *(page 6)*

consensus An agreement about basic beliefs *(page 6)*

government The institution through which the state maintains social order, provides public services, and enforces binding decisions on citizens *(page 8)*

social contract The theory that people surrender to the state the power needed to maintain order, and the state, in turn, agrees to protect its citizens *(page 8)*

DRAWING FROM EXPERIENCE

You probably ride in or drive a motor vehicle at least once a day. Have you ever thought how difficult travel would be without paved roads or traffic signals? Providing services, such as road construction and road safety, is just one of the purposes of government.

This section focuses on the origins and purposes of government.

READING STRATEGIES

Use the circle diagram below to help you take notes about the four essential features of a state.

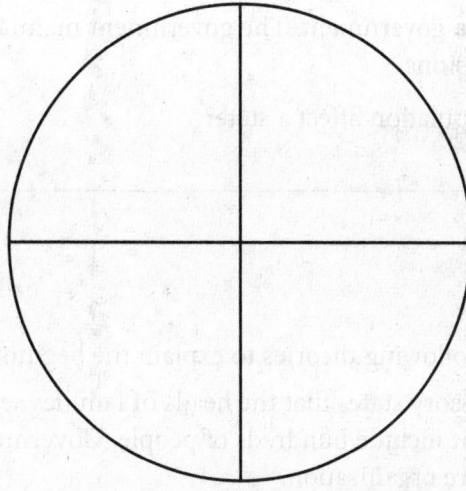

STUDY GUIDE (continued) Chapter 1, Section 1

READS TO LEARN

◉ Introduction (page 5)

Scholars have written about the origins and purposes of government for centuries.

◉ What Is the State? (page 5)

Many words we use to discuss government come from ancient Greece and Rome. For example, the word *state* comes from the Romans' word for "to stand." A *state* has a definite territory and an organized government with the power to make and enforce laws without approval from any higher authority. The United States is one of almost 200 states that exist today. A *nation* is a group of people who share the same race, language, customs, traditions, and, sometimes, religion. In many modern countries, the territorial boundaries of the state and the nation are the same. Countries such as these are sometimes called *nation-states.* This book uses the terms *nation* and *state* interchangeably.

1. What is the difference between a nation and a state?

_____

_____

◉ Essential Features of a State (page 6)

States today share four essential elements.

A. *Population* This is the people living in the state. States are most stable when their people share a political and social *consensus,* or agreement about basic beliefs. Population also affects a state through mobility. For example, since people in the United States are mobile, political power readily shifts from one area to another.

B. *Territory* This means a state has boundaries. Its territory may increase or decrease as a result of war, negotiations with another country, or the purchase by the state of additional territory.

C. *Sovereignty* The state has supreme authority within its territorial boundaries, at least in theory. A sovereign state has complete power to make laws, shape foreign policies, and determine its own course of action.

D. *Government* Every state has a government. The government maintains social order, provides public services, and enforces its decisions.

2. In what two ways does population affect a state?

_____

_____

◉ Origins of the State (page 8)

Scholars have come up with the following theories to explain the beginnings of government.

A. *Evolutionary Theory* This theory states that the heads of families served as the earliest government. These extended families might include hundreds of people. Government emerged gradually as the extended families needed more organization.

STUDY GUIDE (continued) Chapter 1, Section 1

B. *Force Theory* This theory holds that government emerged when all the people in an area were forced to accept the authority of one person or group.

C. *Divine Right Theory* Many civilizations believed that God or gods chose rulers. According to this theory, God created the state and chose those born to royalty to rule it.

D. *Social Contract Theory* According to certain political thinkers, government came about when people agreed to a *social contract.* The people gave the state the power needed to maintain order. The state, in turn, agreed to protect its citizens. John Locke, a political writer in the 1600s, argued that when government failed to preserve the rights of the people, the people could break the social contract. American colonists used Locke's argument to justify the break with their British rulers.

3. On which theory is the government of the United States based? Explain your answer.

_____

_____

_____

_____

◉ Purposes of Government *(page 9)*

A government makes decisions that are binding on all its citizens to carry out the following purposes.

A. *Maintaining Social Order* This means government provides ways to settle disagreements among citizens. For example, it provides courts to help people resolve their differences in an orderly manner.

B. *Providing Public Services* Government provides services needed to make community life possible and to promote the general welfare. For example, government inspectors check meat and vegetables to prevent the sale of spoiled food.

C. *Providing National Security* A government protects its people against attacks from other states or from internal threats, such as terrorism. In addition, the government also handles dealings, such as trade agreements, with other countries.

D. *Making Economic Decisions* A government uses its power to provide its citizens with economic needs and wants, although no government provides its citizens with everything they need and want. A government passes the laws that control the economic environment. For instance, it provides the nation's currency, or money, and helps to distribute benefits and services. For example, the United States government makes payments to farmers who raise certain crops and offers tax advantages to certain industries. A government might also intervene in the economic affairs of another nation by providing aid.

4. List three ways that a government might influence the economy.

_____

_____

_____

_____

STUDY GUIDE  Chapter 1, Section 2

For use with textbook pages 12–17.

THE FORMATION OF GOVERNMENTS

CONTENT VOCABULARY

unitary system A government that gives all key powers to the national or central government *(page 12)*

federal system A government that divides the powers of government between the national government and state or provincial governments *(page 13)*

confederacy A loose union of independent states *(page 13)*

constitution A plan that provides the rules for government *(page 13)*

constitutional government A government in which a constitution has authority to place clearly recognized limits on the power of those who govern *(page 13)*

preamble A statement in the constitution that sets forth the goals and purposes of government *(page 13)*

constitutional law Law that involves the interpretation and application of the U.S. Constitution and state constitutions *(page 14)*

politics The effort to control or influence the conduct and policies of government *(page 14)*

industrialized nation A nation with large industries and advanced technology that provides a more comfortable way of life than developing nations *(page 16)*

developing nation A nation only beginning to grow industrially *(page 16)*

DRAWING FROM EXPERIENCE

Have you ever felt frustrated about community problems, such as the decay of local neighborhoods? The United States system of government provides ways to address problems like this. The more you know about your government, the more likely you are to find solutions.

This section focuses on systems of government in the United States and in other countries.

READING STRATEGIES

Use the graphic organizer below to help you take notes about the causes and results of interdependence among nations.

CAUSES		RESULTS
	→	

STUDY GUIDE (continued)   Chapter 1, Section 2

READvisible TO LEARN

◉ **Introduction** *(page 12)*

Most large countries have several levels of government. These usually include a central or national government, as well as the governments of states or provinces, counties, cities, towns, and villages.

◉ **Government Systems** *(page 12)*

A *unitary system* gives all key powers to a central or national government. The central government has the power to create state, provincial, or other local governments and may give them limited sovereignty. Countries with a unitary system of government are Great Britain, France, and Italy. A *federal system* divides the powers of government between the national government and state or provincial governments. Countries with a federal system are Canada, Switzerland, Mexico, Australia, India, and the United States. To begin with, the United States formed a *confederacy*—a loose union of independent states. But when the confederacy failed, American leaders wrote a constitution that made the national government supreme while preserving some powers for state governments.

    1. Compare the systems of government in Great Britain and the United States.

_____

_____

◉ **Constitutions and Government** *(page 13)*

A *constitutional government* is a government in which a constitution places limits on the powers of those who govern. A *constitution* is a plan that provides guidelines for government. Constitutions are incomplete guides because no written constitution can spell out all the laws, customs, and ideas of a government. However, a constitution does serve the following purposes:

A. It sets forth goals and ideals that the people of a nation believe in and share. These are usually stated in the *preamble.*

B. It establishes the basic structure of government and defines the government's powers and duties. For example, in a federal state, a constitution describes the relationship between the national and state governments.

C. It provides the supreme law for the country. *Constitutional law* involves the interpretation and application of the constitution. It defines the extent and limits of government power and the rights of citizens.

    2. List the purposes of a constitution.

_____

_____

_____

_____

STUDY GUIDE (continued)   Chapter 1, Section 2

◉ Politics and Government (page 14)

People take part in *politics* when they try to control the actions and decisions of government. In the United States, for example, Americans continually struggle over what services the government should provide, how much it should spend, and who should pay the cost. Politics provides peaceful ways for citizens to settle these conflicts. The outcomes of political struggles affect the quality of air and water, jobs and prices, peace and war, rights and freedoms, and other important matters. Some people fear that politics often sacrifices the good of all for the benefit of a few. However, the misuse of politics should not prevent citizens from appreciating the accomplishments of the political system.

   3. Why is politics useful to the citizens of a country?

   _____

   _____

   _____

◉ Governing in a Complex World (page 16)

The United States and about 20 other countries, including Japan, Canada, Australia, and France, are *industrialized nations.* These countries have large industries and advanced technology that provide a more comfortable way of life than many developing nations do. *Developing nations* are only beginning to grow industrially. In the poorest of these countries, widespread hunger, disease, and political unrest are a way of life.

Nations are becoming more and more interdependent. This means that they interact with or depend on one another economically and politically. Thus, what happens in one nation or area of the world affects what happens in other places. Global interdependence is increasing due to growing industrialization and rapid technological advances, such as the Internet. Many developing states are very dependent on industrialized ones for economic aid, medical supplies and services, financial investment, help in handling national disasters, and military aid.

Nonstate groups also play a role in international politics. These nonstate groups fall into four categories:

A. Terrorist groups and quasi-military organizations, such as al-Qaeda

B. Political movements such as the Palestine Liberation Organization (PLO) and the Irish Republican Army (IRA)

C. Multinational corporations such as General Motors, Nabisco, Mitsubishi, and Sony

D. International organizations such as the World Trade Organization (WTO), which is composed of many nations working together for common goals.

   4. What factors have resulted in the growing interdependence among states?

   _____

   _____

   _____

STUDY GUIDE  Chapter 1, Section 3

For use with textbook pages 18–24.

TYPES OF GOVERNMENT

CONTENT VOCABULARY

autocracy A system of government in which the power to rule is in the hands of a single individual *(page 19)*

monarchy An autocracy in which a king, queen, or emperor exercises supreme powers of government *(page 19)*

oligarchy A system of government in which a small group holds power *(page 20)*

democracy A government in which the people rule *(page 20)*

republic A government in which voters hold sovereign power; elected representatives, responsible to the people, exercise that power *(page 20)*

political party A group of individuals with broad common interests who organize to nominate candidates for office, win elections, conduct government, and determine public policy *(page 23)*

free enterprise A system in which individuals have the opportunity to make their own economic decisions *(page 24)*

DRAWING FROM EXPERIENCE

At some time, you and your friends probably have disagreed about how to spend your Friday evening or Saturday together. How do you decide what to do? Most likely you take a vote. On a small scale, this is how democracy—one type of government—works.

This section focuses on the characteristics of different types of government.

READING STRATEGIES

Create a table that lists the *distinguishing feature* of these forms of government: democracy, representative democracy, and republic.

Type of Government	Feature

```
╔══════════════════════════════════════════════════════════════════════════════╗
║ STUDY GUIDE (continued)                          Chapter 1,  Section 3         ║
╚══════════════════════════════════════════════════════════════════════════════╝
```

READ TO LEARN

◉ Introduction (page 18)

The United States has a representative democracy that serves as a model of government for many people around the world. Today, democracies outnumber all other forms of government.

◉ Major Types of Government (page 18)

Autocracy This is probably the oldest type of government. The power and authority to rule are in the hands of a single individual. Totalitarian dictatorship is one form of autocracy in which the government tries to control all aspects of social and economic life. Nazi Germany was an example of a totalitarian dictatorship. *Monarchy* is another form of autocracy. A king, queen, or emperor who exercises the supreme powers of government is an absolute monarch. An example of an absolute monarch is the king of Saudi Arabia. In a constitutional monarchy, a monarch shares governmental powers with an elected legislature or acts mainly as a ceremonial head of state. Great Britain, Sweden, Japan, and the Netherlands have constitutional monarchies.

Oligarchy This is any system of government in which a small group holds power. The government of China is an oligarchy since the Communist Party and the armed forces control the government.

Democracy This is any system of government in which the people rule. In a direct democracy, the citizens govern themselves by voting on issues individually. New England town meetings and some cantons, or states, in Switzerland still practice direct democracy. In a representative democracy, the people elect representatives and give them the power to make laws and run the government. In a *republic,* elected representatives are responsible to the people. *Representative democracy, republic,* and *constitutional republic* mean the same thing to most Americans. However, not every democracy is a republic. For example, Great Britain is a democracy but not a republic.

1. Describe three types of government.

_____

_____

◉ Characteristics of Democracy (page 21)

A. *Individual Liberty* Government in a democracy works to promote the kind of freedom in which all people have an equal opportunity to develop and use their talents to the fullest extent possible.

B. *Majority Rule with Minority Rights* People usually accept decisions made by the majority of voters in a free election. The Constitution helps ensure that the rights of individuals in the minority are protected. However, this is not always the case. For example, the U.S. government imprisoned more than 100,000 Japanese Americans in relocation camps during World War II because it feared they would be disloyal.

C. *Free Elections* Free elections in a democracy have the following characteristics: everyone's vote carries the same weight; all candidates have the right to express their views freely; citizens are free to help candidates or to support issues; legal requirements for voting are kept to a minimum; and citizens may vote by secret ballot.

STUDY GUIDE (continued)   Chapter 1, Section 3

D. *Competing Political Parties* A *political party* is a group of individuals with broad common interests who organize to nominate candidates for office, win elections, conduct government, and determine public policy. Rival parties give voters a choice among candidates. They also help simplify and focus attention on important issues. The political party or parties out of office serve as the "loyal opposition," criticizing policies and actions of the party in power.

2. What are the four characteristics of democracy?

_____

_____

_____

_____

◉ Essential Elements for a Democracy *(page 23)*

Democratic government is more likely to succeed in countries which have the following qualities:

A. *Citizen Participation* Citizens who are able to inform themselves about issues, vote in elections, serve on juries, work for candidates, and run for government office are more likely to maintain a strong democracy.

B. *A Favorable Economy* Democracy succeeds more in countries that do not have extremes of wealth and poverty and have a large middle class. *Free enterprise* also provides a base for making independent economic decisions in the United States. Since people control their economic lives, they are freer to make political decisions.

C. *Widespread Education* Democracy is more likely to succeed in a country with an educated public.

D. *A Strong Civil Society* A *civil society* is a complex network of voluntary associations, economic groups, religious organizations, and many other kinds of groups that exist independently of government. Examples are labor unions, churches, the Red Cross, the Sierra Club, and the National Rifle Association. These organizations give citizens a way to make their views known to government officials and the general public. They also give citizens a means to protect their rights and to learn about participating in democracy.

E. *A Social Consensus.* A country where most people accept democratic values, such as individual liberty and equality, has a social consensus. A democratic country must also have general agreement about the purposes and limits of government.

3. List five ways in which citizens in a democracy participate in government.

_____

_____

_____

_____

STUDY GUIDE  Chapter 1, Section 4

For use with textbook pages 26–30.

ECONOMIC THEORIES

CONTENT VOCABULARY

economics The study of human efforts to satisfy seemingly unlimited wants through the use of limited resources *(page 26)*

capitalism An economic system providing free choice and individual incentive for workers, investors, consumers, and business enterprises *(page 27)*

free market An economic system in which buyers and sellers make free choices in the marketplace *(page 27)*

laissez-faire The philosophy that government should keep its hands off the economy *(page 27)*

socialism An economic system in which the government owns the basic means of production, distributes products and wages, and provides social services such as health care and welfare *(page 28)*

bourgeoisie Capitalists who own the means of production *(page 29)*

proletariat Workers who provide the labor to produce the goods *(page 29)*

communism An economic system in which the central government directs all major economic decisions *(page 29)*

command economy An economic system in which the government controls the factors of production *(page 30)*

DRAWING FROM EXPERIENCE

Recall your last visit to a shopping mall. You probably saw dozens of things you wanted. But probably you could afford to buy only a few. Imagine a country full of people with similar wants. How do they fill them?

This section focuses on how countries try to fill their people's wants and needs.

READING STRATEGIES

Use the graphic organizer below to help you take notes as you read the summaries that follow. Think about the five characteristics of capitalism.

```
┌──────────┐      ┌──────────┐      ┌──────────┐
│          │      │          │      │          │
└──────────┘      └──────────┘      └──────────┘
       ↘              ↓              ↙
            ┌──────────────────┐
            │    CAPITALISM    │
            └──────────────────┘
       ↗                          ↖
┌──────────┐                ┌──────────┐
│          │                │          │
└──────────┘                └──────────┘
```

STUDY GUIDE (continued) Chapter 1, Section 4

READraw TO LEARN

◉ Introduction (page 26)

Economics is the study of human efforts to satisfy seemingly unlimited wants through the use of limited resources. Resources include natural materials, such as land and minerals, as well as human factors, such as skill and knowledge. People in every nation must decide how these resources are to be used.

◉ The Role of Economic Systems (page 27)

An economic system must answer the following questions:

A. What and how much should be produced?

B. How should goods and services be produced?

C. Who gets the goods and services that are produced?

Each economic system—capitalism, socialism, and communism—answers these questions differently.

1. What three questions must an economic system answer?

_____

_____

_____

◉ Capitalism (page 27)

Pure *capitalism* has five main characteristics:

A. Private ownership and control of property and resources

B. Free enterprise, or any productive activity that individuals choose

C. Competition among businesses, workers, and consumers

D. Freedom of choice by consumers

E. The possibility of profits

Capitalism flowered in the eighteenth century. By then Europeans' attitudes toward work and wealth included progress, invention, and the free market. The *free market* means that buyers and sellers make unlimited decisions in the marketplace. Scottish economist Adam Smith described capitalism in 1776. His ideas included *laissez-faire,* which means "let alone." In laissez-faire capitalism, the government's role is limited to those few actions that ensure free competition in the marketplace.

Competition plays a key role in capitalism. Sellers compete with one another to produce goods and services at reasonable prices. Sellers also compete for resources. Buyers compete with one another to buy what they want and need. Workers compete with one another for the best wages or salaries.

No nation in the world has a pure capitalist system. Economists describe the U.S. economy and others like it as mixed market economies. In a mixed market economy, free enterprise is combined with and supported by government decisions in the marketplace.

STUDY GUIDE (continued) Chapter 1, Section 4

2. How does the U.S. economy differ from pure capitalism?

_____

_____

◉ Socialism (page 28)

The main goals of *socialism* are:

A. The equal distribution of wealth and economic opportunity among people

B. Society's control, through government, of all major decisions about production

C. Public ownership of most land, basic industries, and other means of production

In the nineteenth century, industrial capitalism created a class of low-paid city workers. Some socialists favored violent revolution to improve economic conditions. Socialists who believed in peaceful change wanted to work through the democratic political system. They created a system called democratic socialism. Today Tanzania and some Scandinavian countries operate under a form of democratic socialism.

3. Under socialism, who determines the use of resources? What purpose guides their decisions?

_____

_____

_____

_____

◉ Communism (page 29)

In 1848 a German thinker named Karl Marx wrote that people in industrialized nations are divided into the *bourgeoisie*—capitalists who own the means of production—and the *proletariat*—workers who produce the goods. Marx predicted that the workers would revolt and overthrow the capitalists. The goal of this revolution was government ownership of the means of production and distribution. He believed that this socialist government would develop into *communism.* Under communism, property would be held in common, and there would be no need for government.

In communist nations today, government planners decide how much to produce, what to produce, and how to distribute the goods and services produced. This system is called a *command economy* because decisions are made at the upper levels of government and handed down to the people.

4. How does a command economy work?

_____

_____

_____

_____

STUDY GUIDE  Chapter 2, Section 1

For use with textbook pages 35–40.

THE COLONIAL PERIOD

CONTENT VOCABULARY

limited government A system in which the power of the government is limited, not absolute *(page 36)*

representative government A system of government in which people elect delegates to make laws and conduct government *(page 37)*

separation of powers The division of power among the legislative, executive, and judicial branches of government *(page 40)*

DRAWING FROM EXPERIENCE

Does your family have holiday traditions that come from another country? The government of the United States was built on similar traditions.

This section focuses on the origins of representative government in the United States.

READING STRATEGIES

Use the time line below to help you take notes as you read about English and American documents on representative government.

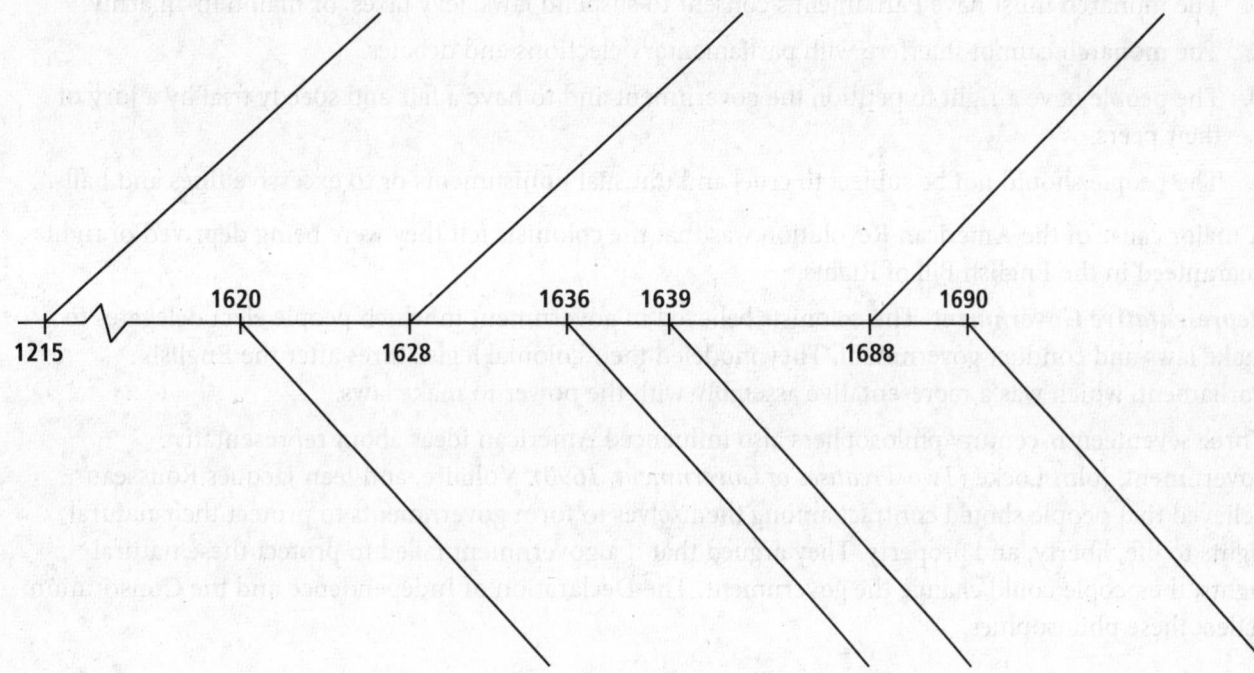

1215   1620   1628   1636   1639   1688   1690

STUDY GUIDE (continued)   Chapter 2, Section 1

READY TO LEARN

◉ Introduction *(page 35)*

Americans today enjoy a legacy of self-government handed down from the English colonists. This legacy enables Americans to voice their opinions without fear of punishment, to choose their own leaders, and to take an active role in shaping their nation and communities.

◉ An English Political Heritage *(page 35)*

English settlers established and governed the original thirteen colonies along the Atlantic coast of North America. The English colonists brought with them two principles at the heart of the English system of government. These principles were limited government and representative government.

Limited Government The English King John was forced by a group of nobles to sign the Magna Carta in 1215. This document established that the power of the monarchy, or royal government, was limited, not absolute. Later generations interpreted the Magna Carta as providing citizens with protection from unjust punishment and the loss of life, liberty, and property except according to the law.

Parliament, England's lawmaking body, forced King Charles I in 1628 to sign the Petition of Right, which further limited the king's power. No longer could a monarch collect taxes without Parliament's approval, imprison people without just cause, house troops in private houses without the permission of the owner, or declare martial law unless the country was at war.

Parliament passed the English Bill of Rights in 1688. The key ideas in this document were:

A. Monarchs do not have absolute authority. They rule with the consent of the people's representatives in Parliament.

B. The monarch must have Parliament's consent to suspend laws, levy taxes, or maintain an army.

C. The monarch cannot interfere with parliamentary elections and debates.

D. The people have a right to petition the government and to have a fair and speedy trial by a jury of their peers.

E. The people should not be subject to cruel and unusual punishments or to excessive fines and bails.

A major cause of the American Revolution was that the colonists felt they were being deprived of rights guaranteed in the English Bill of Rights.

Representative Government The colonists believed in government in which people elect delegates to make laws and conduct government. They modeled their colonial legislatures after the English Parliament, which was a representative assembly with the power to make laws.

Three seventeenth-century philosophers also influenced American ideas about representative government. John Locke *(Two Treatises of Government, 1690)*, Voltaire, and Jean Jacques Rousseau believed that people should contract among themselves to form governments to protect their natural rights to life, liberty, and property. They argued that if a government failed to protect these natural rights, the people could change the government. The Declaration of Independence and the Constitution reflect these philosophies.

STUDY GUIDE (continued)   Chapter 2, Section 1

1. How did John Locke, Voltaire, and Jean Jacques Rousseau affect the government of the United States?

_____

_____

◉ Colonial Governments (page 38)

For many years, the English, later called the British, and the colonists agreed that all colonists owed allegiance to the monarch. But each English colony had its own government consisting of a governor, legislature, and a court system. Colonial governments established the following practices that became key parts of the nation's government:

Written Constitutions In 1620, while still on the ship *Mayflower*, 41 men, representing all the Pilgrim families, drew up the Mayflower Compact. The Pilgrims realized they needed rules if they were going to survive on the New England coast.

Puritans settled the nearby Massachusetts Bay colony. In 1636 this growing community adopted the General Fundamentals. These made up the first basic system of laws in the English colonies. Colonists who left the Massachusetts Bay Colony to settle Connecticut drew up the Fundamental Orders of Connecticut in 1639. This document laid out a plan for government that gave the people the right to elect their governor, judges, and representatives to the legislature. Unlike the General Fundamentals, it did not restrict its rights to church members. Soon after, other English colonies drew up their own plans of government with the same system of limited government and rule by law.

Colonial Legislatures The first legislature in America was established in Virginia in 1619. It was called the House of Burgesses and was made up of elected representatives. Not long after, other colonies set up their own legislatures. Colonial legislatures were an example of government by the consent of the governed because a large number of men were qualified to vote. Although there were property qualifications, land was abundant and most colonists could afford property. Representative government was an established tradition in the United States by 1776.

Separation of Powers Colonial charters divided the power of government. The governor had executive power. The legislatures had the power to pass laws, and colonial courts heard cases. The governors were the king's agents, and the colonial legislatures and courts could be reviewed by a committee of the king's Privy Council. But in practice, the colonies practiced considerable self-government. The principle of *separation of powers* was vital to the United States Constitution because colonial legislatures were the training grounds for the leaders who later wrote the Constitution.

2. Where did the writers of the United States Constitution find out about separation of powers?

_____

_____

_____

STUDY GUIDE Chapter 2, Section 2

For use with textbook pages 42–47.

UNITING FOR INDEPENDENCE

CONTENT VOCABULARY

revenue The money a government collects from taxes or other sources *(page 43)*
embargo An agreement prohibiting trade *(page 44)*

DRAWING FROM EXPERIENCE

Think of a freedom you enjoy at school. Perhaps you are free to talk to your friends during lunch. Imagine the principal banning all talking during school hours. What could you do about the change in the rules? Would you ask your friends to join you in protest? The colonies faced similar questions when their British rulers changed the way they treated the colonies.

This section focuses on the colonial experience just before the American Revolution and how it shaped American ideals of government.

READING STRATEGIES

Use the graphic organizer below to help you take notes as you read the summaries that follow. Track the actions of the British government and the American colonists to show how their relations weakened.

CAUSES	RESULTS
1.	1.
2.	2.
3.	3.
4.	4.
5.	5.

READ TO LEARN

◉ Introduction *(page 42)*

For the most part, Great Britain allowed its colonies to rule themselves for 150 years. Then in the 1760s, the British government began to tighten its control over the colonies.

◉ The Colonies on Their Own *(page 42)*

The American colonies remained loyal to the British government in return for a large measure of self-rule and protection from the French in North America. Two events changed the relationship between the colonists and their rulers. The first was the French and Indian War. The war began as a struggle between the French and British over lands in Pennsylvania and along the Ohio River and lasted from 1756 to 1763. The British eventually won and drove the French out of North America, so the colonists no longer needed British protection.

STUDY GUIDE (continued)   Chapter 2, Section 2

After the war, the British were deeply in debt. King George III, who had just become king in 1760, decided to make the colonies help pay the debt. He and his ministers levied taxes on tea, glass, and other products. Then the Stamp Act of 1765 required colonists to pay a tax on legal documents, pamphlets, newspapers, and even dice and playing cards. Parliament also passed laws to control colonial trade in ways that benefited Great Britain but not the colonies.

Taxes from the colonies increased Britain's *revenue*—the money a government collects from taxes and other sources. But colonists protested the taxes by refusing to buy British goods. This action led to the repeal of the Stamp Act, but the British passed other tax laws, including a tea tax, to replace it. In 1773 a group of colonists dumped chests of British tea into Boston Harbor. This protest became known as the Boston Tea Party.

To get back at the colonists, Parliament passed the Coercive Acts, which the colonists called the Intolerable Acts. One of the acts closed Boston Harbor. Another withdrew the right of the Massachusetts colony to govern itself. The colonists and their British rulers were headed for a showdown.

1. How did the outcome of the French and Indian War change the relationship between the American colonists and the British?

_____

_____

◉ Colonial Unity (page 44)

Harsh new British policies united Americans in their hostility to British authority. For example, in 1765 nine colonies sent delegates to a meeting in New York called the Stamp Act Congress. This was the first meeting organized to protest King George's actions. Delegates at the meeting sent a petition to the king, arguing that only colonial legislatures could impose direct taxes such as the Stamp Act.

By 1773 organizations called committees of correspondence were urging colonists to resist the British. Samuel Adams established the first committee in Boston. Massachusetts alone had 80 such committees, and other colonies soon had their own.

The Intolerable Acts prompted leaders from Virginia and Massachusetts to call a meeting. Delegates from all the colonies except Georgia met in Philadelphia for the First Continental Congress on September 5, 1774. Patrick Henry, George Washington, and other colonial leaders attended.

The delegates imposed an *embargo,* or an agreement prohibiting trade. They vowed not to use British goods. King George responded by announcing that the colonies were "in a state of rebellion." On April 19, 1775, British soldiers clashed with colonists at Lexington and Concord in Massachusetts.

Within weeks of the Battle of Lexington, delegates from all 13 colonies gathered in Philadelphia for the Second Continental Congress. The Congress assumed the powers of a central government and made George Washington commander of the newly organized Continental Army. The Congress purchased supplies, negotiated treaties, and rallied support for the colonists' cause throughout the American Revolution.

2. What was the purpose of the First Continental Congress?

_____

_____

◉ Independence (page 45)

As Congress set to work, the independence movement was rapidly growing. Thomas Paine influenced this growth with his pamphlet *Common Sense*. It argued that monarchy was a corrupt form of government. Many colonists agreed with Paine. Samuel Adams, for example, urged Americans to declare their independence. In June, 1776, Virginian Richard Henry Lee introduced a resolution in the Continental Congress that the "United Colonies are, and of right ought to be, free and independent states."

Congress promptly appointed a committee to prepare a written declaration of independence. The committee asked Thomas Jefferson, a Virginia planter, to write the draft.

On July 2, 1776, the Congress approved Lee's resolution. The colonies had officially broken with Great Britain. On July 4 Congress approved the final draft of the Declaration of Independence. John Hancock, the president of the Congress, was the first to sign the document, which eventually held the signatures of all 56 delegates.

The Declaration is one of the most famous documents in history. Jefferson drew on the ideas of Locke and other thinkers to set out the colonies' reasons for proclaiming their freedom. The purpose of the Declaration was to justify the American Revolution and to put forth the founding principles of the new nation. No government at the time had been founded on the principles of human liberty and consent of the governed.

The Declaration officially recognized the changes that were taking place in the colonies. One of the most important changes was that the colonies began thinking of themselves as states, subject to no higher authority. By the end of 1776, 10 states had adopted written constitutions. Most of the constitutions included a bill of rights defining the personal liberties of citizens. All recognized the people as the sole source of government's power, and all provided for limited government.

3. Why is the Declaration of Independence so famous?

_____

_____

_____

_____

_____

Name _____ Date _____ Class _____

  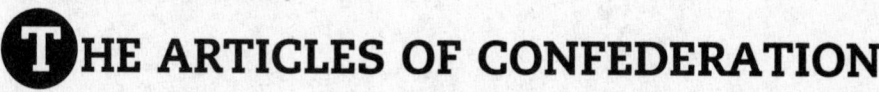

STUDY GUIDE — Chapter 2, Section 3

For use with textbook pages 48–52.

THE ARTICLES OF CONFEDERATION

CONTENT VOCABULARY

ratify To approve *(page 48)*
unicameral Single-chamber *(page 48)*
cede To yield *(page 50)*
ordinance A law *(page 50)*

DRAWING FROM EXPERIENCE

Have you ever belonged to a club? Imagine a club that is powerless to punish members for breaking the club's rules. After the Revolutionary War, the American government was powerless in a similar way.

This section focuses on the United States government under the Articles of Confederation.

READING STRATEGIES

Use an outline similar to the one below to help you take notes about the Articles of Confederation. Add as many points as you find in the section. Think about the weaknesses and achievements of government under the Articles of Confederation.

▣ The Articles of Confederation

I. Government Under the Articles of Confederation

   A.

   B.

   C.

   D.

II. Weaknesses of the Articles

   A.

   B.

III. Achievements

19

STUDY GUIDE (continued)   Chapter 2, Section 3

READx0020TO LEARN

◉ **Introduction** (page 48)

In 1777 a committee appointed by the Congress presented a plan called the Articles of Confederation. By March 1781, all thirteen states had *ratified*, or approved, the Articles of Confederation.

◉ **Government Under the Articles of Confederation** (page 48)

Under the Articles, the plan for the central government included a unicameral, or single-chamber, Congress. A Committee of States made up of one delegate from each state managed the government when Congress was not assembled. There was no federal court system. Congress settled disputes among states.

Each state had one vote in Congress. Every state legislature selected its own representative to Congress, paid him, and could recall him at any time.

Congress had only those powers expressed in the Articles, including the powers to:

A. Make war and peace

B. Send and receive ambassadors

C. Enter into treaties

D. Raise and equip a navy

E. Maintain an army by requesting troops from the states

F. Appoint senior military officers

G. Fix standards of weights and measures

H. Regulate Indian affairs

I. Establish post offices

J. Decide certain disputes among the states

    1. Did the members of Congress under the Articles represent the people? Explain your answer.

_____

_____

◉ **Weaknesses of the Articles** (page 49)

First Congress could raise money only by borrowing or requesting money from the states. Congress could do little if a state refused to provide the money.

Second Congress could not regulate trade. As a result, economic disputes developed among the various states, and difficulty arose in making business arrangements with other nations.

Third Congress could not enforce the laws it passed or the Articles of Confederation.

Fourth Laws needed the approval of nine of the thirteen states. Also, each of the states had only a single vote. So the vote of any five small states could block a measure that eight larger states wanted.

Fifth Amending, or changing, the Articles required the consent of all the states. The Articles were never amended because all the states could never agree on an amendment.

STUDY GUIDE (continued)   Chapter 2, Section 3

Sixth The central government did not have an executive branch. As a result, there was no unity in policy and no way to coordinate the work of different committees of Congress.

Seventh The government had no national court system. So state courts enforced and interpreted federal laws. No court system also made settling disputes between the states difficult for the central government.

2. Which do you consider the greatest weakness of the Articles of Confederation? Explain your answer.

_____

_____

◉ Achievements (page 50)

The greatest achievement of the Confederation was its policy for the development of the lands west of the Appalachian Mountains. The individual states **ceded**, or gave up, their claims to these lands. Then Congress enacted two **ordinances,** or laws, for their organization. The Northwest Ordinance of 1787, for example, established that the land would eventually become states on an equal basis with older states.

Another accomplishment was the peace treaty with Great Britain, signed in 1783. In the treaty, Britain recognized American independence and ceded land from the Atlantic coast to the Mississippi River.

Congress set up the departments of Foreign Affairs, War, Marine, and the Treasury. The Articles also provided that each state respect the legal acts of the other states and the rights of their citizens. Both these achievements were later carried over into government under the Constitution.

3. How did the land policies of the Confederation help to create the present United States?

_____

_____

◉ The Need for Stronger National Government (page 51)

Soon after the war for independence, the states began to quarrel over boundary lines and tariffs. Even worse, both the central government and the states faced growing financial troubles. In 1787 these troubles led to armed rebellion. Daniel Shays, a former captain in the Continental Army, led a raid on the Massachusetts state arsenal. Shays and his followers wanted to force the state to stop courts from foreclosing mortgages on farms. The Massachusetts militia put down Shays's Rebellion. But leaders in Congress feared that the national government was too weak to prevent other such protests.

In 1785 George Washington invited representatives from Maryland and Virginia to discuss their differences. The meeting was so successful that in 1786 Virginia representatives called all states to another meeting called the Annapolis Convention to discuss trade. One of the delegates, Alexander Hamilton, persuaded the others to call still another meeting in Philadelphia for May 1787. The purpose of the meeting was to revise the Articles of Confederation.

4. Why did Shays's Rebellion cause concern in Congress?

_____

_____

STUDY GUIDE  Chapter 2, Section 4

For use with textbook pages 53–58.

❶HE CONSTITUTIONAL CONVENTION

CONTENT VOCABULARY

interstate commerce Trade among the states *(page 55)*

extralegal Not sanctioned by law *(page 57)*

anarchy Political disorder *(page 57)*

DRAWING FROM EXPERIENCE

Remember the last time you did a group assignment. What were the difficulties of working with a group? The problems you faced were probably similar to those faced by the delegates at the Philadelphia convention.

This section focuses on the creation and ratification of the United States Constitution.

READING STRATEGIES

Use the graphic organizer below to list the issues discussed at the Constitutional Convention and how they were settled.

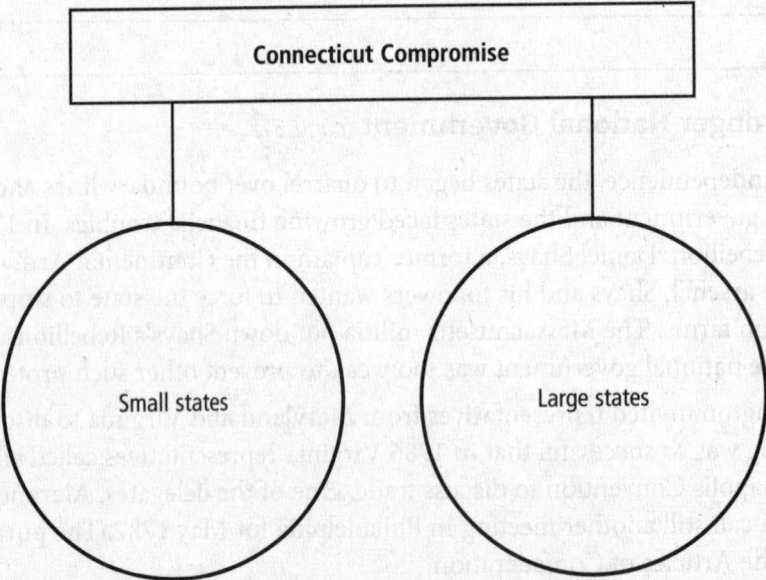

Connecticut Compromise

Small states

Large states

READ TO LEARN

◉ Introduction (page 53)

The Constitutional Convention began on May 25, 1787. Fifty-five delegates from twelve states attended.

◉ The Convention Begins (page 53)

James Madison from Virginia was a brilliant supporter of a strong national government. Madison is often called the Father of the Constitution because he wrote the basic plan of government that the convention eventually adopted. George Washington was chosen to preside over the meetings. The delegates decided to keep the public and press from attending the sessions so they felt free to address issues openly.

The delegates originally intended to revise the Articles of Confederation. They eventually agreed to abandon the former government and begin again. All favored the idea of limited government and separation of powers. They all agreed to strengthen the central government and to limit the power of states.

   1. On what issues did convention delegates agree?

   _____

   _____

◉ Decisions and Compromises (page 54)

The Virginia Plan On May 29, 1787, Edmund Randolph of Virginia introduced 15 resolutions that James Madison had drafted. This Virginia Plan proposed:

A. a strong national legislature with two chambers, the lower chamber to be chosen by the people and the upper chamber to be chosen by the lower;

B. a strong national executive to be chosen by the national legislature; and

C. a national judiciary to be appointed by the legislature.

Delegates from the smaller states objected to the Virginia Plan because it put the larger, more populous states in control of a strong national government. However, after a number of modifications, the Virginia Plan eventually became the basis of the new Constitution.

The New Jersey Plan On June 15, William Paterson of New Jersey proposed an alternate plan. The New Jersey Plan called for a unicameral legislature with one vote for each state. Congress would have the power to impose taxes and regulate trade. Congress would also elect a weak executive, who would appoint a national judiciary. After some discussion, the delegates rejected the New Jersey Plan.

The Connecticut Compromise Roger Sherman and the other delegates from Connecticut came up with the Connecticut Compromise. The compromise suggested that the legislative branch have two parts:

A. A House of Representatives, with state representation based on population. All revenue laws concerning spending and taxes would begin in this house.

B. A Senate, with two members from each state. State legislators would elect senators.

Under the compromise, the larger states would have the advantage in the House of Representatives, but the smaller states would enjoy the advantage in the Senate.

STUDY GUIDE (continued)   Chapter 2, Section 4

The Three-Fifths Compromise Almost one-third of the people in the Southern states were enslaved African Americans. These states wanted the enslaved people counted as free people to give the South more representation, but did not want them counted for levying taxes. The Northern states took the opposite position. The Three-Fifths Compromise settled the issue by having three-fifths of the enslaved people counted for both tax purposes and for representation.

Compromise on Commerce and the Slave Trade The Northern states wanted the government to have complete power over trade with other nations. The Southern states feared that Congress might set up trade agreements that would hurt their agricultural exports and interfere with the slave trade. A compromise settled the issue. Congress could not ban the slave trade until 1808 but could regulate both interstate commerce, or trade among the states, and foreign commerce. Congress was forbidden to impose export taxes.

The Slavery Question The delegates knew that the Southern states would never accept the Constitution if it interfered with slavery, so the Founders compromised on the slavery question. They refused to deal with slavery and thus left it to later generations of Americans to resolve.

Other Compromises The debate over how to elect the president led to another compromise—the present Electoral College system, in which each state selects electors to choose the president. Similarly, the president's four-year term was a compromise between those who wanted a longer term and those who feared a long term would give the president too much power.

2. How did the Connecticut Compromise satisfy both large and small states?

_____

_____

◉ Ratifying the Constitution *(page 56)*

The new Constitution needed the approval of nine states to become law. A great debate raged over the Constitution before it was finally ratified.

A group called the Anti-Federalists claimed that the Constitution was ***extralegal***—not sanctioned by law—because the convention had been authorized only to revise the Articles of Confederation. The Anti-Federalists also argued that the Constitution needed a Bill of Rights. Without this, a strong federal government might take away the human rights won in the Revolution. A group called the Federalists argued that without a strong central government, the country would face ***anarchy,*** or political disorder. The Federalists promised to add a Bill of Rights as the first order of business under a new government.

Many small states quickly ratified the Constitution. It went into effect when New Hampshire became the ninth to ratify on June 21, 1788. But Virginia and New York held out. Washington, Madison, and Randolph persuaded Virginians to ratify on June 25. To win over New York, Hamilton, Madison, and John Jay wrote *The Federalist*—a collection of 80 essays in support of the Constitution. New York finally ratified the Constitution on July 26.

New York City was the new nation's temporary capital. George Washington was elected president and John Adams vice president. Congress met for the first time in New York City's Federal Hall on March 4, 1789. On April 30, Washington took the oath of office as first president.

3. How did Federalists counter the Anti-Federalists' greatest fear?

_____

_____

STUDY GUIDE  Chapter 3, Section 1

For use with textbook pages 63–67.

STRUCTURE AND PRINCIPLES

CONTENT VOCABULARY

article One of seven main divisions of the body of the Constitution *(page 64)*

jurisdiction The authority of a court to rule on certain cases *(page 64)*

supremacy clause The statement establishing the Constitution as the highest law of the land *(page 64)*

amendment A change to the Constitution *(page 65)*

popular sovereignty Rule by the people *(page 65)*

federalism A system in which power is divided between the national and state governments *(page 65)*

separation of powers The division of power among the legislative, executive, and judicial branches of government *(page 66)*

checks and balances The system whereby each branch of government exercises some control over the others *(page 66)*

veto Rejection of a bill *(page 66)*

judicial review The power of the Supreme Court to declare laws and actions of the local, state, or national governments unconstitutional *(page 66)*

DRAWING FROM EXPERIENCE

Remember the first time you used a computer. Did you try to operate it without a manual? If so, you probably had difficulty getting the computer to do what you wanted. Like a manual, the Constitution explains how the government works.

This section focuses on the basic structure and principles of the Constitution.

READING STRATEGIES

Use the graphic organizer below to list the six major principles of government.

Major Principles

STUDY GUIDE (continued) Chapter 3, Section 1

READE TO LEARN

◉ Introduction (page 63)

The Constitution provides citizens with information about their rights and about what they may reasonably expect of their government. An understanding of the Constitution is key to understanding the structure and functions of American government.

◉ Structure (page 63)

The Constitution contains about 7,000 words and is divided into three parts.

The Preamble The Preamble, or introduction, states that the government should provide stability and order, protect citizens' liberties, and serve the people.

The Articles The Constitution contains seven divisions called *articles*. Each article covers a general topic. Most of the articles are also divided into sections.

Article I creates the Congress. It also sets forth details about the House of Representatives and the Senate, explains how to make laws, lists the types of laws Congress may pass, and names powers that Congress does not have.

Article II creates an executive branch, details the powers and duties of the presidency, describes qualifications for the office and how the president is elected, and provides for the vice president.

Article III establishes a Supreme Court to head the Judicial Branch. It also gives the national government the power to create lower federal courts; outlines the *jurisdiction,* or the authority, of the Supreme Court and other federal courts to rule on cases; and defines treason against the United States.

Article IV explains the relationship of the states to one another and to the national government. It requires states to give citizens of other states the same rights as its own citizens, addresses admitting new states, and guarantees that the national government will protect the states against invasion or domestic violence.

Article V spells out the ways that the Constitution can be changed.

Article VI contains the *supremacy clause,* establishing that the Constitution, laws passed by Congress, and treaties of the United States are the highest law of the land.

Article VII addresses ratification of the Constitution.

The Amendments The Constitution has 27 **amendments,** or changes. Amendments provide a way that the document can change along with the changing needs of the nation.

1. Which topics do Articles I, II, and III of the Constitution cover?

_____

_____

_____

_____

STUDY GUIDE (continued)   Chapter 3, Section 1

◉ Major Principles (page 65)

The Constitution rests on the following six major principles of government:

Popular Sovereignty Government's authority flows from the people.

Federalism Power is divided between the national and state governments. Both levels have their own agencies and officials and pass laws that directly affect citizens. Federalism gives the United States flexibility because the national government has the power to act for the country as a whole, and states have power over many local matters.

Separation of Powers This means that the powers of the central government are divided among the executive, legislative, and judicial branches. The Founders hoped this system would prevent any branch from taking too much power.

Checks and Balances Each branch of government exercises some control over the others. For example, Congress passes laws, but the president can check Congress by *vetoing*, or rejecting, a law. This veto power is balanced by the power Congress has to override the veto by a two-thirds vote of each house.

Judicial Review This is the power of the courts to declare law and actions of local, state, or national governments invalid if they violate the Constitution. All federal courts have this power, but the Supreme Court is the final authority on the meaning and interpretation of the Constitution. The Constitution does not explicitly give the judicial branch this power. However, the Supreme Court established this precedent for federal courts in the case of *Marbury* v. *Madison* in 1803.

Limited Government This means that the Constitution limits the actions of the government by specifically listing powers it does and does not have. For example, the first ten amendments place specific limits in the areas of freedom of expression, personal security, and fair trials.

2. Describe one way the president checks the Congress and one way Congress checks the president.

_____

_____

_____

_____

_____

Name _____ Date _____ Class _____

For use with textbook pages 68–75.

THREE BRANCHES OF GOVERNMENT

CONTENT VOCABULARY

expressed powers Powers directly stated in the Constitution *(page 68)*

enumerated powers The expressed powers of Congress that are itemized and numbered 1–18 in Article I, Section 8 of the Constitution *(page 69)*

elastic clause Statement in Article I, Section 8 of the Constitution that gives Congress the right to make all laws "necessary and proper" to carry out the powers expressed in the other clauses of Article I *(page 69)*

federal bureaucracy Departments and agencies of the federal government—mostly the executive branch *(page 72)*

DRAWING FROM EXPERIENCE

Picture yourself entering a dance contest for couples, but being without a partner. What would be your chances of winning the contest? The legislative and executive branches would have the same chances of making effective policy if each operated alone. They have to cooperate with each other to successfully serve the nation's needs.

This section focuses on the powers of the three branches of government.

READING STRATEGIES

Use the graphic organizer below to list the functions of each branch of the federal government.

Legislative	Executive	Judicial

```
╔══════════════════════════════════════════════════════════════════════════╗
║  STUDY GUIDE (continued)        Chapter 3, Section 2                        ║
╚══════════════════════════════════════════════════════════════════════════╝
```

READ TO LEARN

◉ Introduction (page 68)

Article I of the Constitution established the House of Representatives and the Senate. Article II established the executive branch. In 1787 the presidency was an entirely new concept, and the need for the office was hotly debated among the Founders. Article III established the judicial branch. The Constitution set up only the Supreme Court but gave Congress the authority to set up additional courts.

◉ The Legislative Branch (page 69)

The Founders gave Congress *expressed powers,* or the powers directly stated in the Constitution. Most of the expressed powers are itemized in Article I, Section 8. These are called *enumerated powers* because they are numbered 1–18. The final enumerated power is called the elastic clause. This clause gives Congress the right to make all laws "necessary and proper" to carry out the other expressed powers. It allows Congress to "stretch" its powers to meet situations the Founders could not anticipate.

The first Congress introduced 167 bills, and legislating was only a part-time job. Today, a total of 100,000 bills are introduced each year, and members of Congress work nearly year-round in Washington, D.C.

1. Why is the final enumerated power of Congress called the elastic clause?

_____

_____

◉ The Executive Branch (page 70)

Article II of the Constitution states: "The executive power shall be vested in a president of the United States." Under this executive power, the president can fire officials in the executive branch, make agreements with foreign nations, or take emergency measures to save the nation.

Sections 2 and 3 of Article II give the president more specific powers:

A. To command the armed forces and the state militias when they are called into service

B. To appoint heads of executive departments, with Senate approval

C. To pardon criminals, except in cases of impeachment, or to reduce a person's jail sentence or fine

D. To make treaties, with the advice and consent of the Senate

E. To appoint ambassadors, federal court judges, and other top officials, with Senate approval

F. To deliver an annual State of the Union message to Congress and to send Congress other messages

G. To call Congress into special session when necessary

H. To meet with heads of state, ambassadors, and other foreign officials

I. To commission all military officers of the United States

J. To ensure that the laws of Congress are "faithfully executed"

George Washington, the first president, knew his every act would set a precedent. For example, he refused to run for a third term, setting a precedent for future presidents. His responsibilities did not require more than a handful of advisers and staff. Today, presidents direct a White House staff numbering in the hundreds, a military force of millions, and a *federal bureaucracy* made up of all executive branch employees.

STUDY GUIDE (continued)   Chapter 3, Section 2

2. Which powers of the president involve foreign nations?

_____

_____

◉ The Judicial Branch (page 72)

The judiciary of the United States has a dual courts system, or two different sets of courts. One includes federal courts, whose powers come from the Constitution and federal laws. The other includes the state courts, which get their powers from state constitutions and laws. Every court has the authority to hear only certain kinds of cases. This authority is called the jurisdiction of the court. Two factors determine the jurisdiction of federal courts: the subject matter of the case and the parties involved in it.

The first Supreme Court met in a small chamber on the main floor of the Capitol in Washington, D.C. When the Court was not in session, justices had to hear appeals in faraway districts. In 1935 the Supreme Court got its own building. It carved out power in landmark cases such as *Marbury* v. *Madison* of 1803. In that case, Chief Justice Marshall established the Court's power to declare laws unconstitutional. This power, known as judicial review, helps to balance the powers of the other branches.

3. Explain how the Supreme Court can check the power of Congress.

_____

_____

◉ Shared Power and Conflict (page 73)

Relationships among the three branches not mentioned in the Constitution developed over time.

The President as Legislator The executive branch provides plans for much of the legislation Congress considers. Article II gives this power by directing the president to "recommend to their [members of Congress] consideration such measures as he shall judge necessary . . ."

The President vs. Congress At times, presidents charge Congress with trying to take away powers of the executive. At other times, the president and Congress quarrel over the way the president carries out laws. Then the federal courts may be called in to interpret the laws. Often one political party controls the executive and another controls Congress. This can result in compromises or in gridlock, when nothing is accomplished.

Congress vs. the Courts The Constitution gives Congress the power to create lower federal courts and to limit the jurisdiction of the Supreme Court. However, Congress seldom uses this power.

The Supreme Court vs. the President Some Supreme Court decisions require the cooperation of the president. However, a president sometimes disagrees with the Court and refuses to carry out its decision.

4. Describe two kinds of conflicts Congress and the president experience.

_____

_____

STUDY GUIDE  Chapter 3, Section 3

For use with textbook pages 76–81.

MENDING THE CONSTITUTION

CONTENT VOCABULARY

ratify To approve *(page 76)*

petition An appeal *(page 77)*

balanced budget Plan requiring that what the government spends will not exceed its income *(page 77)*

impeach To accuse a public official of high crimes and misdemeanors in office *(page 79)*

treaty An agreement between nations *(page 79)*

executive agreement An agreement made between the president and another head of state *(page 80)*

judicial restraint The philosophy that the Supreme Court should avoid taking the initiative on social and political actions *(page 80)*

judicial activism The philosophy that the Supreme Court should play an active role in shaping national policies by addressing social and political issues *(page 80)*

DRAWING FROM EXPERIENCE

Have you ever written an essay? Did you start with an outline? Most likely, you changed parts of the outline as you did research and wrote the actual essay. In the same way, Americans have changed the Constitution from time to time.

This section focuses on the process of amending, or changing, the Constitution.

READING STRATEGIES

Use the graphic organizer below to explain the kinds of presidential acts that have resulted in changes to the Constitution.

CAUSE

1.

2.

3.

EFFECT

Changes to the Constitution

STUDY GUIDE (continued)   Chapter 3, Section 3

READ TO LEARN

◉ **Introduction** (page 76)

The Constitution can be changed to suit new conditions while the basic form of American government remains unchanged.

◉ **The Amendment Process** (page 76)

Article V provides for making amendments on any topic except equal representation from a state. Amendments are proposed on a national level and ratified, or approved, on a state-by-state basis.

A. One way of proposing an amendment is by a two-thirds vote of each house of Congress. This is the only method that has been used.

B. The other method is by a national convention called by Congress at the request of two-thirds of the states. In 1963 states *petitioned,* or appealed to, Congress for a convention to propose an amendment but failed to get support from the required number of states. Again, between 1975 and 1991, states petitioned Congress to propose an amendment requiring a *balanced budget*—one in which the government's spending never exceeds its income. This effort also failed to win more than two-thirds of the states.

C. Congress can also choose one of two methods for ratifying an amendment. One way is for legislatures in three-fourths of the states to ratify the amendment. If a state rejects an amendment in the state legislature method, lawmakers may reverse their decision and ratify the amendment. The other method is for each state to call a special ratifying convention. This method has been used only once.

D. Congress decides how long states have to ratify an amendment. Recently, the limit has been seven years.

1. What are two ways an amendment can be ratified?

_____

_____

◉ **Indirect Ways the Constitution Changes** (page 78)

Leaders and citizens change the Constitution informally as they fill in the details of government.

Changes Through Law Congress has passed laws that enlarge or clarify many Constitutional provisions. For example, Congress has expanded the executive branch beyond its description in the Constitution by creating cabinet departments, agencies, boards, and commissions.

Changes Through Practices Congress has shaped the Constitution by the way it uses its other powers. For instance, when *impeaching*, or accusing, a federal official, members of Congress decide what the Constitution means by "high crimes and misdemeanors."

2. In what two ways does Congress make informal changes to the Constitution?

_____

_____

STUDY GUIDE (continued)   Chapter 3, Section 3

◉ Informal Presidential Changes (page 79)

In 1841 Vice President John Tyler clarified the constitutional provision for succession to the presidency. When President William Henry Harrison died in office, Tyler took the oath of office and became president rather than just acting as president until the next election. Tyler's precedent guided vice presidents until 1967 when the Twenty-fifth Amendment made it official.

The Constitution specifies a process for making a *treaty*, or an agreement between nations. However, modern presidents usually use executive agreements instead of treaties. An *executive agreement* is made directly between the president and another head of state but does not need Senate approval.

Today presidents often request legislation from Congress. They play a far greater role in American government than most Framers of the Constitution imagined.

3. In what three areas have presidents made informal changes to the Constitution?

_____

_____

_____

◉ Court Decisions (page 80)

Federal courts interpret the meanings of vague words and phrases in the Constitution as they settle cases involving constitutional questions. The most important way the Supreme Court interprets the Constitution is judicial review. However, people disagree about how the Court should practice this power. Some believe the Court should use *judicial restraint.* This means the Court should avoid controversial decisions on social and political issues. Other people believe in *judicial activism*—when the Court helps shape national policies. The Supreme Court under Chief Justice Earl Warren practiced judicial activism when it accepted cases involving civil rights and the rights of the accused.

The Supreme Court has sometimes ruled one way and then reversed its decision years later. In 1896 the Court ruled that separate public facilities for African Americans were constitutional if the facilities were equal. In 1954 the Court reversed its position when it outlawed segregation in public schools.

4. How do federal courts help make the meaning of the Constitution clearer?

_____

_____

◉ Changes Through Custom and Usage (page 81)

Political parties are examples of how government under the Constitution has been enlarged through custom. The Constitution does not mention parties, but they have been an important part of American government since the government was organized. Parties help organize government and conduct elections. The changes to the Constitution achieved through precedent and practice have created a government that responds to the conditions and needs of the time.

5. Describe two ways in which political parties are an important part of American government.

_____

_____

STUDY GUIDE  Chapter 3, Section 4

For use with textbook pages 83–90.

THE AMENDMENTS

CONTENT VOCABULARY

incorporation doctrine The extension of the Bill of Rights protections to state laws *(page 84)*

prior restraint Government censorship of information before it is published or broadcast *(page 84)*

probable cause A reasonable basis to believe a person or premises is linked to a crime *(page 86)*

search warrant An order signed by a judge describing a specific place to be searched for specific items *(page 86)*

arrest warrant An order signed by a judge naming the individual to be arrested for a specific crime *(page 86)*

due process of law Principle in the Fifth Amendment stating that the government must follow proper constitutional procedures in trials and in other actions it takes against individuals *(page 86)*

eminent domain The power of the government to take private property for public use *(page 86)*

lame duck An outgoing official serving out the remainder of a term after retiring or being defeated for reelection *(page 90)*

poll tax Money paid in order to vote *(page 90)*

DRAWING FROM EXPERIENCE

Have you ever heard someone say "It's a free country"? Americans owe many of their freedoms to the first ten amendments to the Constitution.

This section focuses on the amendments to the United States Constitution.

READING STRATEGIES

Use the graphic organizer below to help you take notes as you read the summaries that follow. Think about the categories into which the Constitutional amendments fall.

The Bill of Rights	Civil War Amendments	20th Century Amendments

STUDY GUIDE (continued)   Chapter 3, Section 4

READU TO LEARN

◉ Introduction *(page 83)*

In 1791 Americans ratified the Constitution's first ten amendments, which are called the Bill of Rights.

◉ The Bill of Rights *(page 84)*

The First Amendment protects the right of Americans to worship as they please or to have no religion at all. The First Amendment also protects the freedoms of speech and of the press. As a result, for example, the American press is not subject to *prior restraint,* under which government must approve information before it is published or broadcast. However, freedom of speech and the press has limits.

Spoken or printed lies intended to damage a person's reputation are not protected. In addition, the First Amendment does not protect language that endangers the safety of the nation or individuals. The First Amendment also protects the right to meet in groups, to sign petitions, and to send letters to officials.

The Second Amendment ensures citizens and the nation the right to security. Some people interpret the amendment to mean that they have the right to own firearms.

The Third Amendment prohibits the government from forcing people to provide shelter for soldiers in their homes except under conditions spelled out by law.

The Fourth Amendment protects the right to privacy. Authorities must have a specific reason to search a place or to seize evidence or people. To be lawful, a search or an arrest must be based on *probable cause*. This means that the police must have a reason to believe the person or place is linked to a crime. A search or an arrest usually requires a *search warrant* or an *arrest warrant.*

The Fifth Amendment states that no person can be tried unless a grand jury determines enough evidence exists to justify a trial. The amendment also assures that a person who is found innocent may not be tried again for the same offense. In addition, a person cannot be forced to testify against himself or herself. Finally, the Fifth Amendment states that the government may not deprive any person of life, liberty, or property without *due process of law*. This means that the government must follow proper legal procedures in trials and other actions against individuals. The amendment also defines *eminent domain*—the power of government to take private property for public use.

The Sixth Amendment gives individuals charged with federal crimes the right to a speedy and public trial by an impartial jury. It also gives accused persons the right to know the charges against them, to hear and question witnesses, to compel witnesses to testify in their behalf, and to be defended by an attorney.

The Seventh Amendment gives a person the right to a jury trial in federal court to settle disputes about property.

The Eighth Amendment protects against cruel and unusual punishment and excessive bail—money or property the accused deposits with the court to gain release from jail until trial.

The Ninth Amendment states that the people retain all rights not spelled out in the Constitution.

The Tenth Amendment establishes that whatever powers the Constitution does not give to the national government or deny to the states belong to the states or to the people.

STUDY GUIDE (continued)   Chapter 3, Section 4

1. Describe three freedoms protected by the First Amendment.

_____

_____

_____

◉ Other Amendments *(page 88)*

The *Eleventh Amendment* (passed in 1795) prohibits a state from being sued in federal court by citizens of another state or another country. The *Twelfth Amendment* (1804) corrected problems that arose in elections by providing that the Electoral College use separate ballots for president and vice president.

The Civil War Amendments include the Thirteenth, Fourteenth, and Fifteenth. The *Thirteenth Amendment* (1865) outlaws slavery. The *Fourteenth Amendment* (1868) was intended to protect the legal rights of freed slaves. Today it protects the rights of citizenship by preventing states from depriving any person of life, liberty, or property without due process. The *Fifteenth Amendment* (1870) prevents the government from denying any person's right to vote on the basis of race.

Twentieth century Amendments deal with a range of subjects that reflect changes in modern America. The *Sixteenth Amendment* (1913) gives Congress the power to levy individual income taxes. The *Seventeenth Amendment* (1913) states that the people, not state legislators, elect United States senators. The *Eighteenth Amendment* (1919) prohibited the manufacture, sale, or transportation of alcoholic beverages. In 1933 the *Twenty-first Amendment* repealed the Eighteenth. The *Nineteenth Amendment* (1920) guaranteed women the right to vote. The *Twentieth Amendment* (1933) set new dates for Congress to begin its term and for the inaugurations of the president and vice president. Before this amendment, outgoing officials were *lame ducks*, or had little influence, for several months between the election and when new officials took office. The *Twenty-second Amendment* (1950) limits a president to a maximum of two elected terms. The *Twenty-third Amendment* (1961) allows citizens living in Washington, D. C., to vote for president and vice president. The *Twenty-fourth Amendment* (1964) prohibits *poll taxes*—money paid in order to vote. The *Twenty-fifth Amendment* (1967) establishes a process for the vice president to take over the leadership of the nation when a president is disabled. The *Twenty-sixth Amendment* (1971) lowered the voting age to 18. The *Twenty-seventh Amendment* (1992) makes congressional pay raises effective during the term following their passage.

2. What group of Americans were the Civil War Amendments intended to protect? Explain your answer.

_____

_____

STUDY GUIDE  Chapter 4, Section 1

For use with textbook pages 95–102.

NATIONAL AND STATE POWERS

CONTENT VOCABULARY

delegated powers Powers the Constitution grants or delegates to the national government *(page 95)*

expressed powers Powers directly stated in the Constitution *(page 95)*

implied powers Powers that the government requires to carry out the expressed constitutional powers *(page 96)*

elastic clause A statement in Article I, Section 8 of the Constitution that gives Congress the right to make laws "necessary and proper" to carry out the laws expressed in the other clauses of Article I *(page 96)*

inherent powers Powers that the national government may exercise simply because it is a government *(page 96)*

reserved powers Powers that belong strictly to the states *(page 96)*

supremacy clause The statement in Article VI of the Constitution establishing that the Constitution, laws passed by Congress, and treaties of the United States "shall be the supreme Law of the Land" *(page 97)*

concurrent powers Powers that both the national government and the states have *(page 97)*

enabling act The first step in the state admission procedure *(page 99)*

DRAWING FROM EXPERIENCE

At your school, administrators run the entire school. Yet each teacher runs his or her classroom. The federal system of government is set up in a similar way.

This section focuses on the powers of the central and state governments.

READING STRATEGIES

Use the graphic organizer below to list the powers granted to the national and state governments.

National Powers	State Powers

STUDY GUIDE (continued)   Chapter 4, Section 1

READuTO LEARN

◉ **Introduction** *(page 95)*

National and state powers have been continually redefined through conflict, compromise, and cooperation since the earliest days of the nation.

◉ **The Division of Powers** *(page 95)*

The Constitution divided government authority by giving the national government certain specified powers and reserving other powers to the state or the people. Additional powers are shared by the national and state governments. Some powers are denied to all levels of government.

  1. In what three ways did the Constitution divide government authority?

  _____

  _____

  _____

◉ **National Powers** *(page 95)*

Collectively, the powers that the Constitution grants to the national government are called *delegated powers.* These powers are divided into the following three types:

A. *Expressed powers* are directly stated in the Constitution. They include the powers to levy and collect taxes, to coin money, to make war, to raise an army and navy, and to regulate commerce among the states.

B. *Implied powers* are powers the national government needs to carry out the powers that are expressly defined in the Constitution. For example, the power to draft people into the armed forces is implied by the power given to the government to raise an army and a navy. The basis for the implied powers is in Section 8 of Article I. This is often called the *elastic clause.*

C. *Inherent powers* are those the national government may exercise simply because it is a government. For example, the national government must establish diplomatic relations with other nations.

  2. List five expressed powers of the national government.

  _____

  _____

  _____

  _____

STUDY GUIDE (continued)   Chapter 4, Section 1

◉ The States and the Nation (page 96)

Reserved powers belong strictly to the states. They include powers not delegated to the national government, or denied to the states by the Constitution. The regulation of public school systems is one example.

According to the *supremacy clause* of the Constitution, national law is supreme over state law. This means that no state constitution or state or local law may conflict with national law.

Concurrent powers are those powers that both the national government and the states have. Examples are the powers to tax, to maintain courts, and to define crimes.

Denied powers are those denied to government. For example, the national government cannot tax exports. The Constitution denies several powers to the states. For example, no state can coin money.

    3. What is the difference between reserved powers and concurrent powers?

_____

_____

◉ Guarantees to the States (page 98)

The Constitution requires the national government to:

A. guarantee each state a republican form of government. Congress accomplishes this by allowing senators and representatives from each state to take their seats in Congress.

B. protect states from invasion and domestic violence. The national government has extended its definition of domestic violence to include natural disasters such as floods. When a disaster strikes, the president often orders troops to aid disaster victims. The government also offers victims low-cost loans.

C. respect the territorial integrity of each state. In other words, the national government cannot use the land of an existing state to create a new state unless the state legislature gives its permission.

    4. What three guarantees does the national government owe the states?

_____

_____

_____

◉ Admission of New States (page 99)

The Constitution gives Congress the power to add new states to the union. The procedure for admission begins in Congress. It passes an *enabling act,* which enables the people of a territory interested in becoming a state to prepare a constitution. The completed and approved constitution is submitted to the Congress. Then Congress passes an act admitting the state.

Congress or the president may impose certain conditions before admitting a state. An example is requiring changes in the constitution submitted by the territory.

Once admitted to the Union, each state is equal to every other state. It has the right to control its internal affairs and has the same privileges and obligations as other states.

STUDY GUIDE (continued) Chapter 4, Section 1

5. What three steps make up the process of admitting a new state?

_____

_____

_____

◉ The National Governors' Association *(page 101)*

The National Governors' Association (NGA) supports federalism by helping governors in state policy making and in influencing national policy. In the 1970s, the NGA focused on common problems such as organizing intergovernmental relations. Beginning in the 1980s, however, the governors shifted their attention to national policy concerns such as educational, welfare, and health-care reforms. By joining together, the governors played a part in making national policy.

In addition to the support of the NGA, states perform the following services for national government:

A. Conducting and paying for elections of all government officials

B. Playing a key role in the process for amending the Constitution

6. What two services do states perform for the national government?

_____

_____

◉ The Court as Umpire *(page 102)*

Conflicts frequently arise between national and state governments. The federal court system plays a key role in settling these conflicts. The Supreme Court ruled on the question of national versus state power for the first time in the 1819 case of *McCulloch* v. *Maryland*. The Court held that the national government is supreme in the instance of a conflict between the national government and a state government. In many rulings on this issue since *McCulloch*, the Court's view of the division of powers between the national and state governments has shifted. Since the 1990s, the Court has generally favored states' power. Increasing power of federal judges allows them to serve as umpires of federalism as well, by opening nearly every action by state and local officials to the judges' questioning.

7. What precedent did the Supreme Court set in *McCulloch* v. *Maryland?*

_____

_____

STUDY GUIDE  Chapter 4, Section 2

For use with textbook pages 103–105.

RELATIONS AMONG THE STATES

CONTENT VOCABULARY

extradite To return to the state a criminal or fugitive who flees across state lines *(page 103)*

civil law Law relating to disputes between individuals, groups, or with the state *(page 103)*

interstate compact A written agreement between two or more states *(page 105)*

DRAWING FROM EXPERIENCE

Have you ever shared a room? How did you avoid quarrels with your roommate? You probably learned to cooperate in order to keep the peace. States also have to cooperate to avoid conflicts and jealousies.

This section focuses on relations among the states.

READING STRATEGIES

Use the graphic organizer below to help you take notes as you read about the issues that cause states to make interstate compacts. Use as many answer boxes as issues you identify in the section.

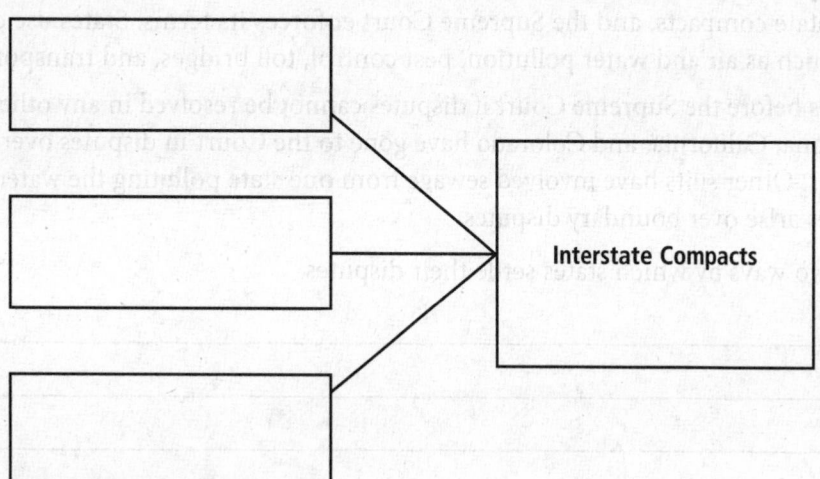

STUDY GUIDE (continued)   Chapter 4, Section 2

READ TO LEARN

● Introduction *(page 103)*

The Constitution set legal ground rules for relations among the states. These rules help to ensure cooperation.

● Interstate Relations *(page 103)*

Article IV of the Constitution requires that each state:

A. give "full faith and credit" to the public acts, records, and judicial proceedings of every other state. Each state must recognize the laws and legal proceedings of the other states. *Public acts* refers to civil laws passed by the state legislatures. *Records* means documents such as mortgages, deeds, leases, wills, marriage licenses, car registrations, and birth certificates. *Judicial proceedings* refers to various court actions, such as judgments to pay debts.

B. provide all the "privileges and immunities" of its citizens to the citizens of every other state. These privileges and immunities include rights to pass through or live in any state; to use the courts; to make contracts; to buy, sell, and hold property; and to marry. On the other hand, states may reasonably discriminate against residents of other states. For example, nonresidents do not have the same right to attend public institutions such as state universities. These institutions usually charge higher tuition to nonresident students.

C. *extradite*—that is, return to another state—criminals and fugitives who flee across state lines to escape justice.

D. settle its differences with other states without using force. The main way states do this is through **interstate compacts.** These are written agreements between two or more states. Congress must approve interstate compacts, and the Supreme Court enforces its terms. States use compacts to deal with matters such as air and water pollution, pest control, toll bridges, and transportation.

E. sue other states before the Supreme Court if disputes cannot be resolved in any other way. For example, Arizona, California, and Colorado have gone to the Court in disputes over water from the Colorado River. Other suits have involved sewage from one state polluting the water in another state. Still other cases arise over boundary disputes.

1. Describe two ways by which states settle their disputes.

_____

_____

_____

_____

STUDY GUIDE  Chapter 4, Section 3

For use with textbook pages 106–110.

DEVELOPING FEDERALISM

CONTENT VOCABULARY

states' rights position An opinion that favors state and local action to deal with problems *(page 107)*

nationalist position An opinion that favors national action to deal with problems *(page 107)*

income tax The tax levied on individual and corporate earnings *(page 108)*

preemption The federal government's ability to take over a state government function *(page 109)*

DRAWING FROM EXPERIENCE

Recall a book you read when you were very young. How did you feel about the story then? Would you feel differently about it if you read it today? You probably would. In the same way, many Americans, including members of the Supreme Court, have changed their views on federalism over the years.

This section focuses on the different views of federalism among government leaders.

READING STRATEGIES

Use a table like the one below to track the positions of states' rightists and nationalists.

	States' Rightists	Nationalists
Relation of Government to People		
Relevant Constitutional Provision of Court Case		

READ TO LEARN

◉ **Introduction** (page 106)

The roles of state and national government officials have been defined during more than 200 years of developing federalism.

◉ **States' Rightists and Nationalists** (page 107)

Throughout American history, people have taken two very different views of how federalism should operate.

The States' Rights Position holds that the Constitution is a compact among the states. States' rightists argue that the states created the national government and gave it only limited powers. Any doubt about whether a power belongs to the national government or is reserved for the states should be settled in the states' favor. Furthermore, they believe that all powers of the national government should be narrowly defined because the national government is an agent of the states.

The Supreme Court accepted this view under Chief Justice Roger B. Taney (1836–1864). The Court often supported states' rights against powers of the national government. The same was true from 1918 to 1936. During that time the Court ruled federal laws unconstitutional that attempted to regulate child labor, industry, and agriculture in the states.

The Nationalist Position argues that the people, not the states, created the national government and the states. Therefore, the national government is not subordinate to the states. Nationalists believe the powers expressly delegated to the national government should be expanded as necessary to carry out the people's will. They look to the national government to take the lead in solving major social and economic problems facing the nation. The Supreme Court established the nationalist position in 1819 in *McCulloch* v. *Maryland,* and the position gained more ground during the Great Depression in the late 1930s. As the Depression grew worse, the Court supported the expansion of national government's powers in order to deal with the nation's terrible economic woes.

1. During what two periods did the Supreme Court accept the states' rights position on federalism?

_____

_____

◉ **Growing National Government** (page 108)

The growth of the national government's powers has been based on the following three constitutional provisions:

War Powers The power to wage war has greatly expanded the federal government's power because national defense depends on such varied factors as the strength of the educational system and the condition of the economy.

Commerce Power The Constitution gives Congress the authority to regulate commerce. The courts today interpret the term *commerce* to mean nearly all activities concerned with the production, buying, selling, and transporting of goods. For example, Congress passed the Civil Rights Act of 1964 forbidding racial discrimination in public places such as hotels and restaurants. The Supreme Court upheld the law

Name _____ Date _____ Class _____

╺◦
STUDY GUIDE (continued)　　　Chapter 4, Section 3
╺◦

because the justices reasoned that racial discrimination restricts people's travel and thus the flow of commerce. So Congress may pass laws against racial discrimination.

Taxing Power Congress has the power to raise taxes and spend money to promote the general welfare. The income tax levied on individual earnings has become the major source of money for the national government. Congress has used its taxing power to increase the national government's power in two ways:

A. *To regulate businesses* For example, Congress has put such high taxes on certain products that it is unprofitable for companies to make them.

B. *To influence states to adopt certain kinds of programs* Federal law allows employers to deduct from their federal taxes any state taxes they pay to support state unemployment programs. As a result, all the states have set up their own unemployment programs.

2. How did the Supreme Court link the power to regulate commerce with civil rights?

_____

_____

◉ Federal Aid to the States *(page 109)*

Congress has developed two major ways to influence the policies of state and local governments. The first is by providing money through *federal grants*, or aid to the states to be spent for a specific purpose. For example, in 1862, Congress gave nearly 6 million acres of public land to the states for support of colleges. Since the 1950s, federal aid to state and local governments has increased tremendously. These grants often help reduce inequalities between wealthy and less wealthy states. However, many federal aid programs provide money only if the state and local governments are willing to meet conditions set by Congress.

Since the mid-1960s, Congress has also gained authority over state governments through *preemption*, the power to assume responsibility for a state function. For example, in 1990 Congress passed the Nutritional Labeling and Education Act to establish national food labeling standards, taking away the power of the states to set their own requirements. Preemption laws limit the authority of state and local governments through restraints and mandates. A *restraint* is a requirement that prohibits a local or state government from exercising a certain power. A *mandate* is an order requiring states to provide a service or activity in a way that meets standards set by Congress. For example, the Americans With Disabilities Act required state and local governments to better accommodate the physically challenged. Advocates of states' rights dislike preemption laws because they can interfere with the laws or priorities of state and local governments. Also, the states, not Congress, are required to pay for new mandates.

3. What are the ways in which Congress can influence the policies of state and local governments?

_____

_____

Name _____ Date _____ Class _____

For use with textbook pages 112–116.

FEDERALISM AND POLITICS

CONTENT VOCABULARY

sunset law A law that requires periodic checks of government agencies to see if they are still needed (*page 112*)

sunshine law A law prohibiting government officials from holding meetings not open to the public (*page 113*)

bureaucracy Organization of government administrators (*page 115*)

DRAWING FROM EXPERIENCE

The layout of your home affects your quality of life. For example, if an entire family has to share one bathroom, life is less convenient than in a household with two bathrooms. The organization of American government also affects Americans' quality of life.

This section focuses on the benefits of federalism.

READING STRATEGIES

Use the graphic organizer below to help you take notes as you read about the ways in which federalism affects political participation.

```
┌──────────────┐
│              │
└──────────────┘ \
                  \
┌──────────────┐   \    ┌──────────────────┐
│              │────────│  How Federalism  │
└──────────────┘   /    │Affects Participation│
                  /     └──────────────────┘
┌──────────────┐ /
│              │/
└──────────────┘ 
                  
┌──────────────┐
│              │
└──────────────┘
```

STUDY GUIDE (continued)   Chapter 4, Section 4

READ TO LEARN

◉ Introduction (page 112)

Federalism affects government policy making, the political party system, the political activities of citizens, and the quality of life in all 50 states.

◉ Federalism and Public Policy (page 112)

A public policy is the course of action a government takes in response to some issue or problem. Federalism affects public policy in the following two ways:

A. *How and where new policies are made in the United States* It allows states and localities to serve as proving grounds where new policies can be developed and tested. For example, Georgia was the first state to allow 18 year olds to vote. The right has since been given to all Americans.

B. *Limits on government policy making* For example, Colorado pioneered the use of sunset laws in 1976. A *sunset law* requires periodic checks of government agencies to see if they are still needed. Another example is when Florida passed the first *sunshine law* in 1967. This kind of law stops public officials from holding meetings not open to the public.

Policy may also start at the national level. Sometimes the national government will impose new policies on states in which local pressure groups have resisted change. For example, the national government forced the states to change civil rights and voting policies in the 1960s.

    1. In what two ways does federalism affect public policy?

_____

_____

_____

◉ Federalism and Political Parties (page 113)

Rival parties are a key element of democratic government. Each political party has a chance to win some elections somewhere in the system. In this way, federalism lessens the chance that one party will gain a monopoly of political power. By providing opportunities for parties to win local, state, and national elections, federalism has helped to keep the two-party system alive.

    2. How does federalism lessen the chance of one political party gaining a monopoly of power?

_____

_____

◉ Political Participation (page 114)

Federalism increases opportunities for citizens to participate in politics at the national, state, and local levels. People have easier access to political office because federalism creates several levels of government. The road to national office often begins at the local or state level. This helps to build political organization from the bottom up. Federalism also gives Americans many points of access to government and increases their opportunities for influencing public policy. For example, citizens vote for state and local officials and on such local issues as mass transit, property taxes, and smoking bans. They may also join interest groups to influence policies on all levels, so more people are likely to participate in politics.

STUDY GUIDE (continued)   Chapter 4, Section 4

3. How does federalism make government in the United States more democratic?

_____

_____

◉ Federalism's Bureaucrats *(page 115)*

In the 1930s, federal programs began to increase in response to national economic problems. The increase created a bureaucracy, or organization of administrators, to carry out the programs. Bureaucrats became experts in a specialized area of government. In other words, they were professional politicians, sometimes called the technocracy. The growth of federal programs also led to organizations that keep state and local officials informed about the programs. An example is the United States Conference of Mayors.

4. How did the federal bureaucracy develop?

_____

_____

◉ Differences Among the States *(page 115)*

Federalism allows each state considerable freedom in arranging its own internal affairs. As a result, some states do more than others to regulate industry, for example, provide more health and welfare services, or protect the environment. Americans have more choices regarding the conditions they live under because states can create different economic and political environments. Political traditions among states also differ, therefore states have different officials, laws, and taxes.

5. What are some of the differences in the political and economic environments of different states?

_____

_____

◉ The Direction of Federalism *(page 116)*

The power balance between national and state governments is constantly evolving in response to new issues. In recent decades, Democrats have generally supported national power, while Republicans have favored states' rights. Because of the relatively even distribution of party seats in recent Congresses, legislation has reflected both positions. For example, Congress has allowed states to set their own highway speed limits, but has also established national food safety standards.

6. How do Republicans and Democrats differ on the issue of federalism?

_____

_____

STUDY GUIDE  Chapter 5, Section 1

For use with textbook pages 123–130.

CONGRESSIONAL MEMBERSHIP

CONTENT VOCABULARY

bicameral legislature A two-chamber legislature *(page 123)*

session A period of time during which a legislature meets to conduct business *(page 123)*

census A population count *(page 124)*

reapportionment The process of reassigning representation based on population after every census *(page 124)*

redistrict To set up new district lines after reapportionment is complete *(page 125)*

gerrymander To draw a district's boundaries to gain an advantage in elections *(page 126)*

at-large As a whole; for example, statewide *(page 127)*

censure A vote of formal disapproval of a member's actions *(page 128)*

incumbent Candidate who is already in office *(page 129)*

DRAWING FROM EXPERIENCE

Have you ever voted in a school election? How did you choose your candidate? You probably voted for the person who wanted the same things that you wanted. Voters choose members of Congress for the same reason.

This section focuses on the nation's representatives in Congress.

READING STRATEGIES

Use the graphic organizer below to help you compare the qualifications for senators and representatives.

Qualifications	
SENATOR	**REPRESENTATIVE**

STUDY GUIDE (continued)   Chapter 5, Section 1

READORY LEARN

◉ **Introduction** (page 123)

The United States Congress is a *bicameral legislature.* It is made up of two houses, the Senate and the House of Representatives. Today Congress plays an important role in policy making by passing laws dealing with everything from health care to tax changes.

◉ **Congressional Sessions** (page 123)

Each term of Congress is divided into two *sessions,* or meetings. A session lasts one year and includes breaks for holidays and vacations. Congress remains in session until its members vote to adjourn. If Congress is adjourned, the president may call it back for a special session.

1. How long does a term of Congress last?

_____

_____

◉ **Membership of the House** (page 124)

The House of Representatives has 435 members. House seats are apportioned, or divided, among the states based on population. Each state has at least one seat, no matter how small its population.

Qualifications The Constitution states that a representative must be at least 25 years of age, a citizen of the United States for at least seven years, and a legal resident of the state that elects him or her. Traditionally, a representative also lives in the district he or she represents.

Term of Office Members of the House of Representatives are elected for two-year terms. Elections are held in November of even-numbered years—for example, 1998, 2000, and 2002. Representatives begin their term of office on January 3 following the November election. Representatives have to run for office every two years, but the House has continuity because 90 percent of all representatives are reelected.

Representation and Reapportionment The Census Bureau takes a national *census,* or population count, every 10 years. The population count of each state determines how many of the 435 seats in the House each state gets—a process called *reapportionment.*

Congressional Redistricting State legislatures set up districts to elect representatives. The process of drawing new district lines after reapportionment is called redistricting. In 2006, the Supreme Court decided a case that allows legislators to redraw districts in the middle of a decade rather than only after a census. This would likely occur only if one party dominated the legislature and governorship. State legislatures have sometimes abused the redistricting power by:

A. creating congressional districts of very unequal populations, and

B. **gerrymandering**—the dominant party in the legislature draws boundaries to gain an electoral advantage. They can try packing a district: drawing lines to include as many voters as possible in one district. Remaining districts will then be safe for their party. They can also try cracking: spreading opposition voters across districts to make it more likely majority party candidates will be elected.

2. How does the census affect members of the House of Representatives?

_____

_____

STUDY GUIDE (continued)   Chapter 5, Section 1

◉ Membership of the Senate (page 127)

The Senate consists of 100 members—2 from each of the 50 states.

Qualifications The Constitution requires a senator to be at least 30 years old, a citizen of the United States for at least 9 years before the election, and a legal resident of the state he or she represents. All voters of each state elect senators **at-large,** or statewide, rather than by districts.

Term of Office Elections for the Senate are held in November of even-numbered years, and senators begin their terms on January 3. The terms last six years, with one-third of the senators running for reelection every two years.

Salary and Benefits The Senate and House set their own salaries. However, the Twenty-seventh Amendment specifies that any new congressional salary increase takes effect after the next election. Members of Congress also enjoy benefits such as free postage for official business, a medical clinic, and a gymnasium, as well as large allowances and annual retirement pensions.

Privileges of Members The Constitution states that members of Congress are free from arrest "in all cases except treason, felony, and breach of the peace" when attending Congress or on their way to or from Congress. They cannot be sued for anything they say on the House or Senate floor. Each house may expel a member for a serious offense, such as treason or accepting bribes, and may censure members who are guilty of lesser crimes. **Censure** is a vote of formal disapproval.

3. When are members of Congress free from arrest?

_____

_____

◉ The Members of Congress (page 128)

Congress includes 535 representatives and senators. It also includes 4 delegates in the House—one each from the District of Columbia, Guam, American Samoa, and the Virgin Islands—and one resident commissioner from Puerto Rico. None of these five can vote, but they attend sessions, introduce bills, speak in debates, and vote in committees.

Nearly half the members of Congress are lawyers. A large number come from business, banking, and education. Members of Congress are typically middle-aged white males. However, Congress is beginning to reflect the diversity of the general population. For example, one recent Congress included 51 women.

In Congress, a large percentage of **incumbents**—those already in office—win reelection. Why? They find it easier to raise campaign funds. Often districts have been gerrymandered to favor the incumbents' party. In addition, incumbents are well known to the voters and use their power to solve voters' problems.

Candidates running for Congress have begun using the Internet as a campaign tool. Nearly all candidates now have election websites that are used as electronic brochures, as voter recruitment tools, to raise campaign contributions, or to broadcast speeches. Some experts predict that candidates will make greater use of Web technologies in the future, to identify important issues, target voters, and improve communication within campaign organizations.

4. Describe a typical member of Congress.

_____

STUDY GUIDE  Chapter 5, Section 2

For use with textbook pages 132–137.

THE HOUSE OF REPRESENTATIVES

CONTENT VOCABULARY

constituents Persons a member of Congress has been elected to represent *(page 133)*

caucus A private meeting of party leaders to choose candidates for office *(page 134)*

majority leader The Speaker's top assistant whose job is to help plan the majority party's legislative program and to steer important bills through the House *(page 134)*

whips Assistants to the party floor leaders in the legislature *(page 135)*

bill A proposed law *(page 135)*

calendars Schedules that list the order in which bills will be considered in Congress *(page 136)*

quorum The minimum number of members who must be present to permit a legislative body to take official action *(page 137)*

DRAWING FROM EXPERIENCE

Do you belong to a sports team? The team probably has a captain. Like leaders in sports, House leaders help House members work as a team.

This section focuses on how the House of Representatives gets laws passed.

READING STRATEGIES

Use the graphic organizer below to help you take notes as you read the summaries that follow. Think about the organization of leaders in the House.

```
                    ┌─────────────────────┐
                    │  Speaker of the House │
                    └─────────────────────┘
                       /               \
        ┌──────────────────┐        ┌──────────────────┐
        │ majority _____.│        │ minority _____.│
        └──────────────────┘        └──────────────────┘
                │                            │
        ┌──────────────────┐        ┌──────────────────┐
        │ majority _____.│        │ minority _____.│
        └──────────────────┘        └──────────────────┘
```

STUDY GUIDE (continued)   Chapter 5, Section 2

READV TO LEARN

◉ Introduction *(page 132)*

The rules of Congress are necessary to ensure fairness, to enable the legislature to carry on business, and to protect the minority.

◉ Rules for Lawmaking *(page 132)*

The House and Senate have many past rulings that serve as the lawmakers' guidelines. Both bodies print their rules every two years. House rules are geared toward moving legislation quickly. For example, House debates rarely last longer than one day. Also, the rules of the House allow its leaders to make key decisions about legislative work without consulting the other members of the House.

Committees do most of the work of the House. Members organize themselves into smaller groups because the House membership is so large. Representatives tend to concentrate on and specialize in a few issues that are important to their *constituents*—the people in the districts they represent.

In many ways, Congress is organized around political parties. For example, the Republicans sit on the right side and the Democrats sit on the left side in both the Senate and the House. In each house, the majority party—the one with the most members—selects the leaders of the body, controls the flow of legislative work, and appoints committee chairs.

In 1995 the House rules were changed to make members more accountable. The new rules provided for fewer committees, fewer staff members, term limits for chairpersons and the Speaker of the House, and an end to absentee voting in committees.

1. Why are committees important in the House of Representatives?

_____

_____

◉ House Leadership *(page 134)*

Leaders of the House serve the following purposes:

A. Organizing and unifying party members

B. Scheduling the work of the House

C. Making certain that lawmakers are present for key floor votes

D. Distributing and collecting information

E. Keeping the House in touch with the president

F. Influencing lawmakers to support the policies of their political parties.

The Speaker's top assistant is the *majority leader.* The majority leader's job is to help plan the party's legislative programs, steer important bills through the House, and make sure that chairpersons of the many committees finish work on bills important to the party. The majority leader has help from the majority whip and deputy *whips,* who serve as assistant floor leaders. They watch how majority-party members intend to vote on bills, persuade them to vote as the party wishes, and see that party members are present to vote. The minority party also has a minority leader and minority whips.

STUDY GUIDE (continued)   Chapter 5, Section 2

2. Describe the job of the majority leader in the House.

_____

_____

⦿ Lawmaking in the House *(page 135)*

The House starts its floor sessions at noon or earlier and is normally in session from Monday through Friday.

All laws start as bills. A proposed law is called a *bill* until both houses of Congress pass it and the president signs it. To introduce a bill in the House, a representative drops it into the hopper—a mahogany box at the front of the chamber. The Speaker of the House sends the bill to the appropriate committee for study, discussion, and review. Bills that survive the committee process are put on one of the House's five calendars. *Calendars* list bills that are up for consideration.

After a committee has considered and approved a major bill, it goes to the Rules Committee, the most powerful committee in the House. The Rules Committee can move the bill ahead quickly, hold it back, or stop it completely.

Major bills that reach the floor of the House for debate and a vote do so by a "rule"—or special order—from the Rules Committee. The chair of the committee that sent the bill to the Rules Committee can ask the Rules Committee to move the bill ahead of other bills to be sent to the House floor. If the Rules Committee agrees, the bill moves ahead. The Rules Committee may also specify how much debate time the bill can have and how much it may be amended on the floor.

The Rules Committee also settles disputes among other House committees. Finally, the Rules Committee often delays and blocks bills that representatives and House leaders do not want to come to a vote. In this way the Rules Committee draws criticism away from members who do not want to take an unpopular stand on a bill if it reaches the floor.

A *quorum* is the minimum number of members who must be present to permit a legislative body to take official action. For a regular session of the House, a quorum consists of 218—a majority of the 435 members. When the House meets to debate and amend legislation, it may often sit as a Committee of the Whole. In that case, only a 100 members make up a quorum. This helps to speed the consideration of important bills. The Committee of the Whole cannot pass bills. It reports a measure back to the full House with whatever changes it has made. The House then passes or rejects the bill.

3. Why is the Rules Committee the most important committee in the House?

_____

_____

STUDY GUIDE  Chapter 5, Section 3

For use with textbook pages 138–140.

THE SENATE

DRAWING FROM EXPERIENCE

Which group has fewer rules: your family or your school? The answer is probably your family because it has fewer members. For the same reason, the Senate has fewer rules than the House of Representatives.

This section focuses on the workings of the Senate.

READING STRATEGIES

Use the graphic organizer below to list the differences in everyday operations of the House and the Senate.

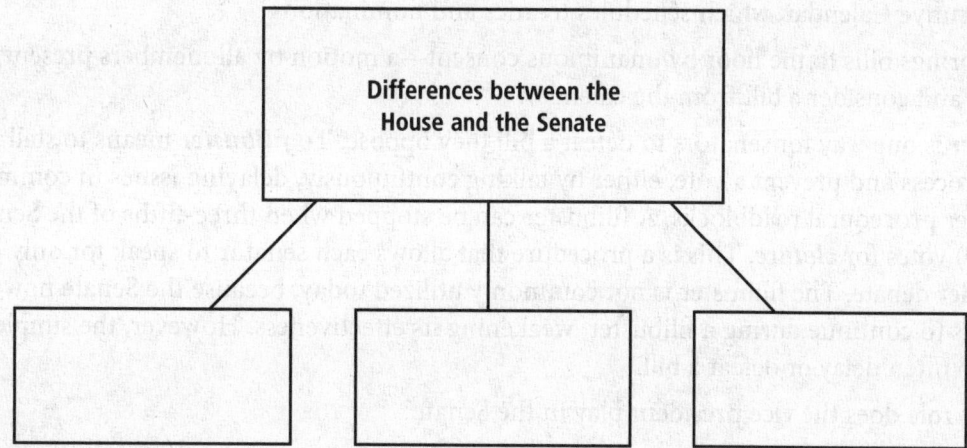

Differences between the House and the Senate

STUDY GUIDE (continued)   Chapter 5, Section 3

README TO LEARN

⊙ **Introduction** (page 138)

Senators handle specific issues in their committees but also deal with many other issues on the floor.

⊙ **The Senate at Work** (page 138)

The Senate usually allows unlimited debate on proposed legislation. Members may debate an issue on and off for weeks or months before taking action. The atmosphere is less formal than in the House because Senate rules are fewer.

The vice president presides in the Senate and may vote to break a tie. The vice president does not take part in debates but may try to influence senators through personal contact. In the absence of the vice president, the president pro tempore presides. The Senate elects this leader, who is from the majority party and is often its senior member.

Majority and minority leaders are the most important officers in the Senate. They are elected by the members of their parties. The main job of the majority leader is to steer the party's bills through the Senate. To do this, the majority leader plans the Senate's work schedule and agenda with the advice of the minority leader. The majority leader also encourages certain majority party members to attend important Senate sessions and to organize support for key bills. The minority leader develops criticism of the majority party's bills and tries to keep senators in the minority party working together. As in the House, whips and assistant whips help the leaders by making sure legislators are present for key votes.

Senate bills can be introduced by any member of the senate. Senate leaders control the flow of bills to committees and to the floor by consulting closely with one another and with other senators. The Senate has only two calendars:

A. The Calendar of General Orders, which lists all the bills the Senate will consider

B. The Executive Calendar, which schedules treaties and nominations

The Senate brings bills to the floor by unanimous consent—a motion by all members present to set aside formal rules and consider a bill from the calendar.

The filibuster is one way for senators to defeat a bill they oppose. To *filibuster* means to stall the legislative process and prevent a vote, either by talking continuously, delaying issues in committee, or using other procedural roadblocks. A filibuster can be stopped when three-fifths of the Senate (60 Senators) votes for *cloture*. This is a procedure that allows each senator to speak for only one hour on a bill under debate. The filibuster is not commonly utilized today, because the Senate now allows other matters to continue during a filibuster, weakening its effectiveness. However, the simple threat of filibuster can often delay or defeat a bill.

   1. What role does the vice president play in the Senate?

   _____

   _____

STUDY GUIDE  Chapter 5, Section 4

For use with textbook pages 141–145.

CONGRESSIONAL COMMITTEES

CONTENT VOCABULARY

standing committee A permanent committee in Congress that oversees bills that deal with certain kinds of issues *(page 142)*

subcommittee A group within a standing committee that specializes in a subcategory of its standing committee's responsibility *(page 142)*

select committee A temporary committee formed to study one specific issue and report its findings to the Senate or the House *(page 143)*

joint committee A committee of the House and Senate that usually acts as a study group and reports its findings back to the House and the Senate *(page 143)*

conference committee A temporary joint committee set up when the House and the Senate have passed different versions of a bill *(page 144)*

seniority system A system that gives the member of the majority party with the longest uninterrupted service on a particular committee the leadership of that committee *(page 145)*

DRAWING FROM EXPERIENCE

Have you ever helped with a school dance? Then you know that the work is divided among committees, such as the decoration and refreshment committees. Congress divides its work among committees, too.

This section focuses on the kinds of committees in Congress.

READING STRATEGIES

Use the graphic organizer below to help you take notes about the different types of congressional committees.

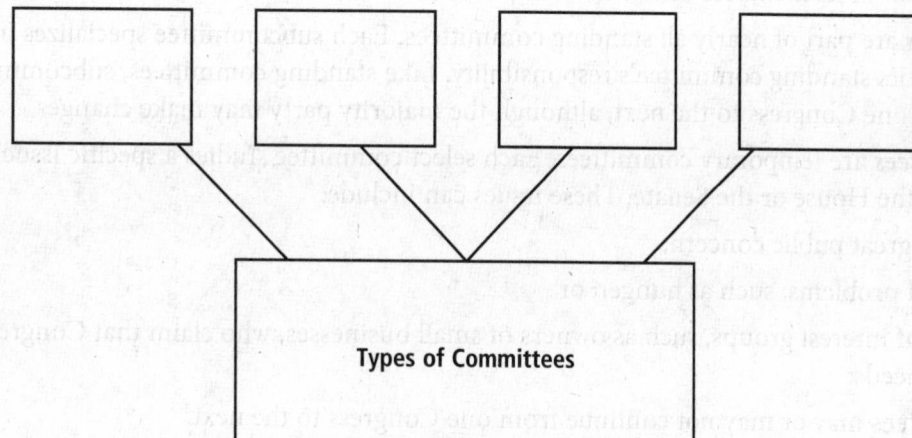

Types of Committees

STUDY GUIDE (continued)   Chapter 5, Section 4

READ TO LEARN

◉ **Introduction** (page 141)

Much of the daily work of considering proposed legislation takes place in committees that meet in congressional offices.

◉ **Purposes of Committees** (page 141)

The committee system allows members of Congress to:

A. divide their work among many smaller groups. As a result, lawmakers become specialists on the issues their committees consider.

B. select the few bills from the many introduced in Congress that are to receive further consideration. Lawmakers in committees listen to supporters and opponents of the bills, work out compromises, and decide which bills will or will not have a chance to become laws. Many bills never make it past the committee stage.

C. instruct the public about national problems and issues such as organized crime, the safety of prescription drugs, and hunger in America.

1. What are the three purposes of the committee system?

_____

_____

◉ **Kinds of Committees** (page 142)

Congress has the following kinds of committees:

Standing committees are permanent committees set up to oversee bills that deal with certain kinds of issues. The committees continue from one Congress to the next. The House and Senate each create their own standing committees. The majority party in each house controls the standing committees. It selects a chairperson from among its members. Committee membership in each party is usually divided in direct proportion to each party's strength in the house. However, the party in power will often have a larger proportion of its members on the most important committees.

Subcommittees are part of nearly all standing committees. Each subcommittee specializes in a subcategory of its standing committee's responsibility. Like standing committees, subcommittees usually continue from one Congress to the next, although the majority party may make changes.

Select committees are temporary committees. Each select committee studies a specific issue and reports its findings to the House or the Senate. These issues can include:

A. matters of great public concern;

B. overlooked problems, such as hunger; or

C. problems of interest groups, such as owners of small businesses, who claim that Congress has not met their needs.

Select committees may or may not continue from one Congress to the next.

Joint committees are made up of members from both the House and the Senate. They may be permanent or temporary. These committees usually act as study groups with responsibility for reporting their findings back to the House and Senate. Joint committees do not have the authority to deal directly with bills or to propose legislation to the Congress.

Conference committees are temporary committees set up when the House and Senate have passed different versions of the same bill. Members of a conference committee, called conferees, usually come from the standing committees that handled the bill in question. The job of the committee is to resolve the differences between the two versions of the bill. The conferees accomplish this by bargaining over each section of the bill. A majority of the conferees from each house must accept the final compromise bill—called a conference report—before it can be sent to the floor of the House and Senate. There it must be accepted or rejected as it comes from the conference committee.

2. How are joint committees and conference committees alike and different?

_____

_____

◉ **Choosing Committee Members** *(page 144)*

The right committee assignment can help a lawmaker in the following ways:

A. By increasing a lawmaker's chances for reelection. For example, a lawmaker might benefit from membership on a committee that deals with bills that help his or her district.

B. By ensuring that the lawmaker will help shape national policy on issues such as education, the budget, and foreign policy.

C. By enabling lawmakers to influence other lawmakers, as a member of the Rules Committee, for instance.

The political parties assign members to the standing committees. However, a lawmaker may request an assignment or a transfer from one committee to another. Each member may only serve on a limited number of committees and subcommittees.

The chairpersons of standing committees decide when their committees will meet, which bills they will consider, and for how long. They also decide when hearings will be held and which witnesses will be called. In addition, they hire committee staff, control the committee budget, and manage the floor debates that take place on the bills from their committee.

Traditionally, the *seniority system* gave the member of the majority party with the longest uninterrupted service on a committee the leadership of that committee. However, in 1995 the House Republicans bypassed several senior members for chairs and ruled that chairpersons of House committees could hold their positions for no more than three consecutive terms.

3. Why are committee chairpersons considered powerful members of Congress?

_____

_____

STUDY GUIDE  Chapter 5, Section 5

For use with textbook pages 146–150.

ⓈTAFF AND SUPPORT AGENCIES

CONTENT VOCABULARY

personal staff The people who work directly for individual representatives and senators *(page 147)*

committee staff The people who work for House and Senate committees *(page 147)*

administrative assistant A member of a lawmaker's personal staff who runs the lawmaker's office, supervises the schedule, and gives advice *(page 148)*

legislative assistant A member of a lawmaker's personal staff who makes certain that the lawmaker is well informed about proposed legislation *(page 148)*

caseworker A member of a lawmaker's personal staff who handles requests for help from constituents *(page 148)*

DRAWING FROM EXPERIENCE

You have probably had school assignments that required a lot of research. Lawmaking requires research, too. It is one of many tasks that staff and support agencies do for lawmakers.

This section focuses on the staff and support agencies that help congressional members.

READING STRATEGIES

Use the graphic organizer below to help you describe the functions of congressional support staff.

Personal Staff	Committee Staff

STUDY GUIDE (continued)   Chapter 5, Section 5

READT TO LEARN

⊙ Introduction (page 146)

Lawmakers and committees need trained staffs to help them do their work effectively. A number of agencies also do important work for members of Congress.

⊙ Congressional Staff Role (page 146)

Lawmakers rely on their staffs to help them handle the growing workload of Congress by communicating with voters, helping to run committee hearings and floor sessions, drafting new bills, writing committee reports, and attending committee meetings. Congressional staffs also help lawmakers get reelected. Staffers get publicity for members of Congress, watch political developments back home, write speeches and newsletters, raise funds for election campaigns, and meet with lobbyists and visitors from home.

1. How do staffs help with the growing workload of Congress?

_____

_____

⊙ Congressional Staff Growth (page 147)

For almost 100 years senators and representatives had practically no aides. After 1946, however, the number of congressional staff members increased dramatically. Why? Lawmaking became more complex after the early 1900s. Lawmakers could not be experts on all the issues that came before their committees or upon which they voted in Congress. Also, constituents increased their demands. Congress members needed large office staffs just to deal with the many letters from the people in their states.

2. Why did the need for office staff increase in the 1900s?

_____

_____

⊙ Personal Staff (page 147)

Personal staff members work directly for individual senators and representatives. **Committee staff** members work for the many House and Senate committees.

The size of senators' staffs vary because the allowances to pay for them are based on the population of the senator's state and distance from the capital. Senators each receive a yearly budget to operate their offices. Most of it is spent on staff salaries. About one-third of the personal staff works in the legislator's home state. The rest work in Washington, D.C. Each member of the House has an allowance to pay for a personal staff. The House and Senate employ thousands of personal staff aides.

An **administrative assistant** (AA) is an aide who runs the lawmaker's office, supervises the lawmaker's schedule, and gives advice on political matters.

A **legislative assistant** (LA) makes certain that the lawmaker is well informed about the many bills with which he or she must deal. The LA does research, drafts bills, studies bills currently in Congress, and writes speeches and articles for the lawmaker. The LA also assists the lawmaker in committee meetings

STUDY GUIDE (continued)   Chapter 5, Section 5

and attends the meetings when the lawmaker cannot be present. LAs also keep track of the work taking place on the floor of Congress, as well as bills that are in committee.

Caseworkers handle the many requests from people in a lawmaker's state or congressional district. They staff offices in key cities of the lawmaker's state and in Washington, D.C.

3. Which kind of personal staff member do you think is most important? Explain your answer.

_____

_____

◉ Committee Staff *(page 149)*

Committee staff members draft bills, study issues, collect information, plan committee hearings, write memos, and prepare committee reports. Some senior committee staff members are very experienced in the area their committee covers, whether it be tax policy, foreign affairs, or health care.

4. What lawmaking responsibilities do committee staffers help with?

_____

_____

◉ Support Agencies *(page 149)*

Congress has created the following important support agencies:

The Library of Congress was created in 1800. The Library has a Congressional Research Service (CRS) with hundreds of employees. Members of Congress use the CRS to answer requests for information from voters and for research on matters related to bills.

The Congressional Budget Office (CBO) was created in 1974. It coordinates the budget-making work of Congress, studies the budget proposals put forward by the president each year, and makes cost projections of proposed new programs. CBO staff members also study economic trends, keep track of how much congressional committees are pending, and prepare a report on the budget each April.

The Government Accountability Office (GAO) was established in 1921. The staffers of the GAO review the financial management of government programs, collect government debts, settle claims, and provide legal service. Many GAO staffers answer requests for information about specific programs from lawmakers and congressional committees.

The Government Printing Office does the printing for the entire federal government. Every day it prints the *Congressional Record*—a record of all the bills introduced in both houses and of the speeches and the testimony presented in Congress. Another valuable publication of the GPO is the *Statistical Abstract of the United States*. It provides statistical information about population, government finances, personal income, business, agriculture, education, law enforcement, national defense, elections, and many other topics.

5. Which support agency helps lawmakers prove that they have supported certain issues? Explain your answer.

_____

_____

STUDY GUIDE  Chapter 6, Section 1

For use with textbook pages 157–165.

CONSTITUTIONAL POWERS

CONTENT VOCABULARY

expressed powers Powers directly stated in the Constitution *(page 157)*

necessary and proper clause Article I, Section 8, of the Constitution, which gives Congress the power to make all laws that are necessary and proper for carrying out its duties *(page 157)*

implied powers Powers that the government requires to carry out the expressed powers *(page 157)*

revenue bill A law proposed to raise money *(page 158)*

appropriations bill A proposed law to authorize spending money *(page 160)*

interstate commerce Trade among the states *(page 161)*

impeachment A formal accusation of misconduct in office against a public official *(page 164)*

DRAWING FROM EXPERIENCE

Do you play baseball or basketball? If you do, then you know that the rules of the game spell out what players can and cannot do. In a similar way, the Constitution states what Congress can and cannot do.

READING STRATEGIES

Use the graphic organizer below to help you list the powers denied Congress by the Constitution.

Congress cannot . . .

STUDY GUIDE (continued)   Chapter 6, Section 1

READ TO LEARN

◉ Introduction *(page 157)*

The Framers of the Constitution intended for Congress to play a central role in governing the nation. That role has developed and changed over time.

◉ Constitutional Provisions *(page 157)*

The Constitution describes the *expressed powers* of Congress in Article I, Section 8, Clauses 1–18. The last clause of Section 8 gives Congress the power to do whatever is "necessary and proper" to carry out its other powers. This *necessary and proper clause* implies that Congress has powers beyond those listed in the first 17 clauses. Because these *implied powers* have allowed Congress to expand its role to meet the needs of the nation, the necessary and proper clause has been called the elastic clause.

The Supreme Court has often been the site of conflict over what is "necessary and proper." For example, those who believe in the "strict construction," or interpretation, of the Constitution, opposed Congress when it created the Second Bank of the United States in 1816. They believed that Congress did not have the power to charter such a bank. The Court supported the "loose constructionists" in Congress who argued that the necessary and proper clause gave them the power to set up the bank.

The Bill of Rights and other parts of the Constitution deny several powers to Congress. Congress may not:

A. suspend the **writ of habeas corpus**—a court order to release a person accused of a crime to determine whether he or she has been illegally detained.

B. pass **bills of attainder**—laws that establish guilt and punish people without allowing them a trial.

C. pass **ex post facto laws**—laws that make crimes of acts that were legal when they were committed.

D. tax exports.

   1. How do expressed powers differ from implied powers?

_____

_____

◉ Legislative Powers *(page 158)*

Congress has expanded its control of the economy by passing laws that involve taxing, spending, and regulating commerce, or trade.

The power to tax and spend allows Congress to influence national policy because no government agency can spend money without congressional authorization. *Revenue bills*—laws for raising money—start in the House and then go to the Senate. Most *appropriation bills*—proposed laws to authorize spending— are requests from the executive branch. Over the years Congress has used its taxing and spending authority to expand its powers to regulate spending. Congress often requires that local officials follow federal regulations as a condition of receiving federal money. Another tactic is to tax products such as cigarettes to discourage their use. Cutting or increasing taxes also helps Congress to control the economy.

Another money power of Congress is borrowing. The most common way for the United States to borrow money is by selling savings bonds, Treasury bills, or Treasury notes. Congress also has the power to coin money and regulate its value. Congress can also punish counterfeiters—people who print postage

STUDY GUIDE (continued)   Chapter 6, Section 1

stamps, paper money, or government securities illegally; to establish a system of weights and measures; and to make laws concerning bankruptcy—when a person cannot pay his or her debts.

The commerce power is given to Congress in Article I, Section 8, Clause 3 of the Constitution. It authorizes Congress to regulate foreign commerce and *interstate commerce,* or trade among the states. The Supreme Court has expanded this power by ruling that commerce goes beyond just buying and selling goods and services. According to Court rulings, broadcasting, banking and finance, air and water pollution, and civil rights come under the "commerce" heading. Congress itself has expanded its power over interstate commerce to include the power to regulate working conditions.

Foreign policy powers of Congress include the power to approve treaties, to declare war, to create and maintain an army and a navy, to make rules governing land and naval forces, and to regulate foreign commerce. Congress shares foreign policy and national defense responsibilities with the president.

The Constitution puts Congress in charge of *naturalization*—the process by which immigrants become citizens. Congress is also authorized to admit states and pass laws to govern territories, military bases, national parks, and historic sites.

Other legislative powers of Congress include the granting of *copyrights*—the exclusive right to publish and sell a literary, musical, or artistic work—and *patents*—the exclusive right of an inventor to manufacture, use, and sell his or her invention.

2. Name three activities covered by the commerce power of Congress.

_____

_____

_____

◉ Non legislative Powers *(page 163)*

Most non legislative powers of Congress require that the House and Senate work together, yet each usually performs a different function:

A. The House chooses a president from the three candidates with the most electoral votes if no candidate for president has a majority of the electoral votes. The Senate chooses the vice president.

B. Both houses of Congress must confirm the appointment when a president appoints a replacement for a vacancy in the office of vice president.

C. The House has the power of *impeachment*—a formal accusation of misconduct in office. A two-thirds vote of the Senators present is required for conviction and removal.

D. The Senate has the power to approve presidential appointments to federal office.

E. The Senate has the power to ratify treaties between the United States and other nations.

F. Amendments to the Constitution may be proposed by two-thirds vote of both houses.

3. Which powers can the Senate carry out with no involvement from the House?

_____

_____

STUDY GUIDE  Chapter 6, Section 2

For use with textbook pages 167–171.

INVESTIGATIONS AND OVERSIGHT

CONTENT VOCABULARY

subpoena A legal order that a person appear or produce requested documents *(page 168)*

perjury Lying under oath *(page 168)*

contempt Willful obstruction of justice *(page 168)*

immunity Freedom from prosecution for witnesses whose testimony ties them to illegal acts *(page 169)*

legislative veto Device that gave Congress ability to review and cancel actions of executive agencies; ruled unconstitutional in 1983 *(page 170)*

DRAWING FROM EXPERIENCE

Imagine finding that your collection of baseball cards is missing. How would you go about finding the cards? You might ask people what they know about their disappearance. In a similar way, when Congress has a problem, it conducts an investigation and asks witnesses what they know.

This section focuses on two powers of Congress not mentioned in the Constitution.

READING STRATEGIES

Use the graphic organizer below to list the possible results of congressional investigations.

CAUSE		EFFECTS
Congress conducts an investigation.	→	1. 2. 3. 4.

READ TO LEARN

◉ Introduction *(page 167)*

Congress has developed the powers of investigation and oversight, not mentioned in the Constitution.

◉ The Power to Investigate *(page 167)*

A standing or select committee may conduct investigations. The committee's staff members collect evidence and schedule witnesses. Dozens of witnesses may be called to testify, sometimes under oath, at committee hearings. Congressional investigations occur for many reasons. The first in 1792 was an investigation of the military. More recently, Congress has investigated charges against its own members.

STUDY GUIDE (continued) Chapter 6, Section 2

Investigations may lead to new legislation to deal with a problem, changes in a government program, or removal of officials from office. Sometimes they damage the reputations of innocent people.

Congressional investigations are not trials. However, like courts, a congressional committee has the power to issue a *subpoena*—a legal order that a person appear or produce requested evidence. Also like courts, congressional committees require witnesses to testify under oath. If witnesses for a committee lie under oath, they can be tried for *perjury.* Committees can punish witnesses who refuse to testify by holding them in *contempt,* or willful obstruction, of Congress. Those held in contempt may be arrested and jailed.

The Supreme Court has ruled that Congress must respect witnesses' constitutional rights, including the Fifth Amendment right not to testify against oneself. Congress has sidestepped this requirement by offering witnesses *immunity,* or freedom from prosecution for witnesses whose testimony ties them to illegal acts. Witnesses with immunity can be forced to testify against themselves. If they refuse, they can be held in contempt.

1. How are congressional investigations like trials?

_____

_____

◉ Legislative Oversight (page 169)

Many congressional investigations are related to the power of legislative oversight. This involves a continuing review of how effectively the executive branch carries out the laws Congress passes. Through its power of legislative oversight, Congress places a check on the executive branch and its agencies.

However, Congress does not continually watch the agencies of the executive branch because:

A. lawmakers do not have enough staff, time, or money to keep track of everything in the executive branch.

B. lawmakers know that voters and the news media are seldom interested in oversight activities unless an investigation turns up a scandal or unusual problem.

C. the language of some laws is so vague that it is difficult to tell exactly what they mean.

D. committees sometimes come to favor the federal agencies they are supposed to oversee.

One way Congress exercises its oversight power is by requiring executive agencies to report on their activities to Congress. Another way is for lawmakers to ask a congressional support agency, such as the General Accounting Office, to study an executive agency's work. The power of Congress to appropriate money is another means of oversight. Each year the House and the Senate review the budgets of all agencies in the executive branch. For years Congress used the *legislative veto* to cancel actions of executive agencies. However, the Supreme Court ruled this practice unconstitutional in 1983.

A final means of oversight is the independent counsel law. It authorizes the House or the Senate judiciary committee to require the attorney general to investigate charges of criminal wrong doing by top officials.

2. List four ways that Congress exercises its power of legislative oversight.

_____

_____

STUDY GUIDE  Chapter 6, Section 3

For use with textbook pages 172–176.

CONGRESS AND THE PRESIDENT

CONTENT VOCABULARY

national budget The yearly financial plan for the national government *(page 175)*

impoundment The president's refusal to spend money Congress has voted to fund a program *(page 175)*

DRAWING FROM EXPERIENCE

Do you ever disagree with a friend about what to do? What happens when neither of you gives in? The answer is "nothing happens," or in other words, gridlock. The government can also experience gridlock when the president and Congress disagree.

This section focuses on dealings between the Congress and the president.

READING STRATEGIES

Use the graphic organizer below to help you take notes on how the 1974 Congressional Budget and Impoundment Control Act affected the president's power.

CAUSE	EFFECT
Congress passed the Congressional Budget and Impoundment Control Act.	

STUDY GUIDE (continued)   Chapter 6, Section 3

READ TO LEARN

◉ Introduction (page 172)

The Constitution's system of checks and balances can result in a stalemate. Many of the president's responsibilities, such as treaty making, require congressional cooperation. When Congress refuses to cooperate, the president is frustrated. On the other hand, all bills Congress passes need the president's signature to become law. When a president refuses to sign, two-thirds of the members in each house must vote to override the veto.

◉ Cooperation and Conflict (page 172)

Presidents have found working with Congress difficult for the following reasons:

Constituents Members of Congress represent voters from a specific area. The president represents all Americans. As a result, members of Congress often differ with the president about what public policies are needed.

Checks and Balances The system of checks and balances gives Congress and the president the power to counteract each other.

Party Politics Political differences affect the relationship between the president and Congress when different parties control the White House and Congress. For example, gridlock occurred in 1996 when Democratic President Clinton disagreed with Republican majorities in both houses.

Organization Rules of procedure in Congress can be used to block legislation that the president supports. Conflicts also occur when the president wants a bill approved and a committee tries to delay, revise, or defeat it.

Different Political Timetables Presidents have little more than three years to develop, present, and move their programs through Congress before they must start running for reelection. At best, presidents get eight years to accomplish anything. Senators and representatives are not limited to two terms as is the president. Most look forward to reelection and do not want to act on legislation that may hurt their chances.

1. When might party politics cause gridlock in government?

_____

_____

◉ The Struggle for Power (page 174)

Presidents increased presidential powers as they dealt with changing social, political, and economic conditions. Congress tried to regain lost power and gain new influence in the following ways:

A. Congress gave President Franklin Roosevelt emergency powers to deal with the Depression and World War II. Later presidents continued exercising these powers until Congress passed the National Emergency Act, ending the 35-year state of emergency in 1976. Now presidents must notify Congress when they intend to declare a state of emergency. The state of emergency cannot last more than one year unless the president repeats the process. Also, Congress may end the state of emergency at any time by passing legislation.

STUDY GUIDE (continued)   Chapter 6, Section 3

B. Presidents assumed the responsibility for planning the national budget—the yearly financial plan for the national government. Then in 1974 Congress increased congressional involvement in the budget by passing the Congressional Budget and Impoundment Act. This act established a permanent budget committee in each house and created a Congressional Budget Office. The act also limited the president's power to impound funds. Impoundment is the president's refusal to spend money Congress has voted to fund a program. The law requires that the funds must be spent unless the president requests and both houses of Congress agree that the money not be spent.

C. Congress has argued that the legislative veto was an important check on the executive branch. Since the Supreme Court ruled against the veto, Congress has been searching for a constitutional way to exercise the same power.

D. The Constitution provides for a presidential veto of entire bills. Many presidents have asked Congress for a line-item veto, enabling them to veto only certain items in a bill. In 1996 President Clinton signed into law the Line Item Veto Act. However, some members of Congress challenged the law in federal court. In 1998 the Supreme Court ruled that the law was unconstitutional.

2. What are the provisions of the National Emergency Act?

_____

_____

STUDY GUIDE  Chapter 7, Section 1

For use with textbook pages 181–188.

HOW A BILL BECOMES A LAW

CONTENT VOCABULARY

private bill A bill dealing with an individual person or place *(page 181)*

public bill A bill dealing with general matters and applying to the entire nation *(page 182)*

simple resolution A statement adopted to cover matters affecting only one house of Congress *(page 182)*

rider A provision included in a bill on a subject other than the one covered in the bill *(page 183)*

hearing A session at which a committee listens to testimony from people interested in the bill *(page 184)*

veto Rejection of a bill *(page 187)*

pocket veto When a president kills a bill passed during the last ten days Congress is in session by simply refusing to act on it *(page 187)*

DRAWING FROM EXPERIENCE

Have you ever built a model? If so, you know the process involves several steps: assembling, gluing, sanding, and painting. Making a law requires even more steps.

This section focuses on how Congress makes laws.

READING STRATEGIES

Use the flowchart below to help you analyze the major steps by which a bill becomes law.

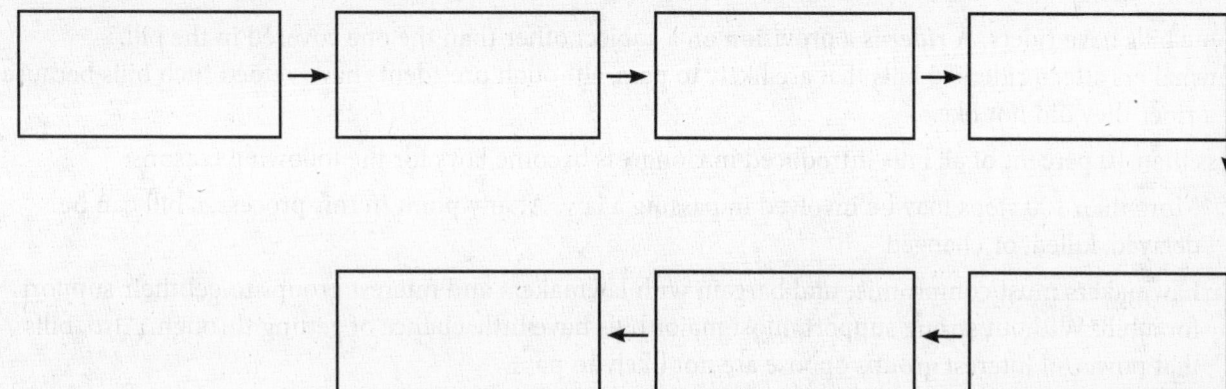

STUDY GUIDE (continued)   Chapter 7, Section 1

READnal TO LEARN

◉ **Introduction** (page 181)

Of the thousands of bills introduced in each session, only a few hundred become laws. Most die in Congress, and some are rejected by the president. If a bill does not pass before the end of a congressional term, it must be reintroduced in the next Congress.

◉ **Types of Bills and Resolutions** (page 181)

Members of Congress introduce the following types of bills:

Private bills deal with individual people or places. They often involve people's claims against the government or their immigration problems. Today private bills account for only a small number of the bills introduced in Congress.

Public bills deal with general matters and apply to the entire nation. They may involve major issues such as raising or lowering taxes, national health insurance, gun control, civil rights, or abortion. Major public bills may be debated for months before they become law.

Congress may also pass the following types of resolutions:

A. A *simple resolution* covers matters affecting only one house of Congress and is passed by that house alone. If a new rule or precedent is needed, it is adopted in the form of a resolution. It is not a law and does not need to be signed by the president.

B. A joint resolution is passed by both houses, requires the president's signature, and has the force of law. A joint resolution may correct an error in an earlier law or appropriate money for a special purpose. When a joint resolution is used to propose a constitutional amendment, it does need the president's signature.

C. Concurrent resolutions cover matters requiring the action of both the House and Senate but on which a law is not needed. For example, a concurrent resolution may set the date for the adjournment of Congress. It does not require the president's signature and is not a law.

Some bills have riders. A *rider* is a provision on a subject other than the one covered in the bill. Lawmakers attach riders to bills that are likely to pass, although presidents have vetoed such bills because of a rider they did not like.

Less than 10 percent of all bills introduced in Congress become laws for the following reasons:

A. More than 100 steps may be involved in passing a law. At any point in this process, a bill can be delayed, killed, or changed.

B. Lawmakers must compromise and bargain with lawmakers and interest groups to get their support for a bill. Without strong support, most major bills have little chance of getting through. Also, bills that powerful interest groups oppose are not likely to pass.

C. Lawmakers sometimes introduce bills they know have no chance of passing. Members of Congress do this to go on record in support of an idea or policy or to attract the attention of the news media. When the bills fail, they can blame a committee or other lawmakers.

STUDY GUIDE (continued)   Chapter 7, Section 1

1. How does a simple resolution differ from a law?

_____

_____

◉ Introducing a Bill (page 183)

The Constitution sets forth a few of the steps a bill must go through to become law. The other steps have developed over the years as Congress and the number of bills have grown.

How Bills Are Introduced The ideas for new bills can come from private citizens, interest groups, the president, or officials in the executive branch. However, only a member of Congress can introduce a bill. In the House, a representative drops the bill into a hopper—a box near the clerk's desk. In the Senate, the presiding officer must first recognize the senator who then presents the bill. Each bill is given a title and a number, printed, and distributed to lawmakers. This process is the first reading of the bill.

Committee Action A new bill is sent to the committee that deals with the subject matter of the bill. The committee chairperson may send the bill to a subcommittee, or the committee can ignore the bill and let it die. This is called "*pigeonholing*." The committee can also kill the bill by a majority vote. If the committee accepts the bill, it can recommend that the bill be adopted as introduced, make changes, or completely rewrite the bill before sending it back to the House or Senate for further action.

Committee Hearings When a committee decides to act on a bill, the committee or subcommittee can hold hearings on the bill. *Hearings* are sessions at which a committee listens to testimony from people interested in the bill. Hearings are supposed to be an opportunity for Congress to gather information on the bill. Skilled chairpersons use them to influence public opinion for or against the bill. Hearings also help focus public attention on a problem. Hearings are also the best point in the lawmaking process for citizens to send letters, telegrams, and e-mails supporting or opposing the bill. Many committees use the Internet to set up interactive hearings with experts outside of Washington, D.C. They can also use the Internet to broadcast hearings, and to make committee reports, documents, and other information publicly available. After hearings, the committee meets in a *markup session* to decide on changes to the bill. A majority vote is required for all changes.

Reporting a Bill After all changes are made, the committee votes to kill the bill or report it. To report the bill means to send it to the House or Senate for action. Along with the revised bill, the committee sends a report by the committee staff. The report explains the committee's actions, describes the bill, lists the major changes, and gives opinions on the bill.

2. What courses of action can a committee take on a new bill?

_____

_____

◉ Floor Action (page 186)

Debating and Amending Bills Only a few lawmakers take part in floor debates. During the floor debate, the bill receives its second reading—a clerk reads the bill section by section. After each section is read, amendments may be offered. Amendments range from the introduction of major changes in a bill to the correction of typographical errors. In both the House and Senate, amendments are added to a bill only if a majority of the members present approves them.

STUDY GUIDE (continued) Chapter 7, Section 1

Voting on Bills After the floor debate, the bill, including any proposed changes, is ready for a vote. A quorum, or majority of the members, must be present. The House or Senate now receives a third reading of the bill. A vote on the bill is taken. Passage of a bill requires a majority of all the members present. House and Senate members can vote on a bill in three ways: a *voice vote*, in which members together call out "Aye" or "No"; a *standing vote* or *division vote*, in which those in favor and then those against stand and are counted; and the *roll-call vote*, in which everyone responds "Aye" or "No" as their names are called. The House can also record members' votes electronically, called a recorded vote.

3. What happens during a floor debate?

_____

_____

◉ Final Steps in Passing Bills *(page 186)*

To become a law, a bill must pass both houses of Congress in identical form. A bill passed in the House often differs at first from a Senate's bill on the same subject.

Conference Committee Action If one house will not accept the version of a bill the other house has passed, a conference committee made up of senators and representatives must work out differences between the versions. The members of the conference committee, called conferees, usually come from the committees that handled the bill originally. A majority of the conferees from each house drafts the compromise bill, called a *conference report*. Once accepted, it is sent to each house of Congress for final action.

Presidential Action on Bills After both houses of Congress approve a bill in identical form, it is sent to the president. The president may:

A. sign the bill, and it becomes law.

B. keep the bill for ten days without signing. If Congress is in session, the bill will become law without the president's signature.

C. veto a bill. In a *veto,* the president refuses to sign the bill and returns it to the house of Congress in which it started.

D. kill a bill passed during the last ten days Congress is in session by refusing to act on it. This is called a *pocket veto.*

Line-Item Veto This allows a leader to reject specific parts of a bill while accepting the main body of the legislation. In 1996, Congress passed a bill that gave the president a line-item veto for spending and tax issues. President Clinton used the line-item veto in 1997 to cancel a provision in an act for increased Medicaid funding to New York state hospitals. New York City challenged the line-item veto in court. As a result, the Supreme Court ruled the line-item veto unconstitutional in 1998.

Registering Laws After a bill becomes law, it is registered with the National Archives and Records Service. The law is labeled as public or private and assigned a number that identifies the Congress that passed the bill and the number of the law for that term. The law is then added to the United States Code of current federal laws. An online information resource called THOMAS also provides access to current information about all legislation being considered by Congress. THOMAS helps to open up the complicated lawmaking process to individual citizens.

4. Explain the ways a president can kill a bill.

_____

_____

STUDY GUIDE  Chapter 7, Section 2

For use with textbook pages 189–192.

Taxing and Spending Bills

CONTENT VOCABULARY

tax The money that people and businesses pay to support the activities of the government *(page 189)*

closed rule A rule that forbids members of Congress to offer amendments to bills from the floor *(page 190)*

appropriation Approval of government spending *(page 191)*

authorization bill A bill that sets up a federal program and specifies how much money may be appropriated for the program *(page 191)*

entitlement A required government expenditure that continues from one year to the next *(page 192)*

DRAWING FROM EXPERIENCE

Where do you get the money you spend? Most likely, you receive an allowance or earn money from a part-time job. The government gets most of the money it spends from taxing people and businesses.

This section focuses on bills that involve taxing and spending.

READING STRATEGIES

Use the Venn diagram below to show the roles of the House and Senate in making and passing tax laws.

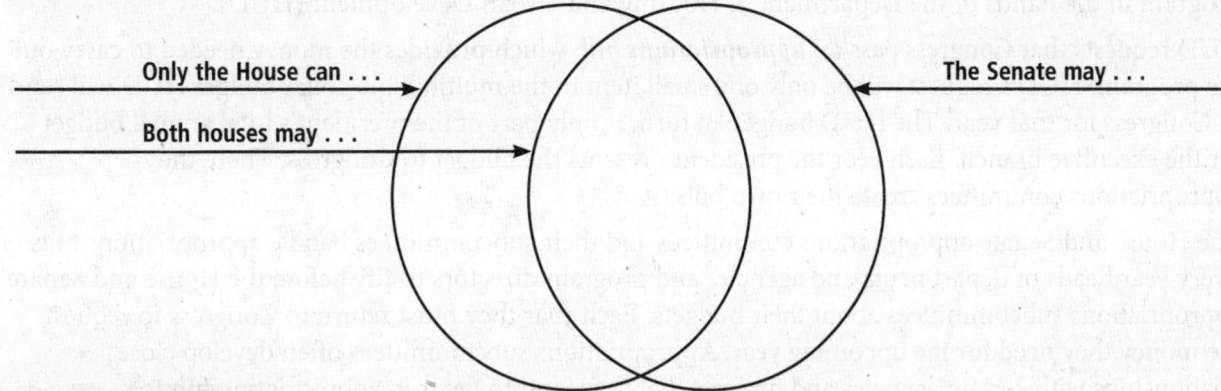

Only the House can . . .

Both houses may . . .

The Senate may . . .

READ TO LEARN

● **Introduction** *(page 189)*

The government could not operate without money to carry out its many programs and services.

Copyright © Glencoe/McGraw-Hill, a division of The McGraw-Hill Companies, Inc.

╔══╗

STUDY GUIDE (continued) Chapter 7, Section 2

╚══╝

◉ Making Decisions About Taxes *(page 189)*

The national government gets most of the money it spends from taxes. *Taxes* are money that people and businesses pay to support the government.

According to the Constitution, only the House of Representatives can start revenue, or tax, bills. Almost all important work on tax bills occurs in the House Ways and Means Committee. This committee decides whether to go along with presidential requests for tax cuts or increases. It also makes the rules that determine who will pay how much tax. For many years the committee's tax bills were debated on the House floor under a *closed rule.* The rule stopped members from offering any amendments to a bill from the floor. This meant that only the Ways and Means Committee could have any say in writing a tax bill. In 1973 the House allowed members to amend tax bills from the floor. Critics complained that tax bills became collections of amendments written to please special interests.

The Constitution allows the Senate to change tax bills. The Senate Committee on Finance has the main responsibility for tax matters. As a result, the chairperson of the Committee on Finance is very powerful.

1. Describe the advantages and disadvantages of the closed rule in the House of Representatives.

_____

_____

◉ Appropriating Money *(page 191)*

The Constitution gives Congress the power of *appropriation,* or approval of government spending. Congress appropriates money in two steps:

An *authorization bill* sets up a federal program and specifies how much money may be spent on the program. For example, it may limit spending for inner city recreation to $30 million a year and place the program in the hands of the Department of Housing and Urban Development (HUD).

HUD requests that Congress pass an *appropriations bill,* which provides the money needed to carry out the program. HUD's request will be only one small item in the multibillion-dollar budget HUD will send to Congress for that year. The HUD budget, in turn, is only part of the president's total annual budget for the executive branch. Each year the president presents the budget to Congress. There the appropriations committees create their own bills.

The House and Senate appropriations committees and their subcommittees handle appropriations bills. Every year heads of departments and agencies and program directors testify before the House and Senate appropriations subcommittees about their budgets. Each year they must return to Congress to request the money they need for the upcoming year. Appropriations subcommittees often develop close relationships with certain agencies and projects that they tend to favor in appropriating funds.

About 70 percent of the money that the federal government spends each year is already committed to certain uses. Therefore, appropriations committees do not control these funds. Examples of required spending are Social Security payments and interest on the national debt. Some of these expenditures are known as *entitlements* because they are social programs that continue from one year to the next.

2. Briefly describe the two steps Congress follows in appropriating money.

_____

_____

STUDY GUIDE  Chapter 7, Section 3

For use with textbook pages 194–198.

INFLUENCING CONGRESS

CONTENT VOCABULARY

lobbyist An interest group representative *(page 198)*

lobbying Direct contact made by lobbyists in order to persuade government officials to support the policies their interest group favors *(page 198)*

DRAWING FROM EXPERIENCE

Have you ever been undecided about something? Did anyone—a parent or a friend, perhaps—try to get you to decide a certain way? In a similar manner, many people try to influence the decisions of Congress.

This section focuses on the individuals and groups who try to influence Congress.

READING STRATEGIES

Use the graphic organizer below to list the different influences on lawmakers in Congress.

Influences on
Congress

STUDY GUIDE (continued) Chapter 7, Section 3

READxTO LEARN

⊙ **Introduction** *(page 194)*

Members of Congress influence the direction of government policies and help shape the public's view of a particular bill or issue. But who influences the lawmakers?

⊙ **Influences on Lawmakers** *(page 194)*

Influences on lawmakers include:

Their personalities Some are more willing than others to make risky choices.

The issues themselves A lawmaker may pay close attention to the desires of people back home in dealing with a controversial issue such as gun control. However, if the issue has little effect on voters back home, a lawmaker is more likely to follow his own beliefs or the advice and opinions of other lawmakers.

Congressional staff members They control the information on which lawmakers base their decisions. They also set the agenda for individual lawmakers and for congressional committees that may favor a certain point of view.

   1. How do staff members influence lawmakers?

_____

_____

⊙ **The Influence of Voters** *(page 195)*

Voters want their lawmakers to follow constituents' wishes on the issues and enact laws that reflect their needs and opinions. In an election campaign, the candidate from the other party and opposing interest groups may demand that the lawmaker explain votes that turned out to be unpopular back home. A legislator running for reelection may also call attention to his or her votes on certain measures to attract constituents' support.

To keep track of their constituents' opinions, most lawmakers use the following methods:

A. Make frequent trips home to learn about local concerns

B. Have staff members screen messages from home to learn what concerns voters (personal letters are considered the most important form of communication; e-mail is ranked low)

C. Send questionnaires to their constituents

D. Hire professional pollsters to conduct opinion surveys

E. Pay close attention to campaign workers and contributors

   2. How do voters who do not follow the day-to-day workings of the Congress find out about their representatives' voting record?

_____

_____

◉ The Influence of Parties (page 196)

Political party membership is one of the most important influences on a lawmaker's voting behavior. Party voting is much stronger on some issues than on others. On issues relating to government intervention in the economy, party members tend to vote the same way. Party voting is much weaker on foreign policy issues because the two parties often do not have fixed positions on international questions.

Party members are likely to share the same general beliefs about public policy. For example, Democrats are more likely than Republicans to favor social-welfare programs. Republicans are more likely to favor lower taxes and less government intervention in the economy. Another reason for party voting is that most lawmakers do not have strong opinions about every issue and rely on the other lawmakers in their party for advice.

On some issues, party leaders pressure members to vote the party position.

3. On what kinds of issues are party members most likely to vote with their party?

_____

_____

◉ Other Influences on Congress (page 197)

Two other influences on lawmakers are:

The president tries to influence Congress to pass laws that he and his party support. Presidents can appear on television to try to influence public opinion and put pressure on Congress. Presidents may also give or withhold favors and support in return for lawmakers' cooperation.

Interest groups have their representatives, or ***lobbyists,*** try to persuade lawmakers to support certain policies. The work these representatives do is called ***lobbying.*** Lobbyists represent a wide variety of interests, such as business organizations, labor unions, education groups, minority groups, and environmental organizations. Lobbyists try to influence lawmakers by:

A. providing information about policies they support or oppose,

B. visiting lawmakers to ask for support, and

C. encouraging citizens to write to members of Congress on the issues they support or oppose.

Interest groups and their lobbyists also focus much of their attention on committees.

Political action committees, known as PACs, are political fund-raising organizations established by corporations, labor unions, and other special-interest groups. They have increased dramatically in recent years. PAC funds come from contributions of company employees, union members, and stockholders. These funds are used to support lawmakers who favor a PAC's positions on issues.

4. In what three ways do lobbyists try to influence lawmakers?

_____

_____

STUDY GUIDE  Chapter 7, Section 4

For use with textbook pages 200–203.

HELPING CONSTITUENTS

DRAWING FROM EXPERIENCE

Have you ever heard the expression "You scratch my back, and I'll scratch yours"? It means that if you do something for someone, that person will do you a favor in return. Many deals in Congress are carried out based on this principle.

This section focuses on how lawmakers and their supporters help each other.

READING STRATEGIES

Use the graphic organizer below to list the purposes of casework.

Purposes of Casework

STUDY GUIDE (continued) Chapter 7, Section 4

READ TO LEARN

◉ Introduction *(page 200)*

To be reelected, legislators must spend much of their time solving problems for voters and making sure their state or district gets its share of federal money and projects.

◉ Handling Problems *(page 200)*

Helping constituents with problems is called *casework.* All lawmakers have staff members called caseworkers. These staffers handle the problems of constituents. When the staffers cannot solve a problem, the lawmaker steps in. Lawmakers spend much of their time on casework for the following reasons:

A. Casework helps lawmakers get reelected. As a result, many lawmakers actually look for casework by encouraging voters to communicate with them.

B. Casework is one way in which Congress oversees the executive branch. Casework brings problems with federal agencies such as Social Security to the attention of congressional members.

C. Casework provides a way for the average citizen to deal with the huge national government.

    1. Why do lawmakers spend time on casework?

_____

_____

◉ Helping the District or State *(page 201)*

Besides providing services to constituents, members of Congress also try to bring federal projects and money to their district or state by:

A. passing laws to appropriate money for local federal projects such as post offices, dams, military bases, harbor and river improvements, federally funded highways, veterans' hospitals, pollution-treatment centers, and mass-transit systems. This is called *pork-barrel legislation.* In order to get federal projects for their areas, lawmakers often agree to support each other's bills. Such agreements are called *logrolling.*

B. winning grants and contracts. These are a vital source of money and jobs that can affect the economy of a state. Agencies of the executive branch award the grants and contracts, so lawmakers try to influence their decisions. They may pressure agency officials to give a favorable hearing to their state's request. They also encourage their constituents to write, call, or e-mail agency officials in order to make their requests for grants and contracts known. Many lawmakers assign one or more of their staff members to act as specialists in contracts and grants. These staffers find out how individuals, businesses, and local governments can qualify for federal money and then help constituents apply.

    2. How can logrolling lead to pork-barrel legislation?

_____

_____

STUDY GUIDE  Chapter 8, Section 1

For use with textbook pages 213–219.

PRESIDENT AND VICE PRESIDENT

CONTENT VOCABULARY

compensation Salary *(page 214)*

presidential succession The order in which officials fill the office of president in case of a vacancy *(page 217)*

DRAWING FROM EXPERIENCE

Think about someone you would be willing to follow. What qualities does he or she possess? Courage? Wisdom? Honesty? These are the kinds of questions voters ask when they choose their president.

This section focuses on the president and vice president of the United States.

READING STRATEGIES

Use the graphic organizer below to list the constitutional requirements for president and vice president.

Constitutional Requirements	
President	**Vice President**

STUDY GUIDE (continued)   Chapter 8, Section 1

READ TO LEARN

⦿ Introduction *(page 213)*

The office of the president has been developing for more than 200 years. The powers of the office have grown along with the nation.

⦿ Duties of the President *(page 213)*

The Constitution gives the president the following duties:

A. overseeing the nation's armed forces as commander in chief,

B. appointing—with the Senate's consent—heads of executive departments, federal court judges, and other top officials,

C. making treaties with the advice and consent of the Senate,

D. meeting with the heads of state and hosting foreign officials,

E. appointing ambassadors to represent the United States in foreign nations,

F. executing the laws of the United States, and

G. delivering a State of the Union address to Congress each year.

The Constitution also gives the president the power to pardon people convicted of federal crimes, except in cases of impeachment. The president may also reduce a person's jail sentence or fine.

1. During the performance of which duty do you think the president proposes policy changes? Explain your answer.

_____

_____

⦿ President's Term and Salary *(page 214)*

George Washington served eight years as president and refused to run for a third term. Other presidents followed his precedent until Franklin Roosevelt ran for third and fourth terms. Concern over too much executive power led Congress to propose and the states to ratify the Twenty-second Amendment in 1951. This amendment limits presidents to two terms. It also allows a vice president who takes over the presidency and serves two years or less of the former president's term to serve two additional terms. Thus, a president may serve up to 10 years.

The Constitution did not specify the amount of **compensation,** or salary, the president would receive. As of 2001, the president receives $400,000 in taxable salary and $50,000 a year for expenses connected with his official duties. The president also receives a nontaxable travel allowance. Other benefits include:

A. the Secret Service, who guard the president and family;

B. the use of *Air Force One,* a specially equipped jet;

C. free medical, dental, and health care; and

D. the White House, which includes a swimming pool, bowling alley, private movie theater, tennis courts, and a domestic staff.

```
STUDY GUIDE (continued)          Chapter 8, Section 1
```

A retired president receives a lifetime pension, free office space, free mailing services, and an allowance to pay office staff.

2. How does the Twenty-second Amendment limit the president of the United States?

_____

_____

◉ Presidential Qualifications *(page 215)*

The Constitution requires that a president or a vice president be:

A. a natural-born citizen of the United States,

B. at least 35 years old, and

C. a resident of the United States for at least 14 years before taking office.

Some informal requirements for presidents are:

A. experience in government,

B. access to large amounts of money to pay for a presidential campaign,

C. moderate positions on most issues,

D. the ability to grow personally.

3. What qualifications for president does the Constitution list?

_____

_____

◉ Presidential Succession *(page 217)*

After the assassination of President Kennedy in 1963, Americans realized that the rules for presidential succession in the Constitution were not enough. So they ratified the Twenty-fifth Amendment in 1967. This amendment establishes the order of succession to the presidency and spells out what happens when the vice presidency becomes vacant. According to the amendment, the vice president becomes president if the president dies or is removed from office. If the office of vice president becomes vacant, the president appoints a vice president. If both the offices of president and vice president become vacant at the same time, the next in line for the presidency is the Speaker of the House. The president *pro tempore* of the Senate is next in line after the Speaker. Next are the cabinet officers, beginning with the secretary of state.

The Twenty-fifth Amendment sets forth these rules to follow when the president becomes disabled:

A. The vice president becomes acting president if the president informs Congress of an inability to perform the office.

B. The vice president becomes acting president if the vice president and a majority of the cabinet or another body authorized by law informs Congress that the president is disabled.

C. The president can resume the powers and duties of office at any time simply by informing Congress that a disability no longer exists. However, the vice president and a majority of the cabinet or other authorized body may insist that the president has not sufficiently recovered to perform properly. Congress must settle the dispute in 21 days or the president can resume office.

4. What is the order of presidential succession if the offices of president and vice president become vacant at the same time?

_____

_____

◉ **The Vice President's Role** (page 218)

The Constitution gives the vice president the following duties:

A. to preside over the Senate and to vote in case of a tie

B. to help decide whether the president is disabled and to act as president should that happen

A vice president's work depends on what responsibilities, if any, the president assigns. Fourteen vice presidents have become president. Of these, nine have succeeded to the office of president when a president died or resigned. Recent presidents have increased their vice presidents' responsibilities. Vice President Richard Cheney consults with President Bush and frequently represents him in meeting with important cabinet members, lawmakers, and foreign dignitaries. He has also led groups developing new policies in key areas such as energy.

5. What determines the work responsibilities of a vice president?

_____

_____

STUDY GUIDE  Chapter 8, Section 2

For use with textbook pages 220–226.

ELECTING THE PRESIDENT

CONTENT VOCABULARY

elector A member of a party chosen in each state to formally elect the president and vice president *(page 220)*

electoral vote The official vote for president and vice president by electors in each state *(page 220)*

DRAWING FROM EXPERIENCE

What determines the winner in an election for class president? The answer probably is a majority of all the votes cast. This is not always true in elections for president of the United States.

This section focuses on how the president is elected.

READING STRATEGIES

Use the graphic organizer below to list the weaknesses of the Electoral College system.

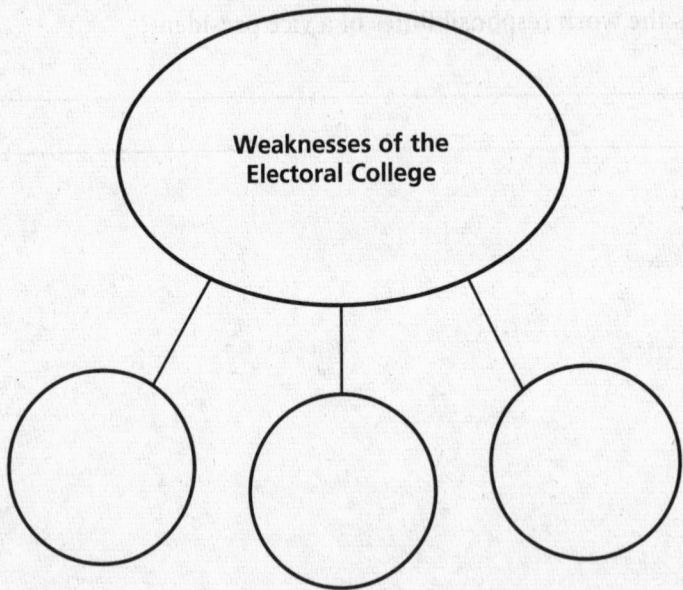

Weaknesses of the Electoral College

STUDY GUIDE (continued)　　Chapter 8, Section 2

READxT TO LEARN

◉ Introduction (page 220)

The Framers of the Constitution came up with more than one way of selecting a president. One idea was that Congress choose the president. Another was that the president be chosen by direct popular vote. The Founders decided on a compromise—an indirect method of election called the Electoral College.

◉ The Original System (page 220)

Article II of the Constitution provided for each state to choose electors by a method the state legislature would set up. Each state would have as many electors as it had senators and representatives. At election time, the electors would meet in their own states and cast votes for president. No popular vote was cast for the early presidential elections. Electoral votes from all the states would be counted in Congress. The candidate with a majority of the votes would become president. The candidate with the second highest number of votes would become vice president. If no one received a majority, the House of Representatives would choose the president or vice president, with each state having one vote. In 1789 and 1792 every elector voted for George Washington as the first president.

    1. How were the first electors in the Electoral College chosen?

_____

_____

◉ The Impact of Political Parties (page 221)

In the presidential election of 1800, the Democratic-Republicans won a majority of the electoral votes, but both their candidates—Thomas Jefferson and Aaron Burr—received 73 votes. The House of Representatives voted 36 times before Jefferson was finally elected president and Burr was elected vice president. To prevent this problem from occurring again, the Twelfth Amendment was added to the Constitution in 1804. It requires that the electors cast separate ballots for president and vice president and that if no candidate receives a majority, the House chooses from the top three candidates. If no candidate for vice president gets a majority of electoral votes, the Senate chooses from the top two candidates for vice president. Since the 1820s, state political parties have chosen electors by popular vote. Parties also began to give the people more of a choice in nominating presidential candidates.

    2. Why was the Twelfth Amendment added to the Constitution?

_____

_____

◉ The Electoral College System Today (page 221)

Parties choose their nominees for president every four years (1996, 2000, 2004, etc.) at conventions held in late summer. Voters cast their ballots for president on the Tuesday after the first Monday in November. The voters actually vote for all of their party's electors in their state. In December these electors will cast the official vote for president and vice president. Thus, a vote for the Democratic candidate is actually a vote for the Democratic electors, and a vote for the Republican candidate is actually a vote for the Republican electors. The Electoral College includes 538 electors—the total of the House and Senate members plus 3 for the District of Columbia. The winning candidate is usually announced on the same evening as the popular election because popular-vote counts indicate who won each state. Most states do not legally require electors to vote for the candidate who wins the popular vote, but electors usually do so.

3. How is the number of electors in the Electoral College determined?

_____

_____

◉ Electoral College Issues (page 223)

Critics point to the three following weaknesses in the Electoral College system:

A. A candidate receives all the state's electoral votes if that person wins the popular vote in a state. The winner-take-all system allows a candidate who loses the popular vote to win the election.

B. A third-party candidate could win enough electoral votes to prevent either major-party candidate from receiving a majority. The third party could then bargain with the major parties.

C. When the House of Representatives must decide an election, each state casts one vote. States with small populations have as much weight as those with large populations. Also, if a majority of representatives cannot agree on a candidate, that state loses its vote. Finally, if some members of the house favor a third-party candidate, no candidate may get the necessary 26 votes.

Critics have proposed the following changes in the Electoral College:

A. Choose electors from congressional districts and add two statewide electors. The candidate winning the most votes in a district would win the electoral vote from that district. The candidate with the most districts in the state would also receive the two statewide electoral votes.

B. Give each candidate the same share of a state's electoral vote as they received of the popular vote. This plan could enlarge the role of third-party candidates and force the election into the House of Representatives.

C. Have the people directly elect the president and vice president. This could rob states of their role in the election. Also, candidates could concentrate their efforts on large cities.

4. Why do some people object to the election of the president by direct popular vote?

_____

_____

◉ Inauguration (page 225)

The new president, called the president-elect until the inauguration, takes office at noon on January 20 following the election. The inaugural ceremony is held outside the Capitol in Washington, D.C., with members of Congress, foreign diplomats, and thousands of citizens attending. The chief justice administers the oath of office, and the new president gives a speech called the Inaugural Address. Then a parade goes from the Capitol to the White House. That evening official parties celebrate the inauguration.

5. When and where does the president-elect take the oath of office?

_____

_____

STUDY GUIDE  Chapter 8 Section 3

For use with textbook pages 228–232.

THE CABINET

CONTENT VOCABULARY

cabinet Secretaries of the executive departments, the vice president, and other top officials that help the president make decisions and policy *(page 228)*

leak The release of secret information by anonymous government officials to the media *(page 230)*

DRAWING FROM EXPERIENCE

Who comes to your aid when you need help? Family members? Friends? The president has a group, called the cabinet, whose main job is to give advice and support.

This section focuses on the members of the cabinet and their roles.

READING STRATEGIES

Use the graphic organizer below to list the major factors that a president must address when appointing cabinet members.

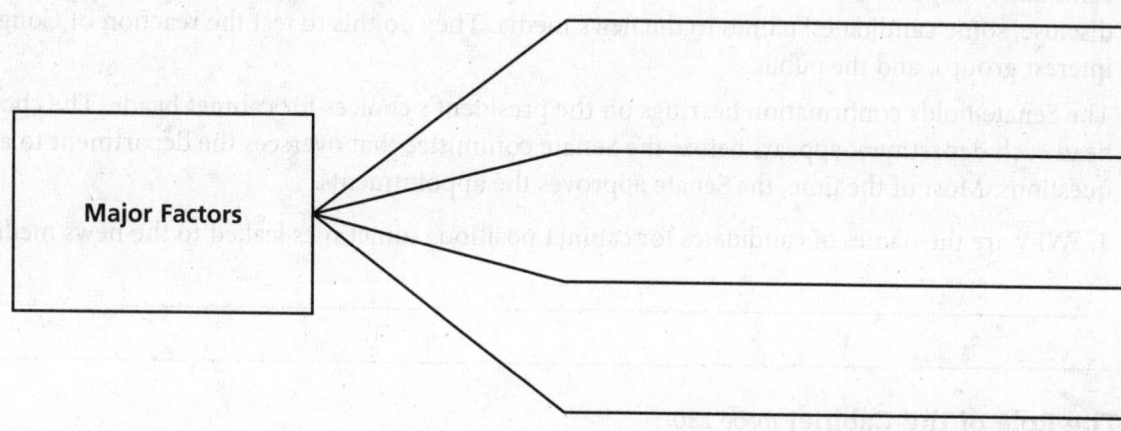

89

STUDY GUIDE (continued)   Chapter 8, Section 3

READU TO LEARN

◉ Introduction *(page 228)*

The president appoints the heads of 15 major executive departments. These department heads—called secretaries—along with the vice president and several other top officials make up the *cabinet*. Cabinet secretaries do more than advise the president; they also administer huge bureaucracies.

◉ The Selection of the Cabinet *(page 228)*

In appointing department heads, the president must balance the following factors:

A. An appointee should have a background that fits the department he or she will head. For example, the head of housing and urban development should have a big-city background.

B. Every cabinet should include women, African Americans, and Hispanics. In others words, the cabinet should be gender and racially balanced.

C. People who accept cabinet appointments often have advanced college degrees. They usually are leaders in business, industry, law, science, or education. They earn much less money as cabinet members than they could outside government, but they take their appointments out of a deep sense of public service.

The selection process includes the following steps:

A. The president-elect draws up a list of candidates for cabinet appointments.

B. Key staff members meet with the candidates to discuss the issues facing the departments the candidates may be asked to head. Members of the president-elect's team may *leak,* or deliberately disclose, some candidates' names to the news media. They do this to test the reaction of Congress, interest groups, and the public.

C. The Senate holds confirmation hearings on the president's choices for cabinet heads. The choice to head each department appears before the Senate committee that oversees the department to answer questions. Most of the time, the Senate approves the appointments.

1. Why are the names of candidates for cabinet positions sometimes leaked to the news media?

_____

_____

◉ The Role of the Cabinet *(page 230)*

Cabinet members meet when the president calls them together. Meetings take place in the cabinet room of the White House and are closed to the public and press. The cabinet's role in decision making depends on how the president defines it. Strong presidents, such as Andrew Jackson and Abraham Lincoln, generally paid less attention to their cabinets than other presidents did.

Several recent presidents have tried to increase the role of the cabinet. Ronald Reagan, for example, wanted his cabinet to be an "inner circle of advisers." Eventually, however, Reagan began to rely more on his White House aides for advice. George H. W. Bush and Bill Clinton used their cabinets as sounding boards for ideas rather than as advisers.

Some cabinet heads work closely with a president because they head departments that are concerned with national issues. These are usually the attorney general and the secretaries of state, defense, and treasury. They are sometimes called an "inner cabinet."

2. Who usually makes up an "inner cabinet"?

_____

_____

◉ Factors Limiting the Cabinet's Role *(page 232)*

The president's use of the cabinet is often limited for the following reasons:

A. Cabinet members answer to the president but also to career officials in their own departments, members of Congress, and special interest groups. Therefore a president does not command the complete loyalty of the cabinet.

B. Disagreements often occur among secretaries. For example, secretaries sometimes battle to influence the president in different directions on policies such as arms control and foreign policy.

C. Keeping secrets is difficult when 15 department heads are involved in a discussion. The president may hesitate to discuss top-secret subjects.

D. Presidents often do not know their cabinet members well. As a result, the president and cabinet have not developed enough trust to discuss tough problems.

3. Why may the president hesitate to discuss top-secret subjects at cabinet meetings?

_____

_____

STUDY GUIDE  Chapter 8, Section 4

For use with textbook pages 234–239.

THE EXECUTIVE OFFICE

CONTENT VOCABULARY

central clearance Office of Management and Budget's review of all legislative proposals that executive agencies prepare *(page 236)*

national security adviser Director of the National Security Council staff *(page 237)*

press secretary One of the president's top assistants who is in charge of media relations *(page 239)*

DRAWING FROM EXPERIENCE

How many people gave you advice and support when you were three years old? Probably just your immediate family. As you and your responsibilities grew, teachers, friends, librarians, police officers, and many others joined your group of advisers and supporters. In a similar way, as the responsibilities of the president have grown, so has the number of people who offer the president help and advice.

This section focuses on the people and agencies in the Executive Office of the President.

READING STRATEGIES

Use the time line below to help you take notes and organize the important events that happened in the history of the Executive Office of the President.

1939   1946   1947

STUDY GUIDE (continued)   Chapter 8, Section 4

READ TO LEARN

◉ Introduction (page 234)

The Executive Office of the President (EOP) includes people and agencies that directly assist the president. Modern presidents have relied on the EOP to provide needed advice and information.

◉ Executive Office Agencies (page 234)

During the 1930s, President Franklin D. Roosevelt felt overwhelmed by all the new programs created to deal with the country's problems. So Congress passed the Reorganization Act of 1939, which created the Executive Office of the President. At the same time, President Roosevelt moved the Bureau of the Budget out of the Treasury into the EOP. Roosevelt also established the White House Office. He intended it to be a small group of advisers who would work directly with the president. Today the Executive Office of the President includes the White House Office and several agencies. These employ more than 1,500 attorneys, scientists, social scientists, and other staff. The EOP has grown for the following reasons:

A. Presidents reorganize it, adding new agencies or expanding existing ones to serve current needs.

B. Presidents want experts to advise them on the complex problems facing the nation.

C. EOP staff members have been added to help executive departments and agencies work together to carry out huge federal programs such as President Bush's national drug control policy in 1989.

The agencies that have played the greatest role in presidential decision making are:

The Office of Management and Budget Once called the Bureau of the Budget, this is one of the oldest agencies. It is also the largest agency in the EOP. The Office of Management and Budget (OMB) prepares the national budget that the president proposes to Congress each year. The OMB's budget indicates what programs the federal government will pay for and how much it will spend on them. So the budget is an important way for a president to influence the government's direction and policies. Each year all executive agencies submit their budgets to the OMB for review. OMB officials suggest to the president where to cut these budgets. The OMB also reviews all legislative proposals that executive agencies make before the proposals go to Congress. It makes sure they agree with the president's goals. This review is called *central clearance*.

The National Security Council Congress created the National Security Council (NSC) in 1947. Its role is to advise the president and coordinate military and foreign policy. The president heads the council, which also includes the secretaries of defense and state. The importance of the NSC has varied with each president's use of it.

The Homeland Security Council President George W. Bush created the Office of Homeland Security and the Homeland Security Council in October 2001, in response to the terrorist attacks of September 11. (Later, in November 2002, a new Cabinet department was created to deal with the same issues: the Department of Homeland Security.) They are responsible for coordinating antiterrorist efforts and advising the president on security issues.

The Council of Economic Advisers Created in 1946, the Council of Economic Advisers helps the president come up with the nation's economic policy. The Council looks at the nation's economic health, predicts future economic conditions, and helps other executive agencies that do economic planning. It also suggests answers to special problems, such as unemployment or inflation.

STUDY GUIDE (continued)   Chapter 8, Section 4

EOP agencies vary from president to president. Some recent EOP agencies have included:

A. The *Domestic Policy Council,* which helps the president plan and carry out long range policies in areas such as farming and energy

B. The *Office of Environmental Policy,* which advises the president on environmental issues and policies

C. The *Office of Science and Technology,* which advises the president on all scientific and technological matters that affect national policies and programs

D. The *National Science and Technology Council,* which advises the president about research and development, including the space program

E. The *Office of the United States Trade Representative,* which helps establish United States trade policy and helps negotiate trade agreements with other nations

F. The *Office of Administration,* which provides data processing, clerical help, and other support services for EOP agencies

1. Which are the three oldest agencies of the Executive Office of the President?

_____

_____

◉ The White House Office *(page 238)*

The president appoints White House staff without Senate approval. Top aides are usually long-time supporters of the president. These top assistants have become an inner circle around the president. The most important are the president's chief of staff, deputy chief of staff, White House counsel, and *press secretary.*

Some White House staffers are policy specialists in certain areas such as foreign policy or energy problems. Other are political strategists. They look at the political impact of decisions the president makes. The White House counsel advises the president on the legal effects of those decisions. Other staff members include:

A. Enforcers, who try to make sure that the executive agencies and departments carry out key orders from the president

B. The press secretary and press staff, who handle the president's relations with White House reporters, set up press conferences, and issue public statements in the president's name

C. The chief assistant for legislative affairs, who advises the president about possible reactions in Congress to White House decisions

D. Other staffers who lobby lawmakers to gain support for presidential programs

E. Aides who decide who and what gets through to the president

2. What are the duties of the White House press staff?

_____

_____

STUDY GUIDE  Chapter 9, Section 1

For use with textbook pages 245–250.

PRESIDENTIAL POWERS

CONTENT VOCABULARY

mandate Expressed will of the people *(page 245)*
forum Medium for discussion *(page 249)*

DRAWING FROM EXPERIENCE

Does your school have student hall monitors? These people get their power to issue passes or to report other students from the principal and faculty. The president gets his power from even higher sources—the Constitution and the people of the United States.

This section focuses on the sources and limits of presidential powers.

READING STRATEGIES

Use the graphic organizer below to list some of the powers given the president by the U.S. Constitution.

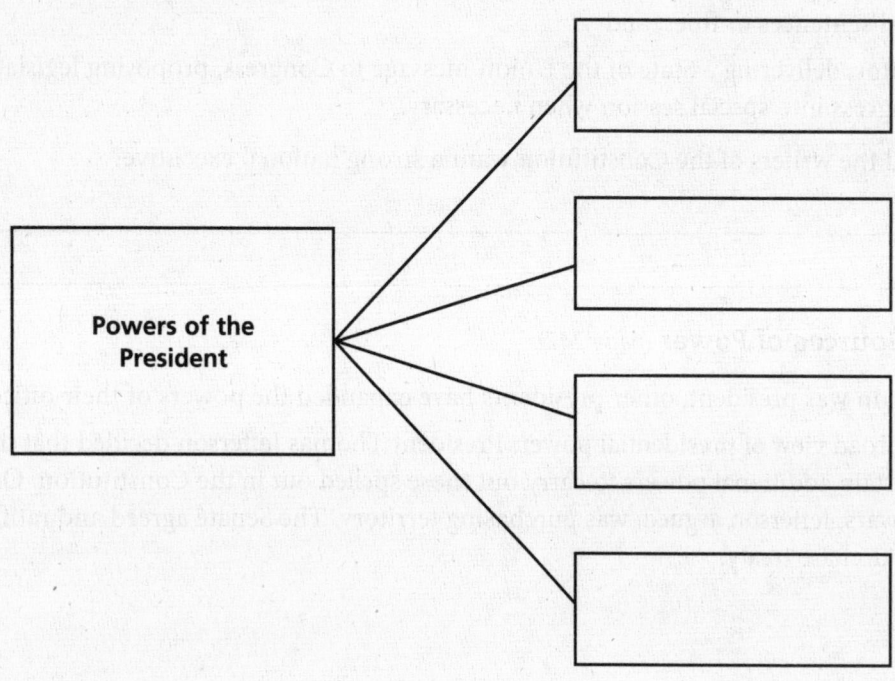

READ TO LEARN

◉ Introduction (page 245)

The Constitution defines the presidency. However, the immediate needs of the nation, the personality of each president, and the *mandate,* or expressed will of the people, have made the office of the presidency what it is today.

◉ Constitutional Powers (page 245)

The Founders of our nation wanted a strong national executive for the following reasons:

A. One of the main weaknesses of the Articles of Confederation was that it lacked an executive to carry out the acts of Congress. This made it difficult for government to enforce laws and to respond quickly to problems.

B. They distrusted direct participation of the people in decision making. Mass democratic movements might try to redistribute wealth and do away with private property.

Article II of the Constitution grants the president broad but vague powers. These include the president's powers as:

A. commander in chief, making the president responsible for national security;

B. head of the executive branch, appointing the heads of executive departments with the approval of the Senate, making treaties and appointing ambassadors with the advice and consent of the Senate;

C. judicial leader, appointing federal court judges, pardoning people convicted of federal crimes, or reducing jail sentences or fines; and

D. chief legislator, delivering a State of the Union message to Congress, proposing legislation, and calling Congress into special session when necessary.

1. Why did the writers of the Constitution want a strong national executive?

_____

_____

◉ Informal Sources of Power (page 247)

Since Washington was president, other presidents have expanded the powers of their office by:

A. taking the broad view of presidential power. President Thomas Jefferson decided that the presidency required certain additional powers to carry out those spelled out in the Constitution. One of these implied powers, Jefferson argued, was purchasing territory. The Senate agreed and ratified Jefferson's Louisiana Purchase treaty.

STUDY GUIDE (continued) **Chapter 9, Section 1**

B. responding to the needs of the nation. During the Civil War, President Abraham Lincoln claimed the Constitution gave him the power to do what was necessary to keep the Union together. During the Great Depression, President Franklin D. Roosevelt persuaded Congress to set up new social and economic programs. After Roosevelt's administration, Americans came to expect the president to take a strong role in directing the nation's economic as well as political life. In 2001, in response to the terrorist strikes on New York City and Washington, D.C., President George W. Bush gained sweeping new authority from Congress to fight terrorism, and his public appeal ratings soared.

C. responding to the people's *mandate*, or strong popular support. This is one of the greatest sources of the president's power. Most presidents have used all forms of media to try to create a mandate. They use radio, television, magazines, newspapers, and the White House Web site to get their message to the people. Television gives presidents great power to put across their ideas and personalities. Major newspapers and magazines also provide presidents with a *forum,* or medium for discussion. White House staff members make sure reporters from these media receive a steady flow of information about the president's activities and ideas.

2. Identify three sources of presidential power in addition to the Constitution.

_____

_____

◉ Limits on Executive Power *(page 249)*

The president's power is limited by:

Congress It has the power to pass legislation over a president's veto with a congressional override—a two-thirds vote in both houses. Other limits include the Senate's power to confirm or reject the president's appointments, the House of Representatives' power of the purse, and the power to impeach a president.

Federal Courts They have the power to review legislative action. For example, during the Great Depression, the Supreme Court ruled some of Franklin Roosevelt's New Deal legislation unconstitutional.

The Bureaucracy Bureaucrats can stand in the way of presidents' programs by failing to provide needed information, by misinterpreting instructions, and by neglecting to complete a task properly.

Public Opinion A president cannot carry out a political program without favorable public opinion. For example, public opinion derailed President Clinton's plan for a health-care system because interest groups raised questions in people's minds. In addition, people usually condemn a president if the president fails to live up to the high standards they set for their leaders.

3. How does Congress limit the president's power?

_____

_____

STUDY GUIDE  Chapter 9, Section 2

For use with textbook pages 252–259.

ROLES OF THE PRESIDENT

CONTENT VOCABULARY

executive order A rule issued by the president that has the force of law *(page 253)*

impoundment The president's refusal to spend money Congress has voted to fund a program *(page 253)*

reprieve The postponement of legal punishment *(page 254)*

pardon A release from legal punishment *(page 254)*

amnesty A group pardon to individuals for an offense against the government *(page 254)*

patronage The practice of granting favors to reward party loyalty *(page 256)*

treaty A formal agreement between the governments of two or more countries *(page 257)*

executive agreement An agreement made between the president and another head of state *(page 257)*

DRAWING FROM EXPERIENCE

In your life, you have different roles. Son or daughter, student, and part-time worker may describe just some of the parts you play. In a similar way, the president plays various roles while in office.

This section focuses on the roles of the president.

READING STRATEGIES

Use the table below to list the roles and duties of the president.

Roles	Duties

STUDY GUIDE (continued)   Chapter 9, Section 2

READ TO LEARN

◉ Introduction (page 252)

The president has seven key duties. Head of state, chief executive, chief legislator, chief diplomat, and commander in chief are based on the Constitution. The roles of economic planner and political party leader have developed over time.

◉ Head of State (page 252)

As head of state, the president represents the nation and performs ceremonial roles. For example, the president serves as hosts to kings and queens, gives awards and medals, and throws out the first ball to begin the major league baseball season. As a symbol of the nation, the president is not just an individual leader but the collective image of the United States.

1. Give an example of a ceremonial duty the president performs as head of state.

_____

_____

◉ Chief Executive (page 253)

As chief executive, the president sees that the laws of Congress are carried out. To do this, the president uses the following tools:

A. Presidents issue *executive orders*—rules with the force of law—to spell out the details of policies and programs Congress enacts. For example, President Carter used an executive order to put thousands of acres of land in Alaska under the control of the National Park Service. He was exercising power under a law that allowed the president to keep certain lands free of business use.

B. Presidents appoint top-level federal officials who share their political beliefs. As a result, the officials at the heads of departments and agencies are more likely to carry out the presidents' policies.

C. Presidents have the right to remove officials they have appointed.

D. Presidents can refuse to allow a federal department or agency to spend the money Congress has appropriated for it. This process is called *impoundment.* Most impoundments are for routine matters. Money is appropriated; the need for spending changes; the president impounds the money, and usually Congress agrees. An exception is when President Nixon impounded huge sums in the 1970s. Groups who would benefit from the funds took the president to court. The court ordered the president to release the money. Then Congress passed legislation to stop the impoundment of large sums of money.

E. Presidents appoint federal judges, including Supreme Court justices, with Senate approval. A president can influence government for many years by appointing justices who hold views similar to the president's.

F. Presidents can grant reprieves and pardons for federal crimes. A *reprieve* postpones a person's punishment. A *pardon* frees a person from punishment altogether.

G. Presidents may also grant amnesty. *Amnesty* is a group pardon. For example, Presidents Ford and Carter granted amnesty to men who fled the draft during the Vietnam War.

2. What limit has Congress placed on the president's power of impoundment?

_____

_____

◉ Chief Legislator (page 254)

Usually the president describes the laws he wants in the annual State of the Union message to Congress. It calls attention to the president's ideas about how to handle important problems facing the nation. To carry out these ideas during the year, the president has a large staff to help write legislation. This legislation determines much of what Congress does each year. The president also presents a suggested budget and an annual economic report.

The president works hard to influence Congress in the following ways:

A. A president often meets with members of Congress to hear their views.

B. A president may hand out political favors to get congressional support. For example, the president may visit the home state of a senator or representative at reelection time.

C. A president may use the threat of a veto to force Congress to stop a bill or change it to fit the president's wishes. Threats often succeed because Congress finds it hard to override a veto.

3. Why is the State of the Union message to Congress important?

_____

_____

◉ Economic Planner (page 256)

The Employment Act of 1946 directed the president to submit an annual economic report to Congress. The law created the Council of Economic Advisers to help the president prepare the report. The law also declared that the government is responsible for promoting high employment, production, and purchasing power. Since 1946 Congress has passed even more laws giving the president power to deal with economic problems. In addition, the president prepares the federal budget each year. The size of the budget and decisions about how government money is spent affect the economy.

4. Describe three provisions of the Employment Act of 1946.

_____

_____

_____

◉ Party Leader (page 256)

The president's party expects the president to be a party leader. This means giving speeches or attending fund raisers to help party members running for office. The president also selects the party's national chairperson and often helps plan election strategies. Presidents are expected to reward persons who support the party with *patronage,* or political appointments.

STUDY GUIDE (continued)   Chapter 9, Section 2

5. How do presidents help party members running for office?

_____

_____

◉ Chief Diplomat *(page 257)*

In this role, the president makes key decisions about the relations the United States has with other countries. Congress and the president continually struggle over who will control the country's foreign policy because Congress also has powers related to foreign policy. However, a president has more information about foreign affairs than most members of Congress. Presidents use this information to plan and justify actions they want to take. Also presidents have the ability to act quickly in foreign affairs. Congress on the other hand, is slow to act.

As chief diplomat, the president has sole power to make *treaties.* These are formal agreements between two or more countries. However, the Senate must approve all treaties before they can go into effect.

The president can also make *executive agreements.* These are pacts between the president and heads of other countries. These agreements have the same status as treaties, but they do not require the Senate's approval. Most presidents prefer executive agreements to treaties.

As chief diplomat, the president decides whether the United States will recognize governments of other countries. To recognize a government means to acknowledge its existence and have dealings with it. For example, since 1961 presidents have refused to recognize the Cuban government of Fidel Castro to show American opposition to the policies of the Cuban government.

6. Why do you think most presidents prefer executive agreements to treaties?

_____

_____

◉ Commander in Chief *(page 258)*

The president shares with Congress the power to make war. For example, in 1991 President George H.W. Bush received congressional approval for military action in Iraq before he ordered an air strike. In addition, the president is responsible for important military decisions. One of these decisions is whether to use atomic weapons. The president may also act at home to support the war effort. For example, Franklin Roosevelt demanded price controls and food and gas rationing for Americans during World War II. The president can also use federal troops to put down rioting in American cities or to keep order in case of a natural disaster.

7. How can the president use federal troops during peace time?

_____

_____

STUDY GUIDE  Chapter 9, Section 3

For use with textbook pages 261–267.

STYLES OF LEADERSHIP

CONTENT VOCABULARY

de facto Existing "in fact" rather than legally *(page 265)*

covert Secret *(page 265)*

executive privilege The right of the president and other high-ranking executive officers to refuse to provide information to Congress or a court *(page 266)*

DRAWING FROM EXPERIENCE

Imagine you are the captain of a team. How will you lead? For example, will you give orders or encouragement to the team members? Presidents have to answer these same questions when they take over the leadership of the nation.

This section focuses on how different presidents lead Americans.

READING STRATEGIES

Use the graphic organizer below to list the reasons for presidential isolation.

Reasons for Presidential Isolation

STUDY GUIDE (continued)   Chapter 9, Section 3

READbox TO LEARN

◉ Introduction (page 261)

Each president has a unique style of leadership. For example, President Ronald Reagan focused on the "big picture" in making policy and let the cabinet, the EOP, and the White House Office work out the details. President Jimmy Carter, on the other hand, spent many hours studying the complex details of policies. Each president used the same tools of power but fulfilled his leadership responsibilities differently.

◉ Increased Responsibilities (page 261)

The Founders thought that Congress would lead the nation. Today, however, the president has the main responsibility for national leadership. Sometimes presidents lead by introducing new ideas. President Truman did this when he ended segregation of whites and African Americans in the military in 1948. More often, presidents lead by responding to crises, problems, or opportunities as they occur. For example, President Nixon took advantage of tension between the Soviet Union and the People's Republic of China to open diplomatic relations between the United States and China.

  1. Name two ways in which presidents lead.

_____

_____

◉ Leadership Qualities and Skills (page 262)

Many presidents have more than one of the following qualities or skills:

Understanding the Public Understanding the people is necessary to gain and hold their support. Public support, in turn, can give a president real power to influence lawmakers. Presidential proposals and policies are better received by Congress when a president is popular. Failure to understand the public, on the other hand, can bring disaster on a president. For example, in 1932, President Herbert Hoover thought that the public did not want government to take an active role when millions of Americans were out of work. As a result, Hoover lost the 1932 presidential election to Franklin D. Roosevelt.

Ability to Communicate Successful presidents must explain their policies clearly and present their ideas in a way that inspires public support. Franklin Roosevelt inspired confidence by broadcasting "fireside chats." A president who cannot communicate may have difficulty leading the nation. President Carter, for example, had problems winning support for his policies due to his uninspiring speeches.

Sense of Timing A successful president knows the right time to introduce a new policy or make a key decision. In the early 1990s, President Bush agreed that American economic aid would encourage democratic reforms in the crumbling Soviet Union. However, he waited until the Soviet situation was more stable to act on this policy. To test a position on a controversial issue, skilled presidents sometimes have assistants leak information to the press or make a statement about the issue. If public and congressional responses are favorable, the president then supports the position. If the reaction is unfavorable, the president may quietly drop the idea or try to shape public opinion in its favor.

STUDY GUIDE (continued) Chapter 9, Section 3

Openness to New Ideas Good leadership requires presidents to be open to new ideas. Presidents who are flexible engage in give-and-take sessions with their staffers. Presidents Roosevelt and Kennedy, for example, liked to hear their staff arguing differing positions.

Ability to Compromise Even the president often must give up something in order to get something in return. Successful presidents realize that sometimes they have to settle for legislation from Congress that gives them only part of what they want. Presidents who do not compromise risk accomplishing nothing at all. President Woodrow Wilson refused to compromise when senators raised objections to the treaty drawn up after World War I. He chose instead to appeal to the public for support of the treaty as it was. During a speaking tour, the president suffered a paralyzing stroke and the Senate rejected the treaty.

Political Courage Sometimes presidents must go against public opinion when they believe the nation's well-being is at risk. President Lincoln showed political courage. He decided to continue the Civil War and to preserve the Union despite many Northerners' demands to make peace with the South.

2. What six qualities and skills should presidents have to lead the country?

_____

_____

_____

◉ Presidential Isolation (page 264)

Presidents need information and good advice to make successful decisions. However, more and more presidents become isolated from information and advice for the following reasons:

A. Modern presidents receive special treatment. It is easy for them to see themselves as deserving only praise and to consider their ideas above criticism.

B. Staff members often feel in awe of the president. Such feelings make it difficult for staffers to present unpleasant news or voice criticism. As a result, presidents sometimes receive one-sided views of issues.

C. Political power in Washington can be measured in access to the president. The people with the most access are the top members of the White House staff. As a result, the president may not get news and advice from a wide variety of viewpoints.

D. Top staff control access to the president. This access reflects a president's preferences, as well as staff decisions about what is best politically. President Reagan was relatively isolated. This helps explain why he was believable when he claimed he was unaware of the *covert*, or secret, activities his National Security staff was conducting.

To offset isolation, former President George H.W. Bush appointed his close friends to the cabinet rather than to the White House staff. In this way, the president had access to a greater variety of views. President Bill Clinton offset the isolation of depending on White House staffers by reorganizing his staff.

3. Why was President Reagan unaware of the activities of his National Security Council?

_____

_____

STUDY GUIDE (continued)   Chapter 9, Section 3

◉ Executive Privilege *(page 266)*

Executive privilege is the right of the president and other high-ranking executive officers with the president's consent, to refuse to provide information to Congress or a court. Presidents since George Washington have claimed that executive privilege is implied in the powers granted in Article II of the Constitution.

Presidents claim that executive privilege also protects their communication with other members of the executive branch. Presidents argue that executive privilege is necessary if they are to get frank opinions and advice from their assistants.

In 1974 the Supreme Court issued a major decision on executive privilege. The Court said that President Nixon had to turn over tapes of conversations with assistants about the Watergate cover-up and that the tapes were not protected by executive privilege. However, the question of how far executive privilege extends to presidential advisers remains unanswered.

4. Why do presidents want to extend executive privilege to conversations with their advisers?

_____

_____

STUDY GUIDE  Chapter 10, Section 1

For use with textbook pages 275—283.

BUREAUCRATIC ORGANIZATION

CONTENT VOCABULARY

bureaucrat A worker in a department or agency of the federal government—civil servant *(page 275)*

embassy An ambassador's official residence and offices in a foreign country *(page 276)*

government corporation A business that the federal government runs *(page 279)*

deregulate To reduce or remove government regulations *(page 281)*

DRAWING FROM EXPERIENCE

How does your family tackle major house cleaning? Many families divide the work. One member cleans the bathrooms. Another cleans the kitchen, and perhaps a third member handles the dusting and vacuuming. The work of government is divided in a similar way among the government bureaus and agencies.

This section focuses on how the government bureaucracy is organized.

READING STRATEGIES

Use the graphic organizer below to list the effects of Republicans pushing for deregulation in the 1990s.

CAUSE		EFFECTS
Republicans push for deregulation.	→	

STUDY GUIDE (continued)   Chapter 10, Section 1

READ TO LEARN

◉ Introduction (page 275)

Most of the departments and agencies of the federal government are part of the executive branch. The people who work for these organizations are called **bureaucrats,** or civil servants. The writers of the Constitution realized the need for federal agencies to carry out the daily business of government. However, they might be shocked by how much this bureaucracy has grown. Today, millions of civilians work for the federal government.

◉ The Cabinet Departments (page 276)

The 15 cabinet departments are a major part of the federal bureaucracy. A secretary, who is a member of the president's cabinet, heads each of the departments. Departments usually have a deputy secretary or under secretary and assistant secretaries, who are also appointed by the president. Under these officials are directors of bureaus, agencies, offices, administrations, and divisions and their assistants. The top officials set overall department policy. The career workers under them provide the ideas and information that give the top people alternatives from which to choose.

The Department of State deals with the overall foreign policy of the United States. Its agencies also protect the rights of American citizens traveling in foreign countries.

The Department of the Treasury manages money in the United States. Some of its agencies are the Bureau of the Mint, which manufactures coins; the Bureau of Engraving and Printing, which produces paper money; the Internal Revenue Service, which operates the nation's tax code and collects taxes each year; and the Bureau of Public Debt, which borrows the additional money needed to operate the federal government.

The Department of the Interior protects public lands and natural resources throughout the country. It also oversees relations with Native Americans. Its divisions include the Bureau of Mines and the National Park Service.

The Department of Agriculture develops conservation programs, provides credit to farmers, and protects the nation's food supply.

The Department of Justice oversees the nation's legal affairs. It includes the Federal Bureau of Investigation (FBI), the U.S. Marshals Service, and the Civil Rights Division, among other agencies.

The Department of Commerce promotes and protects American business. Among its agencies are the Bureau of the Census, which counts the population every ten years, and the Patent and Trademark Office, which issues patents for inventions.

The Department of Labor ensures safe working conditions, a minimum wage, and pension rights. Its agency called the Bureau of Labor Statistics analyzes facts on employment, wages, and salaries.

The Department of Defense protects United States security. Its Joint Chiefs of Staff oversee the Army, Navy, Marines, and Air Force.

The Department of Health and Human Services directs programs concerned with health and social services. It manages the federal Medicare and Medicaid programs. Its Food and Drug Administration inspects food and approves new drugs for medical treatment.

The Department of Housing and Urban Development helps keep up the nation's communities and ensures Americans of equal housing opportunities.

STUDY GUIDE (continued)   Chapter 10, Section 1

The Department of Transportation makes rules for aviation, railroads, highways, and mass transit. This department regulates all aspects of American transportation needs, policy development, and planning.

The Department of Energy plans energy policy and researches and develops sources of energy.

The Department of Education coordinates federal assistance programs for public and private schools.

The Department of Veterans Affairs runs several hospitals as well as educational and other programs for the benefit of veterans and their families.

The Department of Homeland Security coordinates the dozens of federal agencies working to prevent terrorism.

1. Which department of the cabinet do you think conducts medical research? Explain your answer.

_____

_____

◉ Independent Agencies *(page 279)*

The federal bureaucracy also contains more than 100 agencies, boards, and commissions that are not part of any cabinet department. The president appoints the heads of these organizations. A few of these agencies, such as the Environmental Protection Agency (EPA) and the National Aeronautics and Space Administration (NASA), are almost as large as cabinet departments. Other agencies, such as the Small Business Administration and the American Battles Monuments Commission, are much smaller.

Some independent agencies perform services for the executive branch. For example, the Central Intelligence Agency (CIA) gathers information about activities in other countries, evaluates it, and passes it on to the president.

Some independent agencies, such as the Small Business Administration, directly serve the public. Many of the major agencies are *government corporations.* These are businesses the federal government runs. The best-known government corporation is the United States Postal Service (USPS). Government corporations are organized like private businesses. Each has a board of directors and executive officers who direct daily operations. Unlike a private business, however, money from Congress, not investors, supports a government corporation.

2. How are government corporations and private businesses alike and different?

_____

_____

_____

◉ Regulatory Commissions *(page 280)*

Regulatory commissions are independent of the branches of government. The president appoints the commissioners for each commission. However, they do not report to the president and the president cannot fire them.

The purpose of regulatory commissions is to make rules for large businesses and industries that affect people's lives. The regulatory agencies decide questions such as who will operate a radio station or build a natural gas pipeline. The commissions may also hold hearings, collect evidence, and decide punishments for any business that breaks the rules.

Lobbyists for industries that the commissions regulate sometimes try to pressure the agencies to rule favorably for their clients. Critics of the commissions charge that some commissions are more interested in protecting regulated industries than serving the public interest. But others point out that commissions have a good record of protecting the public interest.

In 1976 presidential candidate Jimmy Carter suggested that American society had too many regulations. Congress responded to complaints of overregulation by taking steps to *deregulate,* or reduce the powers of regulatory commissions. For example, in 1978 Congress ordered the Civil Aeronautics Board to cut back on rules concerning airlines. Also, in the 1980s and 1990s, Republicans pushed for regulatory changes. Congress responded by passing deregulation laws dealing with reduced paperwork, risk assessment, and private property rights.

In 1994 Congress eliminated much of the federal regulation of the trucking industry and in 1995 eliminated the Interstate Commerce Commission. Along with demands for deregulation came demands to cut costs in government. The Clinton administration proposed cutting 252,000 jobs from the federal workforce over 6 years.

In 1996 Congress streamlined rules for the traditionally regulated industries of telecommunications and investments. Congress also repealed 300 laws concerning procurement, or purchasing of materials, in the federal government.

3. How did Congress respond to President Carter's suggestion that society was overregulated?

_____

_____

Name _____ Date _____ Class _____

STUDY GUIDE  Chapter 10, Section 2

For use with textbook pages 284–289.

THE CIVIL SERVICE SYSTEM

CONTENT VOCABULARY

spoils system The practice of victorious politicians rewarding their followers with government jobs *(page 285)*

civil service system Practice of government employment based on competitive examinations and merit *(page 286)*

DRAWING FROM EXPERIENCE

At one time or another, you have probably been the only one in a group of friends with a pack of gum. What happens? The others ask if they can share your gum and you hand it out. Many friends and supporters of newly elected officials want something, too—they want jobs.

This section focuses on how federal workers are chosen for their positions.

READING STRATEGIES

Use the graphic organizer below to list the causes and effects of calls to reform the federal bureaucracy in the 1850s.

CAUSE		EFFECT
	→	

STUDY GUIDE (continued)   Chapter 10, Section 2

READ TO LEARN

◉ Introduction (page 284)

Who works for the many departments and agencies that make up the federal bureaucracy? The typical federal bureaucrat is more than 40 years old and has worked for the government for about 15 years. About 30 percent of federal workers belong to minority groups, compared to about 22 percent in the private work force. Women make up about 44 percent of federal workers, roughly the same percentage of women in the total labor force. Federal workers hold a great variety of jobs. About half of federal employees are administrative and clerical workers. The bureaucracy also includes FBI agents, forest rangers, and air traffic controllers as well as engineers, doctors, lawyers, veterinarians, and other professionals.

◉ Origins (page 285)

When Andrew Jackson became president in 1829, he fired about 1,000 federal workers and gave their jobs to his political supporters. Jackson's method of appointing federal workers became known as the *spoils system*—the practice of victorious politicians rewarding their followers with government jobs. For the next 50 years, national, state, and local politicians used the spoils system to fill bureaucratic positions.

As a result, many federal workers who were good at working in campaigns were not as good at their new jobs. Corruption developed. Government employees did favors for interest groups in return for support for their candidates. Jobs were bought and sold. In the 1850s groups of citizens called for reforms. So Congress set up the first Civil Service Commission in 1871. However, Congress failed to appropriate money for the new commission. Then a disappointed office seeker killed President James Garfield in 1881.

The public was outraged by the president's murder. In response, Congress passed the Pendleton Act, which created the current federal *civil service system.* This system requires that government employment be based on open exams that test merit. In other words, job seekers who are best qualified get the jobs. In 1979 the Office of Personnel Management and the Merit System Protection Board replaced the Civil Service commission.

1. How did the spoils system differ from the civil service system?

_____

_____

◉ The Civil Service System Today (page 286)

The Office of Personnel Management is responsible for filling job openings. Most secretarial and clerical jobs require that job applicants take a written test. For jobs such as accountants, social workers, managers, and so on, applicants are judged on their training and experience. Veterans receive special preference.

Government jobs have many benefits such as:

A. salaries about equal to those in private business,

B. 13 to 26 days of paid vacation a year,

C. extensive health insurance and 13 paid sick days,

STUDY GUIDE (continued)   Chapter 10, Section 2

D. retirement at age 55, or earlier with a reduced monthly benefit payment, and

E. job security.

Civil service workers can only be fired after a very long series of hearings. Most supervisors and top officials find putting up with an incompetent worker easier than firing one. As a result, the system that was set up to hire qualified workers actually protects a number of incompetent or inefficient employees.

In 1939 Congress passed the Hatch Act. This law prevents a political party from using federal workers in election campaigns. Otherwise, the workers' promotions and job security might depend on their support of the party in power. Many federal workers argue that the Hatch Act violates freedom of speech. Supporters of the Hatch Act believe it keeps the civil service politically neutral. In 1993 Congress revised the act to tighten on-the-job restrictions while loosening off-duty limitations. The amended Hatch Act prohibits federal employees from working on political activities while on duty. However, it allows them to:

A. hold offices in political parties,

B. participate in campaigns and rallies,

C. publicly endorse candidates, and

D. raise political funds from within their own government agency's political action committee.

However, the Hatch Act forbids federal employees from running for elective office against a member of another party and from collecting contributions from the general public.

2. Why did many federal employees dislike the original Hatch Act?

_____

_____

◉ Political Appointees in Government *(page 288)*

Every new president has the chance to fill about 2,200 top-level jobs in the federal bureaucracy. These jobs are outside the civil service system. Filling these jobs gives a president the opportunity to place loyal supporters in key positions. These political appointees are expected to carry out the president's decisions. Unlike career civil service workers, appointees' jobs usually end when a new president is elected.

Appointees are supporters of the president. They are usually college educated. Most have advanced degrees. Many are lawyers. Most return to jobs outside the government when the president leaves office.

Top political appointees hold their jobs for only a few years. The head of a large agency needs about a year just to learn all the issues, programs, and procedures involved in running the agency. The result is that most of the real power over the daily operations of the agency falls to the lower-level, career civil service officials. Their decisions shape how the national government handles key problems facing the nation.

3. What general qualifications does a president look for in an appointee?

_____

_____

STUDY GUIDE  Chapter 10, Section 3

For use with textbook pages 291–298.

THE BUREAUCRACY AT WORK

CONTENT VOCABULARY

client group Individuals and groups who work with a government agency and are most affected by its decisions *(page 295)*

liaison officer A cabinet department employee who helps promote good relations with Congress *(page 296)*

injunction An order that will stop a particular action or enforce a rule or regulation *(page 297)*

iron triangle A relationship formed among government agencies, congressional committees, and client groups who work together *(page 297)*

DRAWING FROM EXPERIENCE

You shop at the stores that have what you want. The store owners, in turn, benefit from the money you spend. This kind of interaction keeps the economy going. The same kind of mutual assistance takes place among federal agencies, congressional committees, and client groups. Their interaction keeps government moving.

This section focuses on how the bureaucracy works.

READING STRATEGIES

Use the graphic organizer below to help you take notes about three groups who work together to help keep government moving.

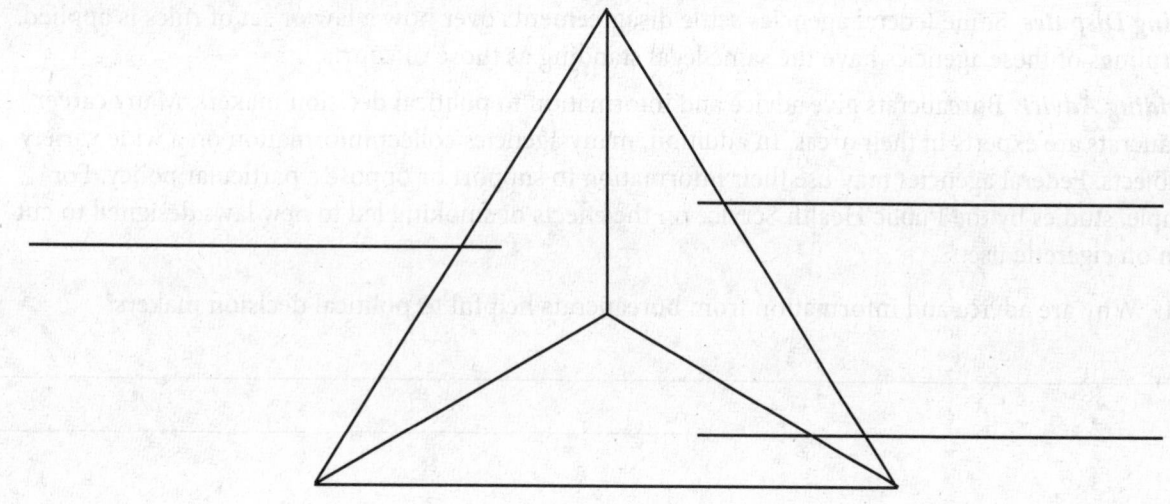

STUDY GUIDE (continued)   Chapter 10, Section 3

READ TO LEARN

◉ Introduction (page 291)

Public policy is whatever action the government chooses to take or not to take. In theory, federal bureaucrats only carry out the policies that the president and Congress make. In practice, the bureaucracy also makes public policy.

◉ Influencing Policy (page 291)

Federal bureaucrats help make policy in the following ways:

Making Rules Congress cannot possibly spell out exactly what needs to be done to enforce a law. The bureaucracy issues rules that put the law into action. For example, Congress established the Social Security system in 1935. The law provides for payments to disabled workers. The Social Security Administration in the Department of Health and Human Services has written 14 pages of rules and regulations defining the word *disability*. The rules ensure that deserving people receive payments. Often rules made by federal agencies have the same force as laws. For instance, builders must follow guidelines from the Department of Housing and Urban Development when working on federally funded building projects.

Paperwork Companies once spent one billion hours per year filling out forms required by rules from federal agencies. In 1995 Congress passed a law to reduce the amount of federal paperwork. The Office of Management and Budget set a goal of reducing paperwork about 35 percent by the year 2001.

Involvement in Lawmaking The bureaucracy shapes lawmaking in the following ways:

A. Helping draft new bills for Congress

B. Testifying about legislation

C. Providing lawmakers with technical information

D. Advising lawmakers about bills related to an agency's area of concern

E. Providing ideas for new laws

Settling Disputes Some federal agencies settle disagreements over how a law or set of rules is applied. The rulings of these agencies have the same legal standing as those of courts.

Providing Advice Bureaucrats give advice and information to political decision makers. Many career bureaucrats are experts in their areas. In addition, many agencies collect information on a wide variety of subjects. Federal agencies may use their information to support or oppose a particular policy. For example, studies by the Public Health Service on the effects of smoking led to new laws designed to cut down on cigarette use.

1. Why are advice and information from bureaucrats helpful to political decision makers?

_____

_____

STUDY GUIDE (continued)   Chapter 10, Section 3

⦿ Why the Bureaucracy Makes Policy *(page 293)*

The federal bureaucracy has grown in size and importance for the following reasons:

National Growth and Technology The government grew as the population grew. The same number of officials who ran a country of 50 million people cannot be expected to govern a country of more than 250 million. Also, rapid advances in technology have made life more complicated. Congress cannot have all the time or knowledge to deal with the nation's many issues—nuclear power, education reform, space exploration, environmental protection, and health care, among others. So the president and Congress establish bureaucracies and give them the money and power to handle these tasks.

International Crises Competition with the Soviet Union and international crises after World War II furthered the growth of the federal bureaucracy. For example, the Soviet Union launched *Sputnik I*, the first space satellite, in 1957. The United States government established NASA in 1958 to direct its own space program. To deal with the Soviet Union and its allies, the government created several other new agencies. These included the Central Intelligence Agency, the Arms Control and Disarmament Agency, the United States Information Agency, and the Peace Corps.

Economic Problems President Franklin D. Roosevelt greatly expanded the size of the federal bureaucracy as he tried to end the Depression during the 1930s. By the 1940s the number of federal workers had almost doubled. Most people accepted the idea that the government should help the ill, disabled, elderly, and neglected. As a result, the government today spends billions of dollars on hundreds of assistance programs. Also as a result of the Depression, the government set up agencies to stimulate and regulate business.

Citizen Demands Congress created the Departments of Agriculture, Commerce, and Labor to meet the increased demands of farmers, business people, and workers. Each agency serves client groups. Clients are the individuals and groups who work with the agency and are most affected by its decisions. For example, a client group of the Department of Defense are the manufacturers that make weapons and military supplies. Client groups often lobby both Congress and the agency itself for more programs and services.

The Nature of Bureaucracy Federal agencies seldom die after they are created. Former president Ford observed: "One of the enduring truths of the nation's capital is that bureaucrats survive. Agencies don't fold their tents and quietly fade away after their work is done. They find something new to do."

2. Give three examples of cabinet departments that were created to meet the demands of citizens.

_____

_____

_____

⦿ Influencing Bureaucratic Decisions *(page 295)*

The president, Congress, the courts, and client groups influence federal agencies. Each cabinet department has ***liaison officers*** who help promote good relations with Congress. Liaison officers keep track of bills that might affect the agency. They also respond to requests from lawmakers for information. Congress influences decision making in federal agencies by using:

A. new legislation to change the rules or regulations a federal agency establishes, or to hold agencies more accountable for their activities, and

B. the budget. Lawmakers can add or cut an agency's budget and even refuse to appropriate money for the agency. More often, however, Congress threatens to eliminate programs important to an agency.

The power of the purse has limits, however. Congress finds it almost impossible to cut the part of an agency's budget used for entitlements. These are basic services required by law.

Citizens directly affected by the actions of federal agencies may challenge those agencies' actions in court. A federal court may issue an *injunction.* This is an order that will stop a particular action or enforce a rule or regulation. However, citizens have not had much success in court cases against the bureaucracy. One study shows that courts do not usually reverse the decisions of federal regulatory commissions.

3. What four individuals or groups influence federal agencies?

_____

_____

_____

_____

◉ The Influence of Client Groups *(page 297)*

Client groups often try to influence agency decisions through lobbyists. These lobbyists testify at agency hearings, write letters, keep track of agency decisions, and take other steps to support their groups' interests.

Congressional committees, client groups, and a federal department or agency often cooperate closely to make public policy. Such cooperation is called an *iron triangle,* or a sub-government. This interaction keeps government business moving. Such a relationship is called a triangle because the three groups have the necessary resources to satisfy each other's needs. The adjective *iron* is used because the relationship is so strong that individuals and groups outside the triangle often find it difficult to influence policy in the area. Public policy in veterans' affairs is an example.

A. The Department of Veterans Affairs (VA) provides important services such as hospital care but needs resources to continue offering such services to veterans.

B. Congressional committees responsible for veterans' affairs supply the VA with money, but the lawmakers on the committees need voters' support to stay in Congress.

C. Client groups, such as the American Legion, provide political support for the lawmakers. Client groups, in turn, need the VA's services to satisfy the demands of their members.

Critics believe that iron triangles allow interest groups too much power in shaping public policy. They think Congress should regulate the interest groups that support iron triangles.

Interactions among agencies also influence policy making in the bureaucracy. For example, rules made by the Occupational Safety and Health Administration about noise standards may conflict with rules by the Environmental Protection Agency. Often interagency task forces or committees settle such disputes.

4. Why is *iron* used to describe the interactions among congressional committees, client groups, and federal agencies?

_____

_____

STUDY GUIDE  Chapter 11, Section 1

For use with textbook pages 305–310.

POWERS OF THE FEDERAL COURTS

CONTENT VOCABULARY

concurrent jurisdiction Authority shared by both federal and state courts *(page 306)*

original jurisdiction The authority of a trial court to be first to hear a case *(page 307)*

appellate jurisdiction Authority of a court to hear a case that is appealed from a lower court *(page 307)*

litigant A person engaged in a lawsuit *(page 307)*

due process clause Fourteenth Amendment clause stating that no state may deprive a person of life, liberty, or property without due process of law *(page 309)*

DRAWING FROM EXPERIENCE

Suppose your family assigned you certain rooms—such as your bedroom and washroom—to keep tidy. This would be your area of responsibility. In a similar way, federal courts are responsible for certain areas of law. These areas are called their jurisdictions.

This section focuses on the work of the federal courts.

READING STRATEGIES

Use the Venn diagram below to list the jurisdictions of the state and federal courts.

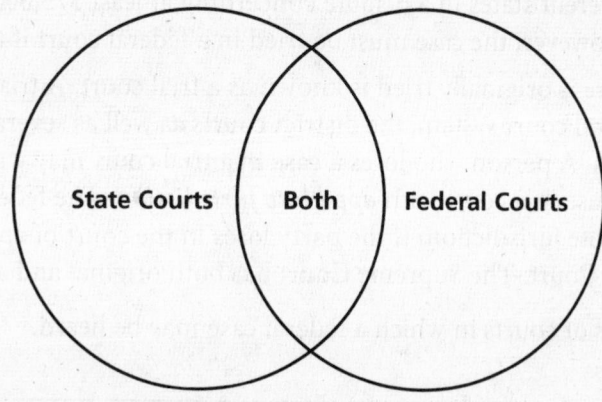

State Courts   Both   Federal Courts

STUDY GUIDE (continued)   Chapter 11, Section 1

READ TO LEARN

◉ Introduction (page 305)

The Supreme Court played only a small role in the United States government until Chief Justice John Marshall was appointed in 1801. He helped to increase the power of the Court. Over the years, the Court's growing role met serious challenges. However, today the judicial branch of government is well established as an equal with the legislative and executive branches.

◉ Jurisdiction of the Courts (page 306)

Each of the 50 states has its own system of courts. Their powers come from state constitutions and laws. The federal court system consists of the Supreme Court and lower federal courts. Federal courts get their powers from the Constitution and federal laws.

The authority to hear certain cases is called the jurisdiction of the court. In the dual court system of the United States, state courts have jurisdiction over cases involving state laws. Federal courts have jurisdiction over cases involving federal laws, treaties with foreign nations, Constitutional interpretations, bankruptcy, and maritime law. Sometimes the jurisdiction of the state and federal courts overlap. Federal courts have the authority to hear cases that involve the following parties or persons:

A. Ambassadors and representatives of foreign governments

B. Two or more state governments

C. The United States government or one of its offices or agencies

D. Citizens that are residents of different states

E. Citizens that are residents of the same state but claim lands under grants of different states

In some instances, called *concurrent jurisdiction*, both federal and state courts have jurisdiction. A case involving citizens of different states in a dispute concerning at least $75,000 may be tried in either a federal or state court. However, the case must be tried in a federal court if the person suing insists.

The court in which a case is originally tried is known as a trial court. A trial court has *original jurisdiction*. In the federal court system, the district courts as well as several other lower courts have only original jurisdiction. A person who loses a case in a trial court may wish to appeal a decision. Then he or she may take the case to a court with *appellate jurisdiction*. The federal court system has courts of appeals with only appellate jurisdiction. If the party loses in the court of appeals, he or she may appeal the case to the Supreme Court. The Supreme Court has both original and appellate jurisdiction.

1. Name three types of courts in which a federal case may be heard.

_____

_____

◉ Developing Supreme Court Power (page 307)

The following principles of the Supreme Court have developed from custom, usage, and history.

STUDY GUIDE (continued)   Chapter 11, Section 1

A. Neither a judge in the federal courts nor a justice in the Supreme Court may seek out an issue and bring it to court. The courts must wait for *litigants*—people engaged in a lawsuit—to come to them.

B. Federal courts will only determine cases. They will not simply answer a legal question, no matter how important the question or who asks it.

C. The Court can review acts of Congress. This is the power of *judicial review.* It was established under Chief Justice John Marshall by the 1803 Supreme Court ruling in *Marbury* v. *Madison.*

D. In 1810 and 1819 the Supreme Court extended its power to review state laws. Supreme Court rulings in 1824 and 1825 also broadened federal power, not just the power of the Supreme Court, at the expense of the states. However, the *Dred Scott* v. *Sandford* (1857) decision supported states' rights on the issue of slavery but damaged the Court in the eyes of the nation.

2. How was the power of judicial review established?

_____

◉ Due Process *(page 308)*

Following the Civil War, the Supreme Court issued several rulings on the Thirteenth, Fourteenth, and Fifteenth Amendments. It often refused to apply the *due process clause* of the Fourteenth Amendment when individuals challenged business or state interests. The due process clause says that no state may deprive any person of life, liberty, or property without the due process of law. The following cases are important rulings related to the Civil War Amendments:

Slaughterhouse Cases Louisiana had granted a monopoly on the slaughtering business to one company. Competing butchers claimed that this grant denied them the right to practice their trade. They claimed that the Fourteenth Amendment guaranteed the privileges and immunities of U.S. citizenship, equal protection of the laws, and due process. In 1873 the Court ruled for the state of Louisiana. It explained that the amendment only protected the rights and privileges of federal, not state, citizenship.

Plessy v. *Ferguson* In the 1896 *Plessy* v. *Ferguson* decision, the Court established the "separate but equal" doctrine. This means that if facilities are equal for both races, the facilities can be separate, or segregated.

The Court and Business In the 1870s, the Supreme Court rejected a challenge to state regulatory laws in the *Granger Cases.* It held that some private property, such as a railroad, was invested with the public interest, so a state could regulate it. More often, the Court sided with business. In *Debs* v. *United States,* it upheld the contempt conviction of labor leader Eugene V. Debs, jailed for disobeying an order to call off a strike. In the 1930s, President Franklin D. Roosevelt was angered when the Supreme Court struck down laws that regulated business. The president tried to pack the court by appointing justices who shared his beliefs. His attempts failed but the Court began to uphold federal and state regulations.

Civil Liberties The Supreme Court under Chief Justice Earl Warren (1953–1969) was a major force in protecting civil freedoms. It overturned the "separate but equal" decision and outlawed segregation in public schools in *Brown* v. *Board of Education of Topeka.* In other cases, the Warren Court extended equal protection in voting rights and applied due process to persons accused of crimes.

3. Give an example of the Supreme Court upholding state regulatory laws over the interests of business.

_____

_____

STUDY GUIDE  Chapter 11, Section 2

For use with textbook pages 312–317.

LOWER FEDERAL COURTS

CONTENT VOCABULARY

grand jury A group that hears charges against a suspect and decides whether there is sufficient evidence to bring the person to trial *(page 312)*

indictment A formal charge by a grand jury *(page 313)*

petit jury A trial jury, usually consisting of 6 or 12 people, that weighs the evidence presented at a trial and renders a verdict *(page 313)*

judicial circuit A region containing a United States appellate court *(page 313)*

senatorial courtesy A system in which the president submits the name of a candidate for judicial appointment to the senators from the candidate's state before formally submitting it for full Senate approval *(page 317)*

DRAWING FROM EXPERIENCE

Imagine you and your friend found a baseball in a field. How would you decide who owned the ball? You might go to a third person to decide for you. In a sense, making decisions is the job of judges and courts.

This section focuses on the kinds of lower federal courts in the United States.

READING STRATEGIES

Use the graphic organizer below to help you take notes as you read the summaries that follow. Think about what happens when a person loses a case in a district court.

CAUSE		EFFECT
A person loses a case in a district court.	→	

STUDY GUIDE (continued)   Chapter 11, Section 2

READ TO LEARN

◉ Introduction (page 312)

The Constitution created the Supreme Court. Congress established the network of lower federal courts. These courts are of two basic types—constitutional federal courts and legislative federal courts.

◉ Constitutional Courts (page 312)

Courts established by Congress under Article III of the Constitution are constitutional courts. These courts include the following kinds:

Federal District Courts Congress created district courts in 1789 to serve as trial courts. Today the United States has 94 district courts. More than 550 judges preside over the district courts with jurisdiction to hear cases involving federal laws. They try both criminal and civil cases. District courts use two types of juries in criminal cases. A *grand jury* of 16 to 23 people hears charges against a person suspected of committing a crime. The grand jury issues an *indictment*, a formal accusation charging a person with a crime, if it believes there is sufficient evidence to bring the person to trial. A petit jury of 6 or 12 people is a trial jury. It weighs the evidence presented at a trial in a criminal or civil case. In a criminal case, a petit jury decides whether a person is guilty or not guilty. In a civil case, the jury finds for either the plaintiff—the person that is suing—or the defendant—the person who is being sued.

The following appointed officials provide support services for district courts:

A. A United States attorney represents the United States in all civil suits brought against the government and prosecutes people charged with federal crimes.

B. A United States magistrate issues arrest warrants and helps decide whether the arrested person should be held for a grand jury hearing.

C. A United States marshal may make arrests, secure jurors, or keep order in the courtroom.

D. A clerk keeps records of court proceedings with deputy clerks, bailiffs, and stenographers.

Federal Courts of Appeals A person who loses a case in a district court may appeal to a federal court of appeals, or in some instances, to the Supreme Court. The United States is divided into 12 *judicial circuits,* or regions, with 1 appellate court in each circuit. The thirteenth court is a special appeals court with national jurisdiction. The courts of appeals have only appellate jurisdiction. Most appeals come from decisions of district courts, the U.S. Tax Court, and various territorial courts. The courts may:

A. uphold the decision,

B. reverse the decision, or

C. send the case back to the lower court to be tried again.

The U.S. Circuit Court of Appeals for the Federal Circuit in Washington, D.C., hears cases from the federal claims court, the Court of International Trade, the U.S. Patent Office, and other executive agencies.

The Court of International Trade This court has jurisdiction over cases dealing with tariffs. Citizens who believe that tariffs are too high bring most of the cases heard in this court.

```
┌─────────────────────────────────────────────────────────────────────┐
│  STUDY GUIDE (continued)        Chapter 11, Section 2                  │
└─────────────────────────────────────────────────────────────────────┘
```

1. Where do most cases heard in courts of appeals come from?

_____

_____

◉ **Legislative Courts** *(page 314)*

The legislative courts help Congress use its powers. For example, the power of Congress to tax led to the creation of the United States Tax Court. Legislative courts include:

United States Court of Federal Claims This court handles claims against the United States for money damages.

United States Tax Court This court hears cases related to federal taxes.

The United States Court of Appeals for the Armed Forces This is the armed forces' highest appeals court. It hears cases involving members of the armed forces convicted of breaking military law.

Territorial Courts These courts are similar to district courts in function, operation, and jurisdiction. They handle civil and criminal cases, along with constitutional cases.

Courts of the District of Columbia This is the judicial system for the nation's capital. The system handles both criminal and civil cases that need to be heard within the District of Columbia.

The Court of Veterans' Appeals This court handles cases arising from veterans' claims for benefits.

Foreign Intelligence Surveillance Court This court is authorized to approve wiretaps and searches of anyone suspected of "terrorism or clandestine activity." Warrants from this court can be issued without probable cause.

2. What kinds of cases does the Court of Appeals for the Armed Forces hear?

_____

◉ **Selection of Federal Judges** *(page 316)*

The Constitution provides that the president, with the advice and consent of the Senate, appoints all federal judges. Judges in constitutional courts serve "during good behavior," which, in practice, is for life. Thus, federal judges are free from public or political pressures when deciding cases.

Presidents favor judges who belong to their own political party. Also, when one party controls both the presidency and Congress, Congress is more likely to create additional judgeships. Because judges serve for life, presidents view judicial appointments as a way to continue their influence beyond the time they spend in the White House.

Presidents commonly follow the practice of senatorial courtesy. A president submits the name of a judicial candidate to the senators from the candidate's state before submitting it for formal Senate approval. If either or both senators oppose the nominee, the president usually withdraws the name and nominates another candidate. Senatorial courtesy is not used with the nomination of a Supreme Court justice because that is considered a national selection rather than a regional one.

Federal judges have held a variety of positions—law professors, members of Congress, attorneys, and state court judges. In recent decades, women, African Americans, and Hispanics have been appointed to more and more federal judgeships.

3. Why do presidents nominate judges who share their views?

_____

STUDY GUIDE  Chapter 11, Section 3

For use with textbook pages 320–326.

THE SUPREME COURT

CONTENT VOCABULARY

riding the circuit Traveling to hold court in a justice's assigned region of the country *(page 320)*

opinion A written explanation of a Supreme Court decision; also, in some states, a written interpretation of a state constitution or state laws by the state attorney general *(page 322)*

DRAWING FROM EXPERIENCE

Suppose your class is ordering pizza. Unfortunately, no one agrees on the toppings. Someone has to have the "final say," or no one will eat. In the federal court system, the Supreme Court has the "final say."

This section focuses on the jurisdiction and justices of the Supreme Court.

READING STRATEGIES

Use the graphic organizer below to list the characteristics of most Supreme Court justices and the qualifications presidents look for when nominating them.

Characteristics of Justices	Qualifications for Presidential Choices

⦿ Introduction *(page 320)*

The Supreme Court has final authority in cases involving the Constitution, acts of Congress, and treaties with other nations. The Court's decisions are binding on all lower courts. Today nomination to the Supreme Court is a high honor. In 1891, justices felt differently. They earned much of their pay **riding the circuit**. This meant they traveled to hold court in their assigned region of the country. This travel was grueling. Now the Court hears all its cases at the Supreme Court building in Washington, D.C.

◉ Supreme Court Jurisdiction (page 321)

The Supreme Court has original jurisdiction in:

A. cases involving representatives of foreign governments, and

B. certain cases in which a state is a party.

The Supreme Court's original jurisdiction cases form an average of only about five cases a year. Most cases fall under the Court's appellate jurisdiction. The Court hears cases that are appealed from lower courts of appeals. It may hear cases from federal district courts where an act of Congress was held unconstitutional. The Court may also hear cases that are appealed from the highest court of a state. In such cases, the court has the authority to rule only on the federal issue involved, not on any issues of state law. For example, a state court may try a person accused of violating a state law. During the trial, the person may claim that the police violated his or her Fourteenth Amendment rights at the time of the arrest. The defendant may appeal to the Supreme Court. The Supreme Court may decide whether the defendant's Fourteenth Amendment rights were violated, but not whether the person violated state law.

   1. In what two kinds of cases does the Supreme Court have original jurisdiction?

_____

_____

◉ Supreme Court Justices (page 321)

The Supreme Court includes the chief justice of the United States and eight associate justices. Although the number of justices is well established at nine, Congress has the power to change the number. Under the Constitution, Congress has the power to remove a justice through impeachment. However, no Supreme Court justice has ever been removed through impeachment.

The main duty of the justices is to hear and rule on cases. This duty involves the following tasks:

A. Deciding which cases to hear from the thousands appealed to the Court each year

B. Deciding the cases itself

C. Determining the Court's opinion, or explanation of its decision

The chief justice has the additional duties of:

A. Presiding over discussions of the cases

B. Acting as leader in the Court's judicial work

C. Helping to administer the federal court system

The justices also have limited duties related to the 12 federal judicial circuits. One Supreme Court justice is assigned to each circuit; three of the justices handle two districts each. Occasionally, justices take on additional tasks. For example, Chief Justice Earl Warren headed the commission that investigated the assassination of President Kennedy. However, justices avoid involvement in activities that might prevent them from dealing fairly with one side or the other in a case. For example, a justice might have a personal or business connection with one of the parties in a case. The justice usually withdraws from the case and it is assigned to another justice.

In 1882 Justice Horace Gray hired the first law clerk. The clerk worked mainly as Gray's servant and barber. Today law clerks help justices with the following jobs:

STUDY GUIDE (continued)   Chapter 11, Section 3

A. Reading all the appeals filed with the Court

B. Writing memos summarizing the key issues in each case

C. Helping prepare the Court's opinions by doing research and writing first drafts

The justices hire their law clerks from among the top graduates from the best law schools in the nation. The clerks usually work for the justices from one to two years. After leaving, many clerks go on to important careers as judges, law professors, and even Supreme Court justices.

More than 100 men and 2 women have served as Supreme Court justices. Most Supreme Court justices have the following characteristics:

A. Law degree and considerable legal experience

B. Experience as a state or federal court judge or attorney general

C. Aged fifty or older, although 10 were younger than fifty

D. Upper class background

E. Native-born citizenship. Only six justices have been born outside the United States, and George Washington appointed three of them

2. What are the three main tasks of Supreme Court justices?

_____

_____

_____

◉ Appointing Justices (page 323)

The Senate does not always approve presidents' choices for justices. The Senate rejected President Reagan's nomination of Robert Bork in 1988. Presidents usually choose a candidate who belongs to the same party and who shares the president's views. However, justices can be unpredictable. President Eisenhower appointed Earl Warren as chief justice because Eisenhower believed Warren would support conservative views. The Warren Court turned out to be the most liberal in the nation's history.

The American Bar Association (ABA) is the nation's largest national organization of lawyers. A special committee of the ABA rates possible candidates as "qualified" or "not qualified." The ratings of the ABA may or may not influence the president or Senate.

Other interest groups try to influence the nominating process. For example, the National Organization for Women (NOW) opposes nominees who are against women's rights. Other interest groups focus on the attitudes of potential justices to *Roe* v. *Wade*, the historic case that sets down the conditions under which a woman can legally obtain an abortion.

Members of the Supreme Court sometimes influence the selection of new justices. They may lobby the president for a certain candidate or write letters of recommendation supporting candidates that have been nominated. For example, in 1981 Sandra Day O'Connor received a strong recommendation from her former law school classmate Justice William Rehnquist.

3. Which groups try to influence the selection of Supreme Court justices?

_____

_____

STUDY GUIDE  Chapter 12, Section 1

For use with textbook pages 331–335.

THE SUPREME COURT AT WORK

CONTENT VOCABULARY

writ of certiorari (SUHR•shee•uh•RAR•ee) An order from the Supreme Court to a lower court to send up the records on a case for review (page 332)

per curiam opinion (puhr KYUR•ee•AHM) A brief, unsigned statement of a Supreme Court decision (page 333)

brief A written statement setting forth the legal arguments, relevant facts, and precedents supporting one side of a case (page 333)

amicus curiae (uh•mee•kuhs KYUR•ee•EYE) Latin for "friend of the court"; a written brief from an individual or group claiming to have information useful to a court's consideration of a case (page 333)

majority opinion The Court's decision expressing the views of the majority of justices (page 335)

dissenting opinion The opinion expressed by a minority of justices in a court case (page 335)

DRAWING FROM EXPERIENCE

Are you swayed by other people's opinions? If you are like many people, the opinions of powerful and respected people influence you most. The opinions of the Supreme Court are so influential that they help shape policy for the whole nation.

This section focuses on how the Supreme Court works.

READING STRATEGIES

Use the graphic organizer below to list the steps that the Supreme Court uses to decide major cases.

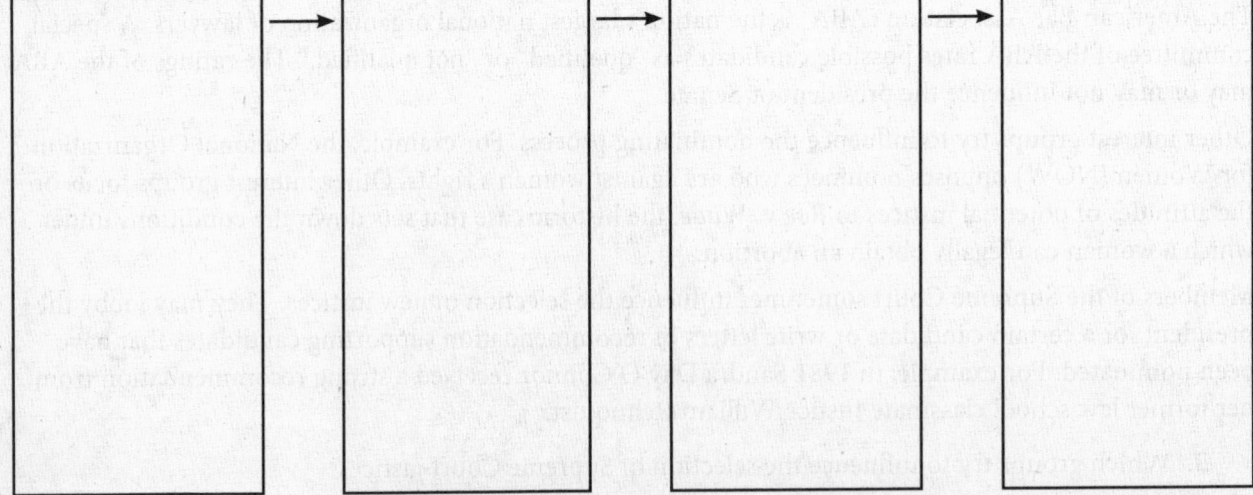

STUDY GUIDE (continued)   Chapter 12, Section 1

READ TO LEARN

◉ Introduction (page 331)

Traditionally, the Supreme Court met for about nine months each year. Each term began the first Monday in October and ran as long as the business before the Court required. Since 1979, however, the Court has been in continuous session throughout the year, taking periodic recesses.

◉ The Court's Procedures (page 331)

During the term, the Court sits for two weeks each month. The justices hear arguments from lawyers on cases before them from Monday through Wednesday. On Wednesday and Friday the justices meet in secret conferences to decide cases. After the two-week sitting, the Court recesses, or takes a break. The justices work on paperwork, consider arguments they have heard, study petitions from plaintiffs who want the Court to hear their cases, and work on opinions. These are written statements on cases they have already decided. In the opinions, the Court sets out general principles that apply to the nation as well as to the parties in the case.

1. Why are the opinions of the Supreme Court important?

_____

_____

◉ Getting Cases to the Court (page 332)

The main route to the Supreme Court is through a *writ of certiorari*. This is an order from the Court to a lower court to send the records on a case for a review. The party seeking review petitions the Court for certiorari. More than 90 percent of the requests for certiorari are rejected. When the Court rejects the request, the decision of the lower court stands.

Certain cases reach the Court on appeal, meaning that the decision of a lower federal or state court has been requested to be reviewed. In most cases, a lower court has ruled a law unconstitutional, or dismissed the claim that a state law violates federal law or the Constitution. When the Court dismisses these cases, the decision of the lower court becomes final.

When a case before the Supreme Court involves the federal government, the solicitor general is appointed by the president to represent the government. Thus, the solicitor general serves as a link between the executive and judicial branches. The solicitor general also plays a key role in setting the Court's agenda by determining whether the federal government should appeal a case to the Supreme Court.

The Supreme Court justices or their clerks identify important cases, and the chief justice puts them on the "discuss list." At the Court's Friday conferences, the chief justice reviews the "discuss list" and the other justices give their views. If four of the nine justices agree to accept a case, the Court will do so. The justices decide whether to ask for more information on a case or to rule quickly on the basis of written materials they already have. If the Court rules without new information, the ruling may be announced with a *per curiam opinion*. This is a brief, unsigned statement of the Court's decision.

2. In what two ways do cases come to the Supreme Court?

_____

_____

Copyright © Glencoe/McGraw-Hill, a division of The McGraw-Hill Companies, Inc.

STUDY GUIDE (continued)   Chapter 12, Section 1

⊙ Steps in Deciding Major Cases *(page 333)*

In hearing important cases, the Supreme Court follows these steps:

Submitting Briefs Lawyers on each side submit *briefs*. These are written statements setting forth the legal arguments, relevant facts, and precedents supporting one side of a case. Parties not directly involved in a case may also submit amicus curiae briefs. These are mostly useful for indicating which interest groups are on either side of an issue.

Oral Arguments A lawyer for each side is asked to present an oral argument before the Court. Justices often challenge a statement or ask for further information during a lawyer's argument.

The Conference On Wednesdays and Fridays the justices meet in secret conference to discuss the cases they have heard. Each decision gets about 30 minutes of discussion. Then the justices vote. A majority of justices must be in agreement to decide a case. At least six justices must be present to make a decision. If a tie occurs, the lower court's decision is left standing.

Writing the Opinion The Court's opinion states the facts of the case, announces the Court's ruling, and explains its reasoning in reaching the decision. The Court issues the following kinds of opinions:

A. In a unanimous opinion, all justices vote the same.

B. A *majority opinion* expresses the views of the majority of the justices on a case.

C. A concurring opinion is written by justices who agree with the majority's conclusions about a case, but do so for different reasons.

D. A *dissenting opinion* is the opinion of the justices on the losing side in a case.

If the chief justice has voted with the majority on a case, he or she assigns someone in the majority to write the opinion. When the chief justice is in the minority, the most senior associate justice among the majority assigns one of the justices on that side of the case to write the majority opinion. When the justices do not accept the first draft of a majority opinion, a bargaining process begins. Justices try to influence or satisfy one another as new versions of the opinion are written. Weeks or months may go by as the justices bargain and rewrite their opinions. Finally, the case is settled and the decision is announced during a sitting. Meanwhile, the Court selects and hears new cases.

3. What are the main steps in deciding important cases?

_____

_____

_____

_____

STUDY GUIDE  Chapter 12, Section 2

For use with textbook pages 336–341.

SHAPING PUBLIC POLICY

CONTENT VOCABULARY

judicial review The power of the Supreme Court to declare laws and actions of local, state, or national governments unconstitutional *(page 336)*

impound Refuse to spend money *(page 337)*

stare decisis (STEH•ee dih•SY•suhs) A Latin term meaning "let the decision stand"; the principle that once the Court rules on a case, its decision serves as a precedent on which to base other decisions *(page 338)*

precedent A model on which to base later decisions or actions *(page 338)*

advisory opinion A ruling on a law or action that has not been challenged *(page 339)*

DRAWING FROM EXPERIENCE

Have you ever worked with clay? Fingers, paperclips, and rolling pins are some tools you might have used to shape the clay. The Supreme Court also uses tools to shape public policy.

This section focuses on the Supreme Court's powers and limits in shaping public policy.

READING STRATEGIES

Use the graphic organizer below to list the criteria the Court uses to decide which cases to hear.

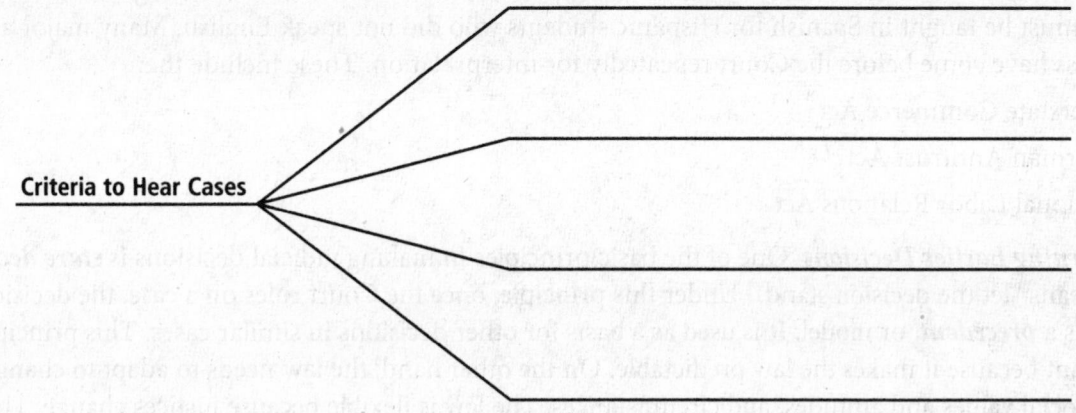

Name _____ Date _____ Class _____

READ TO LEARN

◉ **Introduction** (page 336)

The Supreme Court is a legal institution because it settles disputes and interprets the meanings of laws. It is also a political institution because it determines national policy when it applies the law to specific cases.

◉ **Tools for Shaping Policy** (page 336)

The Supreme Court determines policy in the following ways:

Judicial Review The Supreme Court's power to examine the laws and actions of local, state, and national governments and to cancel them if they violate the Constitution is called *judicial review.* The Supreme Court established this power in the 1803 case of *Marbury* v. *Madison.* Since then, the Court has invalidated about 150 provisions of federal laws. These decisions discourage the passage of similar laws.

Some rulings have even taken the country in a particular direction. For example, the decision in the *Dred Scott* case created tension that led to the Civil War.

The Supreme Court also reviews presidential policies. For example, in the case of *Train* v. *City of New York* (1974), the Court limited the president's power to *impound,* or refuse to spend, money that Congress had appropriated. The Supreme Court exercises judicial review most frequently at the state and local levels. In recent years, the Court has used judicial review to influence public policy at the state level in the areas of racial segregation, reapportionment of state legislatures, and police procedures. For example, the Court's decision in *Miranda* v. *Arizona* (1966) brought major changes in law enforcement across the nation.

Interpretation of Laws Congress often writes its laws in very general language. Disputes over the meaning of the language often end up in federal court. For example, the Civil Rights Act of 1964 forbids discrimination on the grounds of "race, color, or national origin." In the case of *Lau* v. *Nichols* (1974), the Court interpreted the law to require schools to instruct immigrant students in English. Because a Supreme Court decision is the law of the land, judges across the nation took the ruling to mean that classes must be taught in Spanish for Hispanic students who did not speak English. Many major acts of Congress have come before the Court repeatedly for interpretation. These include the:

A. Interstate Commerce Act

B. Sherman Antitrust Act

C. National Labor Relations Act

Overturning Earlier Decisions One of the basic principles in making judicial decisions is *stare decisis.* This means "let the decision stand." Under this principle, once the Court rules on a case, the decision serves as a *precedent,* or model. It is used as a basis for other decisions in similar cases. This principle is important because it makes the law predictable. On the other hand, the law needs to adapt to changing times, social values and attitudes, and circumstances. The law is flexible because justices change. They not only change their minds but also retire or die. New appointees bring different legal views that can shift the Court's position on issues. For example, in *Olmstead* v. *United States* (1928), the Court ruled that wiretaps were legal. However, in *Katz* v. *United States* (1967), the Court overturned the *Olmstead* decision.

STUDY GUIDE (continued)   Chapter 12, Section 2

1. What laws have come before the Supreme Court repeatedly for interpretation?

_____

_____

◉ Limits on the Supreme Court (page 339)

The Supreme Court deals with limited issues. Most Supreme Court decisions have dealt with civil liberties, economic issues, federal legislation and regulations, due process of law, and suits against government officials. Civil liberty cases make up the largest part of the Court's cases. For example, appeals from prisoners to challenge their convictions make up about one-fourth of the Court's decisions. The Court also decides cases involving disputes between the national government and the states and disagreements between the states themselves.

Rules and customs limit the Court's power to form policy. The Court will hear only cases in which:

A. the decision will make a difference. For example, it refused to decide whether Idaho could take back its approval of the Equal Rights Amendment because, even with Idaho, the amendment did not have enough support to pass. Furthermore, the Supreme Court will not give *advisory opinions.* These are rulings on laws or actions that have not been challenged.

B. the person or group bringing the case must have suffered real harm, such as denial of civil liberties or economic loss.

C. an important federal question is involved. The issue in the case must affect many people or the operation of the political system itself.

D. the question involved cannot be resolved by the executive or legislative branches.

With few exceptions, the Supreme Court can decide only cases that come from elsewhere in the legal system. However, the Court signals its interest in an issue by taking on a specific case. For example, the court showed its interest in legislative reapportionment by agreeing to hear *Baker* v. *Carr* (1962). In this case, the court reversed its 1946 position that drawing state legislative districts was a political decision.

A fourth factor limiting the Court's power to shape public policy is the Court's limited ability to enforce its rulings. The president may refuse to carry out a Court ruling. Or lower court judges may simply ignore a Supreme Court decision. However, most Court decisions are accepted and generally enforced.

The legislative and executive branches have ways to check and balance the power of the Court. These include the president's power to appoint justices, the Senate's power to approve appointments, and Congress's power to impeach and remove judges.

2. To which issues are most Supreme Court cases limited?

_____

_____

STUDY GUIDE 📖 Chapter 12, Section 3

For use with textbook pages 343–348.

INFLUENCING COURT DECISIONS

CONTENT VOCABULARY

bloc A coalition that promotes a common interest *(page 344)*
swing vote The deciding vote *(page 344)*

DRAWING FROM EXPERIENCE

Suppose students have a rally scheduled for a Tuesday evening. Can they provide reasons that will persuade their teacher to postpone the deadline for an assignment due on Wednesday? Like the students in this example, individuals and groups try to influence the decisions of the Supreme Court.

This section focuses on the forces that shape Supreme Court decisions.

READING STRATEGIES

Use the graphic organizer below to list the forces inside and outside the Court that influence its decisions.

Influences Inside the Court	Influences Outside the Court

READ TO LEARN

◉ Introduction *(page 343)*

The decisions that the Court makes are shaped by the following forces:

A. Existing laws

B. Personal views of the justices

C. Justices' interactions with one another

D. Social forces and public attitudes

E. Congress and the president

STUDY GUIDE (continued) Chapter 12, Section 3

⦿ Basing Decisions on the Law (page 343)

Justices must base their decisions on principles of law. Laws and the Constitution are not always clear in their meaning. Where the meaning of a law or section of the Constitution is not clear, the justices of the Court must:

A. Interpret the language

B. Determine what it means

C. Apply it to the circumstances of the case

In interpreting a law logically, the justices must relate their interpretations:

A. To the Constitution itself

B. To laws that are relevant to the case

C. To legal precedents

1. What three things must justices do when the language of a law is unclear?

_____

_____

⦿ Views of the Justices (page 344)

Most justices take the same position again and again in areas of personal concern. So voting **blocs,** or groups of justices with similar views, exist on certain kinds of issues. Generally, one bloc of justices tends to be liberal and another tends to be conservative. The size and power of each bloc changes as justices retire and new appointees take their place. When the Court is badly split on an issue, a justice whose views are neither liberal nor conservative may represent a **swing vote.** This means a deciding vote.

2. How could a majority voting bloc on the Supreme Court become a minority voting bloc?

_____

_____

⦿ Relations Among the Justices (page 344)

Relations among the justices influence the Court's decision making. Justices who can work easily with one another are more likely to find common solutions to problems. Justices try to avoid conflict even when they are at odds. However, at times personal conflicts have seriously divided the Court.

The chief justice can influence the Court's decisions in the following ways:

A. By directing decisions and framing alternatives while presiding over the Court during oral arguments and in conference

B. By making up the discuss list and assigning the writing of opinions to the justices

3. How can the chief justice influence the Court's decisions?

_____

_____

◉ **The Court and Society** (page 345)

The justices are interested in keeping as much public support as possible. They realize that the Court's authority and power depend on public acceptance of its decisions. They know that when the Court moves too far ahead of or lags too far behind public opinion, it risks losing valuable public support and may weaken its own authority.

The values and beliefs of society influence Supreme Court justices. As society changes, attitudes and practices that were acceptable in one period may become unacceptable in another. For example, in *Plessy* v. *Ferguson* (1896), the Court upheld a law that required African Americans to "have equal but separate accommodations." It ruled that any facility, although separate, was equal to those available to whites. However, in *Brown* v. *Board of Education of Topeka* (1952), the Court overturned its "separate but equal" ruling. Chief Justice Warren declared that separate was always unequal and that it violated the equal protection clause of the Fourteenth Amendment.

4. Why did the Warren Court overturn the *Plessy* decision of 1896?

_____

_____

◉ **Balancing the Court's Power** (page 347)

Presidents influence the Court in the following ways:

A. Using the power to appoint justices to bring the Court closer to their own point of view

B. The way they enforce Court decisions. Presidents may enforce Court decisions vigorously or with little enthusiasm, depending on their views of the issues.

Congress has tried to control the court's appellate jurisdiction by:

A. limiting the Court's ability to hear certain cases;

B. passing laws to limit the Court's choices of solutions to problems;

C. reenacting a law the Court has rejected in a different form, hoping that the justices will change their minds;

D. proposing a constitutional amendment to overturn a Court ruling. This method has been used successfully several times. For example, in 1895 the Court ruled that a tax on incomes was unconstitutional. However, in 1913 the Sixteenth Amendment passed and allowed Congress to levy an income tax.

Congress also tries to influence the Court by exercising its power to set the justices' salaries and to set the number of justices on the Court. Finally, Congress uses its confirmation power to shape the Court's position. For example, the Senate questioned two of President Bush's appointees on sensitive social issues in Senate confirmation hearings.

5. What occasions do both presidents and Congress use to help shape the Court's position?

_____

_____

Name _____ Date _____ Class _____

For use with textbook pages 355–357.

CONSTITUTIONAL RIGHTS

CONTENT VOCABULARY

human rights Fundamental freedoms *(page 355)*

incorporation A process that extended the protections of the Bill of Rights against the actions of state and local governments *(page 357)*

DRAWING FROM EXPERIENCE

Have you ever been grounded *and* had your phone privileges taken away? Life becomes very limited when you cannot speak or get together with other people. It gives you a taste of life in a country without First Amendment freedoms.

This section focuses on why basic constitutional rights are protected throughout the nation.

READING STRATEGIES

Use the graphic organizer below to describe the freedoms guaranteed by the First Amendment.

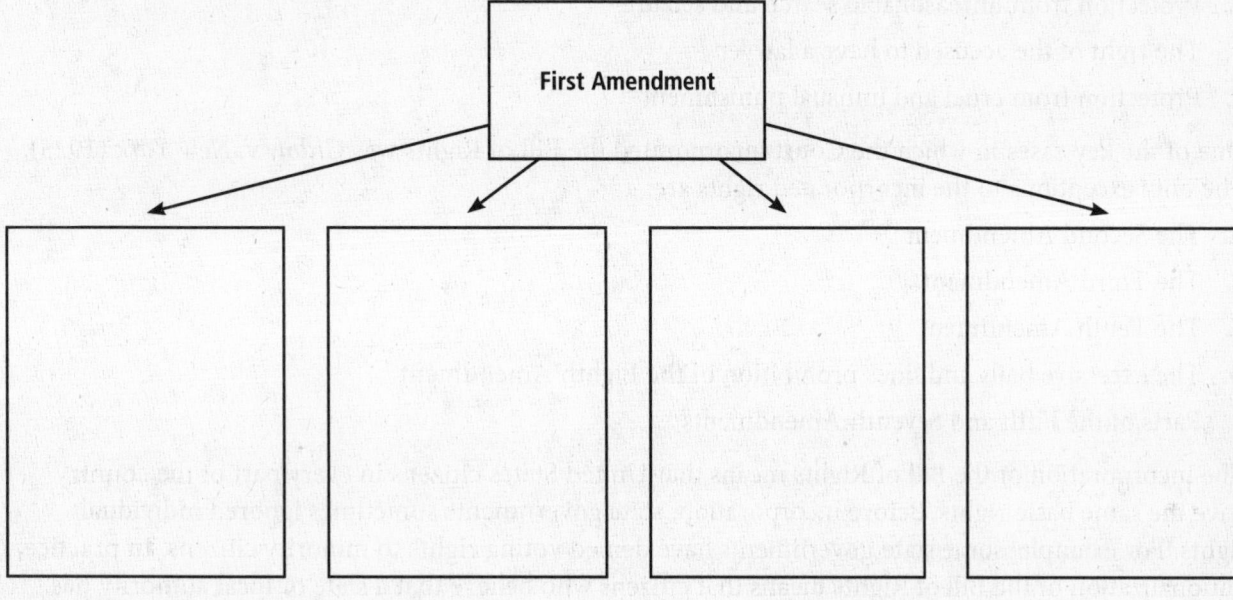

STUDY GUIDE (continued)   Chapter 13, Section 1

READY TO LEARN

◉ Introduction (page 355)

Human rights, or fundamental freedoms, lie at the heart of the United States political system. They enable citizens and noncitizens to worship as they wish, speak freely, and read and write what they choose. The Constitution guarantees the rights of United States citizens.

◉ Constitutional Rights (page 355)

The Constitution guarantees basic rights in the Bill of Rights—the first 10 amendments—and in several other amendments. The Bill of Rights was originally intended to protect people against the actions of the federal government.

The addition of the Fourteenth Amendment in 1868 started a process called *incorporation.* This process extended the Bill of Rights to protect persons from all levels of government in the United States. Over the years the Supreme Court has interpreted the due process clause of the Fourteenth Amendment to apply the guarantees of the Bill of Rights to state and local governments. As a result, no state can deprive any person of their First Amendment rights:

A. Freedom of speech

B. Freedom of the press

C. Freedom of religion

D. Freedom of assembly

Also according to the Supreme Court, the Fourteenth Amendment guarantees people in all states:

A. Protection from unreasonable search and seizure

B. The right of the accused to have a lawyer

C. Protection from cruel and unusual punishment

One of the key cases in which the Court incorporated the Bill of Rights was *Gitlow* v. *New York* (1925). The only exceptions to the incorporated rights are:

A. The Second Amendment

B. The Third Amendment

C. The Tenth Amendment

D. The excessive bails and fines prohibition of the Eighth Amendment

E. Parts of the Fifth and Seventh Amendments

The incorporation of the Bill of Rights means that United States citizens in every part of the country have the same basic rights. Before incorporation, state governments sometimes ignored individual rights. For example, some state governments have denied voting rights to minority citizens. In practice, nationalization of the Bill of Rights means that citizens who believe that a state or local authority has denied them their basic rights may take their case to a federal court.

1. How did incorporation happen?

_____

_____

STUDY GUIDE  Chapter 13, Section 2

For use with textbook pages 358–364.

FREEDOM OF RELIGION

CONTENT VOCABULARY

establishment clause The First Amendment guarantee that "Congress shall make no law respecting establishment of religion" *(page 358)*

free exercise clause The First Amendment guarantee that prohibits government from unduly interfering with the free exercise of religion *(page 358)*

parochial school A school operated by a church or religious group *(page 359)*

secular Nonreligious *(page 360)*

abridge Limit *(page 363)*

precedent A model on which to base later decisions or actions *(page 364)*

DRAWING FROM EXPERIENCE

Imagine a law that requires you to attend a certain church. Worshipping as you please could then mean going to jail. Thanks to the First Amendment, most people do not have to choose between their beliefs and prison.

This section focuses on the parts of the First Amendment that guarantee religious freedom.

READING STRATEGIES

Use the graphic organizer below to list cases related to the establishment clause and the free exercise clause.

Establishment Clause Cases	Free Exercise Clause Cases

STUDY GUIDE (continued)   Chapter 13, Section 2

READ TO LEARN

⊙ Introduction *(page 358)*

The ***establishment clause*** in the First Amendment states that "Congress shall make no law respecting an establishment of religion." The ***free exercise clause*** prohibits government from interfering with the free exercise of religion. The interpretations of these clauses have led to a continuing debate in American politics.

⊙ The Establishment Clause *(page 358)*

The Founders believed that the First Amendment built "a wall of separation between Church and State." Religion has long been part of public life in the United States. Defining the proper distance between the two often results in controversy. The task of deciding falls to the Supreme Court.

For example, *Everson* v. *Board of Education* (1947) involved a challenge to a New Jersey law allowing the state to pay for busing students to parochial schools. Parochial schools are operated by a church or religious order. The Court ruled the law constitutional because the law benefited students rather than a religion directly. However, in *Wolman* v. *Walter* (1977), the Court banned state-supported bus transportation for parochial school field trips.

Why are some forms of aid constitutional and others not? The answer is the so-called *Lemon* test. Since the 1971 case of *Lemon* v. *Kurtzman,* the Court decides whether such aid violates the establishment clause by using a three-part test. To be constitutional, state aid to church schools must:

A. have a clear secular, nonreligious purpose;

B. neither advance a religion nor discourage the practice of a religion; and

C. avoid "excessive government entanglement with religion."

In *Mitchell* v. *Helms* (2000), the Court upheld the part of a federal law that provided funds for equipment and materials to public and private schools. Because students at all schools benefited, the law passed the Court's three-part test.

Can public schools release students from school to attend classes in religious education? In *Zorach* v. *Clauson* (1952), the Court decided that a release-time program of religious instruction was constitutional if it was carried on in private facilities, not in the public schools.

The Supreme Court has passed down several controversial decisions affecting prayer and Bible reading in public schools. For example, in *Engel* v. *Vitale* (1962), the Court ruled that a nondenominational prayer used in New York public schools was unconstitutional. In two 1963 cases the Court banned school-sponsored Bible reading and saying the Lord's Prayer in public schools. The Court reasoned that these acts violated the First Amendment because tax-paid teachers led the activities in public buildings. However, in 1990 the Court ruled the Equal Access Act constitutional. This law allows student religious groups to hold meetings for Bible reading in public schools. According to the Court, a student-led religious club that meets after school like any other student group does not show state approval of a particular religion.

The Supreme Court also has applied the establishment clause to classroom instruction. In *Edwards* v. *Aguillard* (1987), the Court ruled that a law requiring the teaching of creationism violated the establishment clause, because its main purpose was to endorse a certain religious belief.

STUDY GUIDE (continued)   Chapter 13, Section 2

Other establishment clause issues concern Christmas displays and prayers at government meetings. In 1989 the Court ruled that a publicly funded Nativity scene by itself violated the Constitution. That same year, however, the Court upheld placing a menorah—a Jewish religious symbol—alongside a Christmas tree at city hall. In regards to prayer at government meetings, the Court approved. It claimed that such prayers did not sway legislators as easily as students. Besides, prayer at government meetings is a centuries-old tradition.

1. Why did the Court allow groups to meet for Bible reading in public schools?

_____

_____

◉ The Free Exercise Clause (page 363)

The First Amendment forbids laws "prohibiting the free exercise of religion." However, the Supreme Court has never permitted religious freedom to justify any behavior. For example, George Reynolds had been convicted of polygamy, or having more than one wife. Because Reynolds was a Mormon and polygamy was a Mormon tradition, he claimed that the law against polygamy *abridged,* or limited, freedom of religion. In *Reynolds* v. *United States* (1879), the Court upheld Reynolds's conviction. The Court explained that people are not free to worship in ways that violate laws protecting the health, safety, and morals of the community. The Court also has ruled that other restrictions violate the free exercise clause. For example, in *Wisconsin* v. *Yoder* (1972), the Court decided that the state could not require Amish parents to send their children to public school beyond the eighth grade. To do so, the Court determined, would threaten to undermine the Amish community.

Two of the most discussed free exercise cases concerned whether children should be forced to salute the flag. Jehovah's Witnesses believe that saluting the flag violates the Christian commandment against bowing down to graven images. In *Minersville School District* v. *Gobitis* (1940), the Court ruled that requiring children to salute the flag did not infringe on religious freedom. But in 1943, The Court overturned this decision. West Virginia required that a student pledge allegiance to the flag or be expelled. A Jehovah's Witness appealed the state's requirement in *West Virginia State Board of Education* v. *Barnette.* The Court concluded that patriotism could be taught without forcing people to violate their religious beliefs. The Court usually follows *precedent,* decisions made on the same issue in earlier cases. However, when the Court thinks it is in error, it feels no need to follow precedent.

2. Why did the Court uphold the law against polygamy even though the Mormon religion permitted marriage to more than one wife?

_____

_____

STUDY GUIDE 📖 Chapter 13, Section 3

For use with textbook pages 366–370.

FREEDOM OF SPEECH

CONTENT VOCABULARY

pure speech The verbal expression of thought and opinion before an audience that has chosen to listen *(page 366)*

symbolic speech Using actions and symbols to express opinions—also called expressive conduct *(page 366)*

seditious speech Speech urging resistance to lawful authority or advocating the overthrow of the government *(page 367)*

defamatory speech False speech that damages a person's good name, character, or reputation *(page 369)*

slander False speech intended to damage a person's reputation *(page 369)*

libel False written or published statements intended to damage a person's reputation *(page 369)*

DRAWING FROM EXPERIENCE

Has anyone ever told lies about you? Did the lies make you look bad to other people? This kind of gossip is called slander. It is one of several kinds of speech the First Amendment does not protect.

This section focuses on the kinds of speech the First Amendment does and does not protect.

READING STRATEGIES

Use the graphic organizer below to list the types of speech that are protected and that are not protected by the First Amendment.

Protected	Not Protected

STUDY GUIDE (continued) Chapter 13, Section 3

READwd TO LEARN

◉ Introduction (page 366)

The First Amendment exists to protect ideas that may be unpopular or different from those of the majority.

◉ Types of Speech (page 366)

According to the Supreme Court, the First Amendment protects two kinds of speech:

Pure speech is the spoken expression of thought and opinion before an audience that has chosen to listen. It is the most common form of speech. Traditionally, the Supreme Court has provided the strongest protection of pure speech against government control.

Symbolic speech involves using actions and symbols, in addition to or instead of words, to express opinions. For example, protesters sometimes burn the flag to show their displeasure with the government. A government may place more limits on symbolic speech than pure speech. For example, the Supreme Court has ruled that the first Amendment does not permit symbolic speech that unnecessarily blocks sidewalks or traffic, trespasses, or endangers public property. In *United States* v. *O'Brien,* the Court ruled that a government can regulate or forbid symbolic speech if the regulation:

A. falls within the constitutional power of the government,

B. furthers an important government interest that is unrelated to limiting free speech, and

C. leaves open other ways to communicate.

Since the O'Brien decision, the Supreme Court has ruled that the First Amendment protects the rights to wear black armbands and to burn flags. However, the Court held that a city may limit picketing in front of a private home and placed the right to privacy ahead of protesters' right to symbolic speech.

    1. How does symbolic speech differ from pure speech?

_____

_____

◉ Regulating Speech (page 367)

The Supreme Court realizes that freedom of speech must have limits. So justices have developed the following guidelines.

Clear and Present Danger The First Amendment does not protect speech that clearly presents an immediate danger. Justice Oliver Wendell Holmes, Jr., developed the "clear and present danger" test in *Schenck* v. *United States* (1919). Schenck was convicted for printing and distributing leaflets that urged soldiers to obstruct the war effort during World War I. When Schenck appealed to the Supreme Court, it upheld his conviction. Ordinarily, the First Amendment would protect Schenck's speech. During wartime, however, his actions threatened the well-being of the nation.

The Bad Tendency Doctrine In *Gitlow* v. *New York* (1925), the Supreme Court ruled that speech could be restricted even if it had only a tendency to lead to illegal action. However, since the 1920s, this bad tendency doctrine has lost support from the Supreme Court.

STUDY GUIDE (continued)   Chapter 13, Section 3

The Preferred Position Doctrine This test was developed in the 1940s. It holds that First Amendment freedoms are more basic than other freedoms. So any law limiting these freedoms should be ruled unconstitutional unless the government can show the law is absolutely necessary.

Sedition Laws Congress and state legislatures have often outlawed *seditious speech.* This is any speech urging resistance to lawful authority or advocating the overthrow of the government. However, since the late 1950s, the Court has distinguished between urging people to believe in an action and urging them to take action. For example, in *Brandenburg* v. *Ohio* (1969), the Court ruled in favor of a Ku Klux Klan leader who refused a police order to end a rally and cross burning. The Court explained that talking about the use of force may not be forbidden unless the speaker is trying to provoke immediate acts of violence.

2. What are the Supreme Court's four guidelines for limiting free speech?

_____

_____

_____

◉ Other Unprotected Speech (page 369)

The First Amendment also does not protect these other forms of speech:

Defamatory Speech This is false speech that damages a person's good name, character, or reputation. Defamatory speech can be either *slander*—spoken words—or *libel*—written words. A person who makes false statements about someone else may be sued in civil court and ordered to pay damages. However, the Court allows some defamatory speech about public officials. Otherwise, criticism of government, a basic constitutional right, might be silenced. Recently, the Court has extended this protection of statements about politicians to statements about all public figures, such as athletes and entertainers.

"Fighting Words" In *Chaplinsky* v. *New Hampshire* (1942), the Supreme Court ruled that the First Amendment does not protect words that are so insulting that they lead to immediate violence.

Student Speech In *Bethel School District* v. *Fraser* (1986), the Supreme Court ruled that the First Amendment does not prevent school officials from suspending students who use indecent language at school events. Two years later in *Hazelwood School District* v. *Kuhlmeier,* the Court held that school officials have the right to regulate student speech in school-sponsored newspapers, stage productions, and other activities.

3. Why did the Court decide that defamatory statements about politicians are protected speech?

_____

_____

STUDY GUIDE  Chapter 13, Section 4

For use with textbook pages 371–375.

FREEDOM OF THE PRESS

CONTENT VOCABULARY

prior restraint Government censorship of information before it is published or broadcast *(page 371)*

sequester To keep isolated *(page 373)*

gag order An order by a judge barring the press from publishing certain types of information about a pending court case *(page 373)*

shield laws A law that gives reporters some means of protection against being forced to disclose confidential information or sources in state courts *(page 374)*

DRAWING FROM EXPERIENCE

Do you read the newspaper or watch television news? Then you enjoy the benefits of a free press. This section focuses on prior restraint and other free press issues.

READING STRATEGIES

Use the Venn diagram below to help you analyze how trial judges deal with a conflict between freedom of the press and a defendant's right to a fair trial.

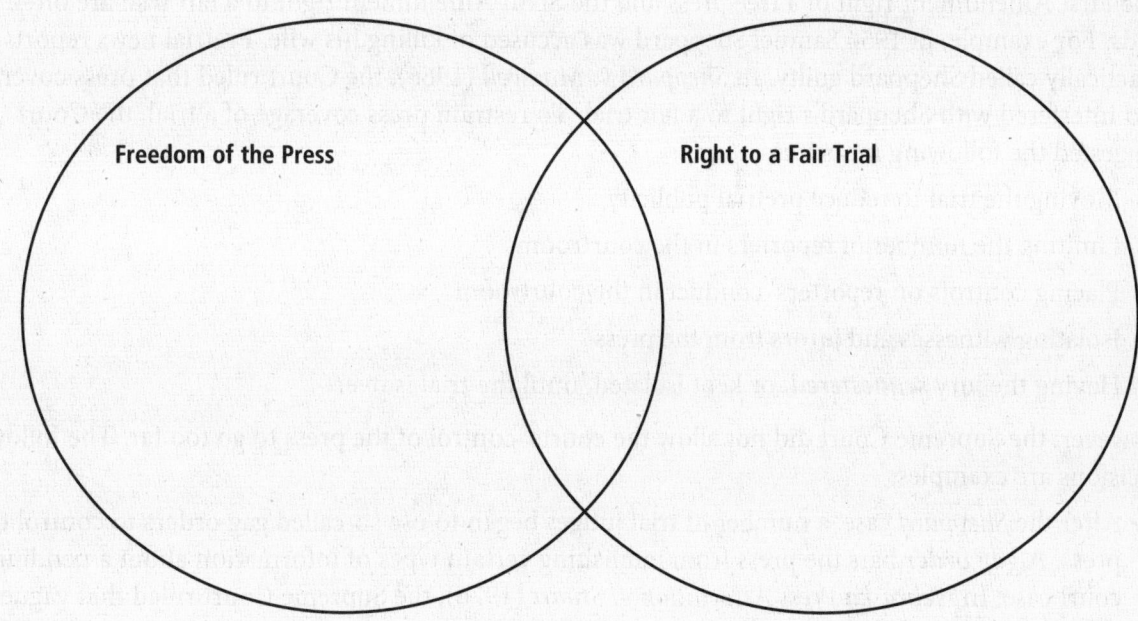

Freedom of the Press

Right to a Fair Trial

STUDY GUIDE (continued)   Chapter 13, Section 4

READ TO LEARN

◉ Introduction (page 371)

Freedom of the press moves free speech one step further by allowing opinions to be written and circulated or broadcast. The press today includes magazines, radio, television, and the Internet as well as newspapers because each has a role in spreading news and opinions.

◉ Prior Restraint Forbidden (page 371)

Prior restraint is censorship of information before it is published. It is a common way for governments in many nations to control information and limit freedom. In the United States, however, the Supreme Court has ruled that the press may be censored in advance only in cases relating directly to national security.

For example, in 1971 the *New York Times* published parts of a secret government report on the American involvement in the Vietnam War. The government tried to stop future publication of other parts of the report, claiming that national security was endangered. In *New York Times Co.* v. *United States,* the Court rejected the government claims because the report showed that government officials had lied to the American public. Justice William O. Douglas noted that the main purpose of freedom of the press was to stop the government from withholding embarrassing facts from the public.

    1. According to the Supreme Court, when can the press be censored in advance?

_____

_____

◉ Fair Trials and Free Press (page 372)

The First Amendment right of a free press and the Sixth Amendment right to a fair trial are often at odds. For example, in 1954 Samuel Sheppard was accused of killing his wife. Pretrial news reports practically called Sheppard guilty. In *Sheppard* v. *Maxwell* (1966), the Court ruled that press coverage had interfered with Sheppard's right to a fair trial. To restrain press coverage of a trial, the Court suggested the following measures:

A. Moving the trial to reduce pretrial publicity

B. Limiting the number of reporters in the courtroom

C. Placing controls on reporters' conduct in the courtroom

D. Isolating witnesses and jurors from the press

E. Having the jury *sequestered,* or kept isolated, until the trial is over

However, the Supreme Court did not allow the courts' control of the press to go too far. The following decisions are examples:

A. After the *Sheppard* case, a number of trial judges began to use so-called gag orders to control the press. A *gag order* bars the press from publishing certain types of information about a pending court case. In *Nebraska Press Association* v. *Stuart* (1976), the Supreme Court ruled that vague and overbroad gag orders were unconstitutional.

STUDY GUIDE (continued)   Chapter 13, Section 4

B. In *Richmond Newspapers, Inc.* v. *Virginia* (1980) and other cases, the Court ruled that trials, jury selections, and preliminary hearings must be open to the press and the public except under limited circumstances.

Many reporters argue that freedom of the press gives them the right to refuse to reveal confidential sources. In three 1972 cases, the Supreme Court held that reporters have no such right, but added that Congress and states can give reporters this protection. Thirty states have passed *shield laws* which protect reporters from disclosing confidential information or sources in state courts. In 2005, questions were raised about whether reporters can be forced to disclose their notes when national security is at stake. The issues remain controversial. There is still no federal shield law, but even state laws set limits on reporters.

2. On what basis did Samuel Sheppard appeal his conviction to the Supreme Court?

_____

◉ Free Press Issues (page 374)

Technology has created the following new issues regarding freedom of the press:

Radio and Television Radio and television do not enjoy as much freedom as other press media because they use public airwaves. Stations must obtain a license from the Federal Communications Commission (FCC), a government agency that regulates their actions. The FCC requires that stations follow certain guidelines in presenting programs. The FCC may also punish stations that broadcast indecent language. To what extent do free speech guidelines apply to cable television? In 1997, the Court ruled that cable television has more First Amendment protection from government regulation than other broadcasters, but not as much as the publishers of newspapers and magazines.

Movies In *Burstyn* v. *Wilson* (1952), the Supreme Court ruled that the First and Fourteenth Amendments guarantee motion pictures "liberty of expression." However, the Court also ruled that movies may be treated differently than books or newspapers.

E-Mail and the Internet In *Reno* v. *American Civil Liberties Union* (1997), the Court ruled that Internet speech deserves the same free speech protection as other print media.

Other modern issues concerning freedom of the press are:

Obscenity In *Miller* v. *California* (1973), the Court ruled that communities should set their own standards for obscenity in speech, pictures, and written material. However, the Court has since stepped in to overrule specific local acts, making it clear that a community's right to censor is limited.

Advertising Advertising is considered commercial speech. This is speech with a profit motive. It is given less First Amendment protection than purely political speech. The government has controlled and regulated advertising for a long time. In the mid-1970s, the Supreme Court began to relax controls. For example, in *Bigelow* v. *Virginia* (1975), the justices permitted newspaper advertisements for abortion clinics. Since then it has struck down bans on advertising medical prescription prices, legal services, and medical services. It has also limited regulation of billboards, "for sale" signs, and lawyers' advertisements.

3. Why do radio and television enjoy less freedom than other press media, and who sets their guidelines?

_____

STUDY GUIDE  Chapter 13, Section 5

For use with textbook pages 376–382.

Freedom of Assembly

CONTENT VOCABULARY

picketing Patrolling an establishment to persuade workers and the public not to enter it *(page 378)*

Holocaust The mass extermination of Jews and other groups by the Nazis during World War II *(page 379)*

heckler's veto Public veto of free speech and assembly rights of unpopular groups by claiming demonstrations will result in violence *(page 379)*

DRAWING FROM EXPERIENCE

Have you taken part in a walkathon? Or signed a petition to save a local wilderness from development? Then you have exercised the freedom of assembly.

This section focuses on the constitutional protections of and the limits on the right to assemble.

READING STRATEGIES

Use the graphic organizer below to list the ways by which the government can regulate freedom of assembly.

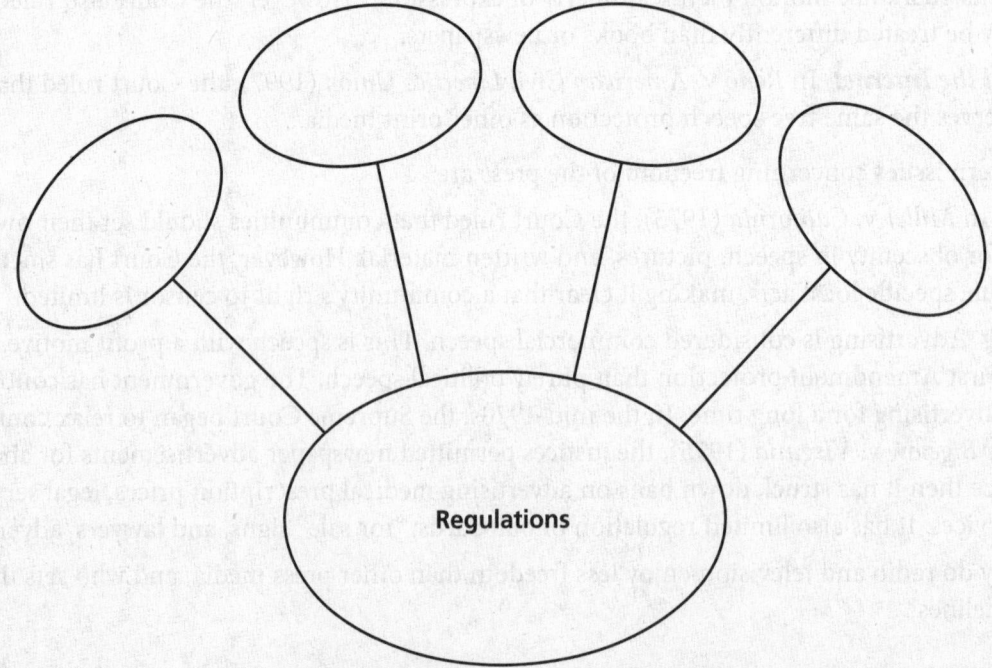

STUDY GUIDE (continued)　　　Chapter 13, Section 5

READ TO LEARN

⊙ Introduction (page 376)

The First Amendment freedom of assembly applies to meetings in private homes and in public places. It also protects the right to make views known to public officials through petitions, letters, lobbying, carrying signs in parades, and marching.

⊙ Protecting Freedom of Assembly (page 376)

Freedom of assembly is closely related to freedom of speech because most gatherings involve some form of protected speech. Political parties and interest groups that influence government would be impossible without freedom of assembly.

In *DeJonge* v. *Oregon* (1937), the Supreme Court established the following two principles:

A. The right of assembly was as important as the rights of free speech and free press.

B. The due process clause of the Fourteenth Amendment protects freedom of assembly from state and local governments.

Freedom of assembly includes the right to parade and demonstrate in public. These forms of assembly may interfere with the rights of others because they usually occur in parks, streets, or on sidewalks. Verbal and physical clashes might occur when the parades and demonstrations advocate unpopular causes. As a result, parades and demonstrations are subject to greater government control than exercises of pure speech and other kinds of assembly.

In *Cox* v. *New Hampshire* (1941), the Supreme Court upheld a law that required a permit for a parade. The Court ruled that the law was not designed to silence unpopular ideas. Rather, it was intended to ensure that parades would not interfere with other citizens using the streets.

Demonstrations may occur in airports, libraries, courthouses, and schools. However, the Court has set limits. For example, in *Cox* v. *Louisiana* (1965), the Court upheld a law that banned demonstrations and parades near courthouses if they could interfere with trials. The Court also required that limits on freedom of assembly apply evenly to all groups. For instance, in *Police Department of Chicago* v. *Mosely* (1972), the Court voided a law that banned demonstrations around schools, except for picketing by labor unions. *Picketing* is patrolling an establishment to persuade workers and the public not to enter it.

The right to assemble does not allow a group to use private property for its own use, even if the property is open to the public. For example, in *Lloyd Corporation* v. *Tanner* (1972), the Court ruled that a group protesting the Vietnam War did not have the right to gather in a shopping mall. The Court has also upheld laws that create a fixed buffer zone around abortion clinics. These zones are intended to keep anti-abortion demonstrators from blocking the entrances to the clinics.

1. What was decided in *Lloyd Corporation* v. *Tanner*?

_____

_____

⊙ Assembly and Disorder (page 378)

People have a right to assemble regardless of the views they hold. However, police have a hard time protecting this right when assemblies threaten public safety. For example, in 1977 the American Nazi

STUDY GUIDE (continued)　　Chapter 13, Section 5

Party announced plans to hold a rally in Skokie, Illinois. The many Jewish residents of Skokie were outraged. Many were survivors of the Holocaust—the mass killing of Jews and other groups by the Nazis during World War II. The city required the Nazis to pay a $300,000 bond to get a parade permit. The Nazis claimed the high bond interfered with free speech and assembly. A federal appeals court ruled that no community could use parade permits to interfere with free speech and assembly. The Skokie case is an example of the *heckler's veto.* The public vetoes the free speech and assembly rights of unpopular groups by claiming demonstrations will end in violence.

Amid other circumstances, the Supreme Court decides that public safety overrides the right to free speech. In *Feiner* v. *New York* (1951), the Court upheld the conviction of a man who refused a police order to stop speaking, even though the listeners were angry and threatening violence. The Court argued that the police had acted to keep the peace and not to stop free speech. However, in *Gregory* v. *City of Chicago* (1969), the Court overturned the convictions of peaceful demonstrators who had been arrested because hecklers were throwing rocks and eggs at them.

2. Why did the Supreme Court uphold the conviction of the speaker in *Feiner* v. *New York?*

_____

_____

◉ Protecting Labor Picketing *(page 380)*

Picketing sends a message, so it is a form of speech and assembly. But labor picketing does more. It tries to persuade customers and workers not to deal with a business. In *Thornhill* v. *Alabama* (1940), the Supreme Court ruled that peaceful picketing was a form of free speech. However, in *Hughes* v. *Superior Court* (1950), it refused to overturn California's ban on picketing at a supermarket to force it to hire African American workers. According to Justice Felix Frankfurter, the Court ruled this way because picketing "produces consequences different from other modes of communication."

3. How is labor picketing different from other kinds of picketing?

_____

_____

◉ Freedom of Association *(page 381)*

The right to freely assemble includes the right of individuals to freedom of association. This means the freedom to join a political party, an interest group, or any other organization. However, in 1927 the Court limited the freedom of association by its decision in *Whitney* v. *California.* It argued that joining the Communist party presented a clear and present danger to the nation because the party promoted the violent takeover of private property. In later cases, however, the Court ruled that only actual preparation for use of force against the government was a just reason for limiting freedom of association.

4. Explain freedom of association.

_____

_____

STUDY GUIDE  Chapter 14, Section 1

For use with textbook pages 387–391.

Ⓐ NATION OF IMMIGRANTS

CONTENT VOCABULARY

amnesty A group pardon to individuals for an offense against the government *(page 390)*

alien A person who lives in a country where he or she is not a citizen *(page 391)*

resident alien A person from a foreign nation who has established permanent residence in the United States *(page 391)*

nonresident alien A person from a foreign country who expects to stay in the United States for a short, specified period of time *(page 391)*

enemy alien A citizen of a nation with which the United States is at war *(page 391)*

refugee A person fleeing a country to escape persecution or danger *(page 391)*

undocumented alien A person without legal permission to be in a country *(page 391)*

DRAWING FROM EXPERIENCE

Are you the descendant of immigrants? Most likely, you are. Most American families began as immigrants from other countries.

This section focuses on the laws that control immigration.

READING STRATEGIES

Use the table below to help you take notes and track changes in U.S. immigration policy.

Major Immigration Legislation	Basic Features of Law
1886 Chinese Exclusion Act	Restricted Chinese immigration, barred citizenship
1924 Immigration Act of 1924	

STUDY GUIDE (continued)   Chapter 14, Section 1

READ TO LEARN

◉ **Introduction** *(page 387)*

An American historian once wrote that "immigrants are American history."

◉ **Immigration Policy** *(page 387)*

Congress controls immigration policy, which practically did not exist until 1882. Since 1882, U.S. immigration policy has gone through the following stages:

1882–1924 In 1882 Congress barred the immigration of people such as the mentally disabled, convicts, and penniless people. That same year Congress passed the Chinese Exclusion Act. It restricted the admission of Chinese laborers and prevented all foreign-born Chinese from becoming citizens. This law marked the first time a federal law had restricted either immigration or citizenship on the basis of nationality or ethnicity. The number of restrictions grew but so did the number of immigrants. Between 1880 and 1920, about 25 million immigrants entered the United States.

1924–1965 In 1924 the Johnson Act lowered the number of immigrants allowed into the country to less than 165,000 a year. Immigration from each country was limited to 2 percent of the 1890 census.

Immigration Reform Act of 1965 This legislation got rid of the national origins system. It set up the following classes of citizens:

A. those who could come from Europe, Asia, and Africa and

B. those who could come from Canada, Mexico, and the nations of Central and South America.

Congress fixed the number of immigrants from Western Hemisphere countries at 120,000 per year and the number from other countries at 170,000 per year. The law also set up preference categories of immigrants, such as immigrants with skills.

Immigration Reform and Control Act of 1986 The major provisions of this law are:

A. Illegal aliens who have resided in the United States since before 1982 can apply for amnesty. This is a general pardon offered by the government. Then they can eventually become permanent residents.

B. Aliens may apply for United States citizenship after five years of permanent American residence.

C. Employers are forbidden to hire illegal aliens.

D. Employers must ask applicants for documents such as passports or birth certificates to prove they are either citizens or otherwise qualified to work in the United States.

Later Immigration Acts The Immigration Act of 1990 reintroduced the countries of origin system. Only up to 7 percent of all visas granted could go to one country. It permitted about 675,000 immigrants per year and encouraged immigration of workers with special skills. The law also established a category for special immigrants, who fall into three groups: refugees displaced by war, close relatives of United States citizens, and those admitted through private laws passed by Congress. A private law is one that applies to a particular person.

The Immigration legislation of 1996 addressed illegal immigration by: enlarging the border patrol and establishing stiffer penalties for people who created false citizen papers or smuggled illegal workers.

STUDY GUIDE (continued)   Chapter 14, Section 1

1. Under which law—the Johnson Act or the Immigration Act of 1990—could more Irish, English, and French immigrants be allowed into the country per year? Explain your answer.

_____

_____

◉ Current Political Debate *(page 390)*

Since 1990, the debate over illegal immigration from across the southwestern border of the United States has intensified. Employers in agriculture and construction do not want to loss the flow of low-cost labor. Other Americans want to limit undocumented workers because they believe these workers will lower their wages.

Late in his second term, President George W. Bush backed a bill to create a guest-worker program and strengthen border control. It also did not propose deporting undocumented workers, something opponents said amounted to amnesty, or forgiveness, for undocumented immigrants. The bill would have fined undocumented workers and required them to fulfill certain obligations before they could apply for U.S. citizenship. The Senate voted down the bill in June of 2007.

◉ Aliens *(page 390)*

An *alien* is a person who lives in a country where he or she is not a citizen. An immigrant is a person who comes to a country intending to live there permanently.

United States law puts aliens into the following categories:

A. A *resident alien* is a person from a foreign nation who has established permanent residence in the United States. Thus, immigrants are resident aliens until they become American citizens.

B. A *nonresident alien* is a person from another country who expects to stay in the United States for a short, specified time. An example is a Nigerian reporter who comes to the United States to write about a presidential election.

C. An *enemy alien* is a citizen of a nation with which the United States is at war.

D. Refugees are people fleeing to escape persecution or danger in their own countries.

E. An *illegal alien* is a person who comes to the United States without a legal permit, such as a passport, visa, or entry permit.

The Bill of Rights protects aliens as well as citizens. The Supreme Court has repeatedly struck down state laws that have tried to limit the rights of aliens. For example, in 1982 the Supreme Court ruled that the state of Texas could not deny free public education to the children of illegal aliens. In recent years, debate over whether such rights should be limited has increased because the number of illegal immigrants has grown significantly. Aliens are expected to pay taxes, obey the law, and be loyal to the government. They cannot vote and usually do not have to serve in the military or on juries. Unlike citizens, aliens cannot travel freely in the United States. They must notify the Immigration and Naturalization Service when they change residences.

2. What is the difference between an enemy alien and an illegal alien?

_____

_____

STUDY GUIDE  Chapter 14, Section 2

For use with textbook pages 392–397.

THE BASIS OF CITIZENSHIP

CONTENT VOCABULARY

naturalization The legal process by which a person is granted citizenship *(page 392)*

jus soli (YOOS SOH•LEE) Latin phrase meaning "law of the soil"; the principle that grants citizenship to nearly all people born in a country *(page 393)*

jus sanguinis (YOOS SAHN•gwuh•nuhs) Latin phrase meaning "law of blood"; the principle that grants citizenship on the basis of the citizenship of one's parents *(page 394)*

collective naturalization A process by which a group of people become U.S. citizens through an act of Congress *(page 395)*

expatriation Giving up one's citizenship by leaving to live in a foreign country *(page 395)*

denaturalization The loss of citizenship through fraud or deception during the naturalization process *(page 395)*

DRAWING FROM EXPERIENCE

How did you become a citizen? Most American citizens, but not all, were born in the United States. This section focuses on the different sources of U.S. citizenship.

READING STRATEGIES

Use the table below to help you take notes and list the conditions of U.S. citizenship in column 1. In column 2, list the responsibilities of all U.S. citizens.

Conditions of Citizenship	Responsibilities

STUDY GUIDE (continued) Chapter 14, Section 2

READ TO LEARN

◉ Introduction (page 391)

The members of a nation are called citizens. United States citizens have duties and responsibilities. Their duties include obeying the law, paying taxes, and being loyal to the American government. The responsibilities are being informed, voting, respecting the rights and property of others, and respecting different opinions and ways of life.

◉ Who Determines Citizenship (page 392)

The nation's Founders left the job of deciding who was a citizen to the states. The exceptions were African Americans and immigrants who became citizens through *naturalization.* This is the legal process by which a person is granted the rights and privileges of a citizen.

In *Dred Scott* v. *Sandford* (1857), the Supreme Court decided that African Americans could not be citizens. Only descendants of people who were state citizens at the time the Constitution was written, or immigrants who became citizens through naturalization, were United States citizens.

In 1868 the Fourteenth Amendment overturned the *Dred Scott* decision. The amendment guaranteed that people of all races born in the United States and subject to its government are citizens. State citizenship became an automatic result of national citizenship.

1. What is the definition of citizenship that the Fourteenth Amendment established?

_____

_____

◉ Gaining Citizenship (page 393)

The two sources of citizenship by birth are:

Jus Soli This is a Latin phrase that means "law of the soil." This principle grants citizenship to nearly all people born in the United States. However, people born in the United States who are not subject to the jurisdiction of the United States government are not granted citizenship. For example, a foreign diplomat's child who is born in the United States is not an American citizen.

Jus Sanguinis This Latin phrase means "law of blood." It grants citizenship to people born of American parents. However, the rules of jus sanguinis make these exceptions:

A. If an individual is born in a foreign country and both parents are United States citizens, the child is a citizen provided one of the parents has been a legal resident of the United States or its possessions at some time.

B. If only one of the parents is a U.S. citizen, that parent must have lived in the United States or one of its possessions for at least 5 years, 2 of which had to occur after age 14.

All immigrants who wish to become citizens must go through naturalization. Immigrants need the following qualifications to apply:

A. Applicants must have entered the United States legally.

B. They must be of good moral character.

STUDY GUIDE (continued)   Chapter 14, Section 2

C. They must declare their support of the principles of American government.

D. They must prove they can read, write, and speak English. However, applicants over 50 who have lived in the United States more than 20 years do not have to meet the English-language requirement.

E. They must show some basic knowledge of American history and government.

2. Explain the basic idea of jus soli.

_____

_____

3. Briefly sum up the qualifications needed for naturalization.

_____

_____

The naturalization process requires the following steps:

A. An applicant must file a petition requesting citizenship. Anyone who is at least 18 years old and who has lived as a legal resident alien in the United States for 30 months out of the previous 5 years and in the state from which the petition is filed for at least 3 months may apply for citizenship. The wife or husband of an American citizen needs to live in the United States only 3 years before applying.

B. The Immigration and Naturalization Service conducts an investigation and holds a preliminary hearing. The hearing is a test of the applicant's qualifications.

C. An applicant who makes it through the first hearing must attend a final hearing. There a judge administers the United States oath of allegiance. Then the judge issues a certificate of naturalization that declares the person a citizen of the United States.

A less common process is ***collective naturalization.*** In this process, a group of people living in the same area become American citizens through an act of Congress. For example, Congress granted citizenship to all people living in Hawaii in 1900. In another exception to regular naturalization, Congress made all Native Americans citizens in 1924. Congress also does away with naturalization requirements in special cases, such as that of a 99-year-old Russian immigrant who wanted to die a U.S. citizen.

4. What is the third step in the naturalization process?

_____

_____

Only the federal government can both grant citizenship and take it away. The three ways to lose citizenship are:

Expatriation　The simplest way to lose citizenship is through ***expatriation.*** This is the voluntary or involuntary giving up of one's native country to live in a foreign one. A person who becomes a naturalized citizen of another country voluntarily gives up his or her citizenship. A child of expatriates involuntarily loses his or her citizenship.

Punishment for a Crime　A person may lose citizenship when convicted of certain federal crimes, such as treason, taking part in a rebellion, or trying to overthrow the government through violence.

Denaturalization　The loss of citizenship through fraud or deception during the naturalization process is called ***denaturalization.*** This could also occur if an individual joins a Communist or totalitarian organization less than five years after becoming a citizen.

5. Describe voluntary expatriation.

_____

_____

◉ Citizen Responsibilities *(page 395)*

Enjoying one's rights as a citizen depends on accepting the following responsibilities:

A. Learning about rights and laws at school or from legal aid societies, consumer protection groups, or other organizations

B. Participating in political life by campaigning for a candidate, distributing leaflets for a political party, or working at the polls on election day

C. Voting helps Americans to share responsibility for how their society is governed.

6. How does a citizen help to assure his or her rights by voting?

_____

_____

STUDY GUIDE  Chapter 14, Section 3

For use with textbook pages 398–402.

EQUAL PROTECTION OF THE LAW

CONTENT VOCABULARY

suspect classification A classification made on the basis of race or national origin that is subject to strict judicial scrutiny *(page 399)*

fundamental right A basic right of the American system or one that is indispensable in a just system *(page 399)*

discrimination Unfair treatment of individuals based solely on their race, gender, ethnic group, age, physical disability, or religion *(page 399)*

Jim Crow law Law requiring racial segregation in such places as schools, buses, and hotels *(page 400)*

separate but equal doctrine A policy which held that if facilities for different races were equal, they could be separate *(page 400)*

civil rights movement The efforts to end segregation *(page 401)*

DRAWING FROM EXPERIENCE

Suppose your teacher passes only students with green eyes. Why is this unfair? Because the teacher is making an unreasonable distinction among students. Fortunately, the Constitution protects against this kind of injustice.

This section focuses on the meaning of *equal protection*.

READING STRATEGIES

Use the time line below to help you take notes and list the major 1960s and 1970s civil rights laws beginning with the Equal Pay Act of 1963.

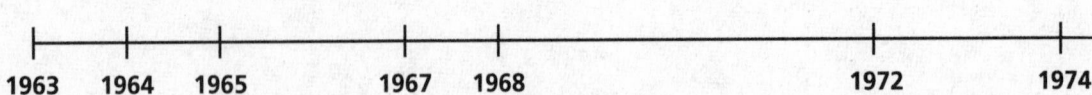

1963   1964   1965   1967   1968   1972   1974

STUDY GUIDE (continued)   Chapter 14, Section 3

READE TO LEARN

◉ Introduction (page 398)

The democratic ideal of equality means people are entitled to equal rights and treatment before the law.

◉ What Is Equal Protection? (page 398)

The Fourteenth Amendment includes an equal protection clause. It forbids state and local governments from drawing unreasonable distinctions among different groups of people. Many laws classify or draw distinctions among people. For example, a cigarette tax taxes smokers but not nonsmokers. When a citizen challenges a law because it violates the equal protection clause, the issue is not whether a distinction has been made. The issue is whether the distinction is reasonable.

The rational basis test provides that the Supreme Court will uphold a state law when the state can show a good reason for the classification applied in the law. The Court usually puts the burden of proving that a law is unreasonable on the people challenging the law. However, a special case arises when the state law involves one of the following:

A. A *suspect classification* is made on the basis of race or national origin. For example, a law that requires African Americans but not whites to ride in the back of the bus would be a suspect classification. The state must show the Court that there is some important public interest to justify the law and its classifications.

B. *Fundamental rights* go to the heart of the American system. The Court looks at state laws dealing with fundamental rights very closely. For example, a state law that limits the right to travel freely between states would be ruled unconstitutional because freedom to move among states is fundamental.

   1. What must a state show to persuade the Supreme Court to uphold a state law of suspect classification?

   _____

   _____

◉ Proving Intent to Discriminate (page 399)

Laws that classify people unfairly are said to "discriminate." *Discrimination* exists when individuals are treated unfairly solely because of their race, gender, ethnic group, age, physical disability, or religion.

In *Washington* v. *Davis* (1976), the Supreme Court ruled that to prove a state guilty of discrimination, one must prove that the state intended to discriminate. The case arose over a District of Columbia police department examination that more African American recruits failed than white recruits.

Since the *Washington* case, the Supreme Court has applied the intent to discriminate to other areas. For example, the Court upheld an Illinois ordinance that permitted only single-family homes in an area, prohibiting housing projects. The justices believed there was no intent to discriminate.

   2. List the different kinds of discrimination.

   _____

   _____

STUDY GUIDE (continued)   Chapter 14, Section 3

◉ The Equal Rights Struggle *(page 400)*

For almost 100 years, the courts upheld discrimination against and segregation of African Americans. Racial discrimination is treating members of a race differently simply because of race. Segregation is separation of people from the larger social group. By the late 1800s, half the states had adopted *Jim Crow laws.* These laws required racial segregation in such places as schools, public transportation, and hotels.

The Supreme Court justified Jim Crow laws in *Plessy* v. *Ferguson* (1896). The Court said that the Fourteenth Amendment allowed separate facilities as long as they were equal. However, in *Brown* v. *Board of Education of Topeka* (1954), the Court overturned the *separate-but-equal doctrine.*

This decision marked the beginning of a long, difficult battle to desegregate the public schools. Though public schools were no longer segregated by law, housing patterns in many areas created segregated school districts that were largely either African American or white. In *Swann* v. *Charlotte-Mecklenburg Board of Education* (1971), the Court declared that children should be bused to schools outside their neighborhoods to ensure integrated schools.

After the *Brown* decision, many African Americans and whites worked together to end segregation through the *civil-rights movement.* African Americans deliberately broke laws supporting racial segregation. When arrested, they were almost always found guilty. They then could appeal and challenge the constitutionality of the laws. The most important leader of the civil rights movement was Dr. Martin Luther King, Jr., a Baptist minister from Georgia. Influenced by the civil rights movement, Congress passed the Civil Rights Act of 1964 and other laws to ensure voting rights and equal job opportunities for African Americans.

3. How did the *Brown* decision affect American schools?

_____

_____

STUDY GUIDE  Chapter 14, Section 4

For use with textbook pages 404–410.

CIVIL LIBERTIES CHALLENGES

CONTENT VOCABULARY

affirmative action Government policies that award jobs, government contracts, promotions, admissions to schools, and other benefits to minorities and women in order to make up for past discriminations *(page 404)*

security classification system The provision that information on government activities related to national security and foreign policy may be kept secret *(page 408)*

DRAWING FROM EXPERIENCE

Have you ever tried to make up for hurting another person? The government tries something similar when it uses policies like affirmative action to make up for discrimination against people.

This section focuses on government and civil liberties.

READING STRATEGIES

Use the graphic organizer below to help you take notes and list the challenges to civil liberties.

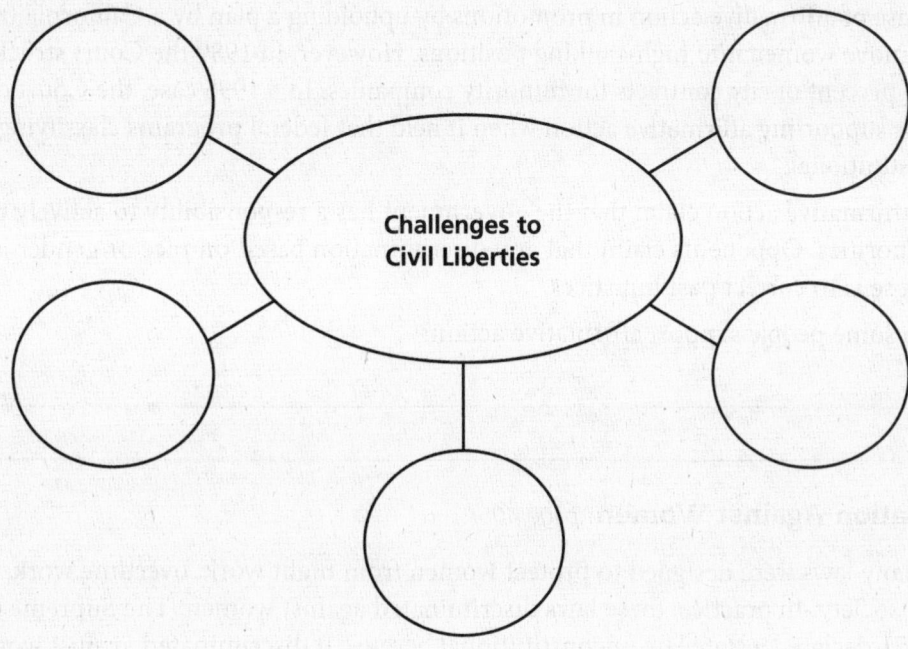

STUDY GUIDE (continued) Chapter 14, Section 4

READE TO LEARN

◉ Introduction (page 404)

Changing ideas, social conditions, and technology raise new civil liberties issues. These issues involve affirmative action, discrimination against women, the right to know about government actions, privacy, and the fight against terrorism.

◉ Affirmative Action (page 404)

Affirmative action refers to policies that directly or indirectly award jobs, government contracts, promotions, admissions to schools and training programs, and other benefits to minorities, women, or the physically challenged in order to make up for past discrimination. Most affirmative action programs are required by federal government regulations and court decisions. Others are voluntary efforts.

One of the most important applications of affirmative action has been in the field of education. In *Regents of the University of California* v. *Bakke* (1978), the Supreme Court ruled that colleges and universities could take race into account when admitting students. In *Grutter* v. *Bollinger* (2003), the Court upheld an admissions policy at the University of Michigan that gave preference to minorities who applied to its law school by considering race as a "plus factor" along with other characteristics such as special talents. With this decision, the Court endorsed the idea that universities have a special mission to consider race in admissions in order to provide diverse, well-trained graduates. However, the Court has also made it clear that not all forms of affirmative action in college admissions are acceptable. For example, colleges cannot set aside a certain quota of slots for minority candidates (*Bakke*), or use a point system that automatically gives extra points to minority applicants (*Gratz* v. *Bollinger*, 2003).

The Court's attitude towards affirmative action in other areas has been less clear. In 1987 the Court supported the use of affirmative action in promotions by upholding a plan by a California transportation department to move women into high-ranking positions. However, in 1989 the Court struck down a plan setting aside 30 percent of city contracts for minority companies. In a 1995 case, the Court overturned earlier decisions supporting affirmative action when it held that federal programs classifying people by race are unconstitutional.

Supporters of affirmative action claim that the government has a responsibility to actively promote more equality for minorities. Opponents claim that any discrimination based on race or gender is wrong even when the purpose is to correct past injustices.

1. Why do some people support affirmative action?

_____

_____

◉ Discrimination Against Women (page 406)

Before 1970, many laws were designed to protect women from night work, overtime work, heavy lifting, and dangers in society. In practice, these laws discriminated against women. The Supreme Court for the first time in 1971 declared a state law unconstitutional because it discriminated against women. In *Reed* v. *Reed*, the Court ruled that a law that automatically preferred a father over a mother as executor of a son's estate violated the equal protection clause of the Fourteenth Amendment.

STUDY GUIDE (continued) — Chapter 14, Section 4

The *Reed* case established a new standard for judging constitutionality in sex discrimination cases. The Court said that any law that classifies people based on gender "must be reasonable . . . and must rest on some ground of difference." The difference must serve "important governmental objectives" and be substantially related to those objectives.

All of the following standards result from Court decisions that bar distinctions based on gender:

A. States cannot set different ages at which men and women become legal adults.

B. States cannot set different ages at which men and women are allowed to purchase alcohol.

C. States cannot exclude women from juries.

D. Employers cannot require women to take a pregnancy leave from work.

E. Girls cannot be kept off Little League baseball teams.

F. Private clubs and community service groups cannot exclude women from membership.

G. Employers must pay equal retirement benefits to men and women.

H. States cannot bar women from state-supported military colleges.

The following standards are based on Court decisions that allow differences based on gender:

A. All-boy and all-girl public schools are allowed to exist as long as the enrollment is voluntary and quality is equal.

B. A state can give widows a property tax exemption not given to widowers.

C. A state may prohibit women from working in all-male prisons.

D. Hospitals may bar fathers from the delivery room.

Congress has also protected women from discrimination by passing the following laws:

A. The Civil Rights Act of 1964 banned job discrimination on the basis of gender.

B. The 1972 Equal Employment Opportunity Act strengthened earlier laws by banning gender discrimination in activities ranging from hiring and firing to promotion, pay, and working conditions.

C. In 1976 Congress required all schools to give boys and girls an equal chance to take part in sports programs.

D. In 1991 the Civil Rights and Women's Equity in Employment Act required employers to justify any gender distinctions in hiring.

   2. What are three Supreme Court decisions that barred distinctions based on gender?

_____

_____

◉ Citizens' Right to Know *(page 408)*

The right of citizens and the press to know what government is doing is an essential part of democracy. However, the national government's *security classification system* keeps secret information on government activities related to national security and foreign policy.

In 1966 Congress passed the Freedom of Information Act requiring federal agencies to show citizens public records on request. Exceptions are granted for national defense materials, confidential personnel and financial data, and law enforcement files. People can sue the government if it denies their request to see materials.

The Sunshine Act of 1976 required that government meetings and hearings be open to the public. The law applies to about 50 federal agencies, boards, and commissions. These meetings must also be announced one week in advance. Some closed meetings are allowed, but then a *transcript,* or summary record, of the meeting must be made. If necessary, people can sue to force public disclosure of the proceedings of a meeting.

3. What does the Freedom of Information Act require?

_____

_____

◉ Citizens' Right to Privacy *(page 408)*

The Constitution does not mention a specific right to privacy. However, in *Griswold* v. *Connecticut* (1965), the Supreme Court ruled that personal privacy is one of the rights protected by amendments to the Constitution.

In many later decisions, the Court has recognized the right to privacy in areas of personal behavior, such as child rearing and abortion. However, the Court has also held that the right to personal privacy is limited when the state has a "compelling need" to protect society.

Widespread use of the Internet is creating many new challenges to the right to privacy. One concern is online surveillance by the government. Online privacy is also being threatened by the ability of Web sites, hackers, and marketers to gather personal information about people as they "surf" the Web and store it in "data warehouses," where it becomes available to nearly anyone willing to pay for it.

War and other national emergencies create tension between the need to maintain individual rights and the need to protect the nation's security. In response to the September 11, 2001, terrorist attacks, Congress passed the USA Patriot Act, which greatly increased the federal government's power to detain, investigate, and prosecute people suspected of terrorism. For example, it allows the government to seize a person's private records without showing "probable cause." The Act also broadened the scope of who could be considered a terrorist, allowed the FBI to share evidence collected in criminal probes, and gave the attorney general sweeping new powers to detain and deport people.

Though Americans strongly supported the Patriot Act at the time of its passage, concerns later arose over whether the Act poses a threat to civil liberties. Many legal experts have noted that the law could lead to changes in basic principles of the American legal system, such as the right to a jury trial, the privacy of attorney-client communications, and protections against preventative detention. By 2004, more than 140 U.S. cities and towns had passed resolutions critical of the Patriot Act. In 2002, however, the Act survived a court challenge when a federal appeals court overturned attempts to limit new surveillance tactics. In March 2006, the Act was renewed although a few limits were placed on the government's powers.

4. What new powers did the Patriot Act give to the federal government?

_____

_____

STUDY GUIDE  Chapter 15, Section 1

For use with textbook pages 415–430.

SOURCES OF AMERICAN LAW

CONTENT VOCABULARY

law Set of rules and standards by which a society governs itself *(page 415)*

constitutional law Law that involves the interpretation and application of the U.S. Constitution and state constitutions *(page 416)*

statute A law written by a legislative branch *(page 417)*

ordinance A law or statute passed by city council *(page 417)*

statutory law A law that is written down so that everyone might know and understand it *(page 417)*

administrative law Law that spells out the authority, procedures, rules, and regulations to be followed by government agencies *(page 417)*

common law Law made by judges in the process of resolving individual cases *(page 418)*

equity A system of rules by which disputes are resolved on grounds of fairness *(page 418)*

due process Principle in the Fifth and Fourteenth Amendments stating that the government must follow proper constitutional procedures in trials and in other actions it takes against individuals *(page 419)*

substantive due process Certain rights of individuals in the application of laws, some that are specified in the Constitution (like free speech) and some that are not specified (like the right of privacy in making personal decisions) *(page 419)*

procedural due process Principle that prohibits arbitrary enforcement of law and also provides safeguards to ensure that constitutional and statutory rights are protected by law enforcement *(page 419)*

adversary system A judicial system in which opposing lawyers present their strongest cases *(page 419)*

presumed innocence The presumption that a person is innocent until proven guilty *(page 420)*

DRAWING FROM EXPERIENCE

Do you like playing card games? The rules for many popular card games go back hundreds of years. The sources for the rules, or laws, that govern the United States go back hundreds of years, too.

This section focuses on the beginnings of American law.

READING STRATEGIES

Use the time line below to help you take notes as you read the summaries that follow. Think about the sources of American law.

| 1792 B.C. | A.D. 534 | | 1765–1769 | 1776 | 1804 |

Copyright © Glencoe/McGraw-Hill, a division of The McGraw-Hill Companies, Inc.

READ TO LEARN

⦿ Introduction (page 415)

Law is the set of rules or standards by which a society governs itself. Law is used to solve problems, protect rights, limit government, promote general welfare, set social goals, and control crime. In democratic societies, both the government and its citizens are subject to the law. Government decisions are made according to established laws. No person is above the law, regardless of his or her position.

⦿ Early Systems of Law (page 415)

One of the earliest known written sets of laws was the Code of Hammurabi. The king of Babylonia collected these laws from 1792 B.C. to 1750 B.C. The code spelled out relationships among individuals as well as punishments in areas that we now call property law, family law, civil law, and criminal law. Another set of early laws that influenced our legal system was the Ten Commandments. The Ten Commandments were one of the sources of law for the ancient Israelites. According to the Hebrew Bible, Moses received these commandments from God on Mount Sinai. The Ten Commandments' emphasis on social justice and individual and communal responsibility has become a model for ethical laws. These ideals have been adopted by much of the world.

    1. What two early sets of laws influenced our legal system?

    _____

    _____

⦿ Our Legal Heritage (page 416)

The laws that govern our lives and protect our rights are divided into the following types:

Constitutional Law This type of law establishes our country as a representative democracy. It also outlines our structure of government and sets forth our basic rights. **Constitutional law** deals with the formation, construction, and interpretation of constitutions. For the most part, cases dealing with constitutional law decide the limits of the government's power. They also decide the rights of individuals.

Statutory Law A **statute** is written by a legislative branch of government. Statutes passed by city councils are called **ordinances.** An example of a statute that limits individuals is a law that sets speed limits. Statutes also grant rights and benefits such as Social Security payments and drivers' licenses. Statutory law is sometimes called "Roman law" because it is based on the way ancient Romans made their laws. The laws of Rome were written down so that everyone might know and understand them. In the A.D. 530s the Roman emperor Justinian had all the laws of Rome organized into a single system called the Justinian Code. In 1804 the French emperor Napoleon Bonaparte updated the Justinian code. His version is still used in France, the state of Louisiana, and the Canadian province of Quebec.

Administrative Law This kind of law spells out the authority and guidelines followed by government agencies. It also includes the rules and regulations these agencies issue. Most administrative agencies either regulate people's behavior or provide or deny government benefits such as welfare payments and medical insurance. Thus, many administrative law cases deal with problems of fairness and due process.

STUDY GUIDE (continued) Chapter 15, Section 1

Common Law This is the single most important basis of the American legal system. Common law, also called case law, is made by judges in the process of resolving individual cases. Common law originated in England. Judges followed earlier rulings, or precedents, if the case before them was similar to cases already decided and in the record books. The English colonists used common law in America. The practice of common law continues across the United States today, except in Louisiana, where legal procedures are based on the Napoleonic Code.

Equity This system of rules settles disputes on the grounds of fairness. Equity was used in medieval times in place of common law. An equity court might issue an injunction to stop a neighbor from building a fence across your property. Today a single court hears cases in equity and common law.

2. What are the different types of laws used in the United States?

_____

_____

◉ Legal System Principles *(page 419)*

Federal and state courts operate under the following four basic principles:

Equal Justice Under the Law This refers to the goal of the American court system to treat all people alike. The equal justice principle grants all Americans rights, such as the right to a trial by a jury.

Due Process of Law has both a substantive part and a procedural part. **Substantive due process** refers to certain rights guaranteed in the Fifth and Fourteenth Amendments. An example of a law that violates substantive due process is one that limits dwellings to single families. This would prevent grandparents from living with grandchildren. Cases about the way a law is carried out involve **procedural due process.** Procedural due process requires:

A. Notice to a person that he or she has done something wrong and that the government intends to take a specific action that will affect the person

B. Giving the affected person the right to respond or be heard concerning the accusation of wrongdoing

The Adversary System Under this system, lawyers for opposing sides try to present their strongest cases. The judge in the court has an impartial role. Critics of the adversary system claim that it encourages lawyers to ignore evidence unfavorable to their side and to be more concerned about victory than justice. Supporters of the system insist that it is the best way to bring out the facts of a case.

Presumption of Innocence In the United States system of justice, an accused person is innocent until proved guilty. This notion of **presumed innocence** is deeply rooted in the English legal heritage. The burden of proving an accusation against a defendant falls to the accuser.

3. Why do some people dislike the adversary system?

_____

_____

STUDY GUIDE 📖 Chapter 15, Section 2

For use with textbook pages 422–427.

CIVIL LAW

CONTENT VOCABULARY

civil law Rules governing disputes among two or more individuals or between individuals and the government *(page 422)*

contract A set of voluntary promises, enforceable by the law, between two or more parties *(page 422)*

expressed contract A contract in which the terms are specifically stated, usually in writing *(page 422)*

implied contract A contract in which the terms are not expressly stated but can be inferred from the actions of the people involved and the circumstances *(page 422)*

real property Land and whatever is attatched to or growing on it *(page 423)*

personal property Movable belongings such as clothes and jewelry, as well as intangible items like stocks, bonds, copyrights, and patents *(page 423)*

mortgage A loan taken out to pay for a house *(page 423)*

tort A wrongful act, other than breach of contract, for which an injured party has the right to sue *(page 432)*

plaintiff A person who brings charges in court *(page 433)*

defendant The person against whom a civil or criminal suit is brought in court *(page 433)*

injunction An order that will stop a particular action or enforce a rule or regulation *(page 433)*

complaint A legal document filed with the court that has jurisdiction over the problem *(page 433)*

summons An official notice of a lawsuit that includes the date, time, and place of the initial court appearance *(page 433)*

answer A formal response by a defendant to the charges in a complaint *(page 433)*

discovery Process when both sides prepare for a trial by gathering evidence to support their case *(page 433)*

mediation A process in which each side is given the opportunity to explain its side of the dispute and must listen to the other side *(page 434)*

affidavit A written statement to prove statements of fact signed by a witness under oath *(page 435)*

DRAWING FROM EXPERIENCE

What would you do if you slipped and broke your leg on a neighbor's icy driveway? You could sue the neighbor for money.

This section focuses on the kinds of civil law and the steps in a civil case.

READING STRATEGIES

Use the graphic organizer below to help you take notes and list the steps in a civil case that does not go to trial.

[ ] → [ ] → [ ] → [ ]

STUDY GUIDE (continued) Chapter 15, Section 2

READptto LEARN

◉ Introduction *(page 430)*

Civil law covers disputes among two or more individuals or between individuals and the government. In civil law cases, one party believes it has suffered an injury at the hands of another party or wants to prevent a harmful action from taking place.

◉ Types of Civil Law *(page 430)*

Four of the most important branches of civil law are:

Contracts A *contract* is a set of voluntary promises between parties who agree to do or not do something. A contract is enforceable by law. In an *expressed contract*, the parties spell out the terms in writing. In an *implied contract*, the terms are not spelled out but inferred from the actions of the people involved and the circumstances of the contract. The characteristics of a valid contract are:

A. All parties to the contract are mentally able and in most cases legal age adults.

B. The contract cannot involve doing or selling anything illegal.

C. The contract must include an offer, acceptance, and in most cases a consideration. An offer is a promise that something will or will not happen. For example, an auto shop may offer to repair a bumper for $500. The other party's written or oral agreement to have the bumper fixed is the acceptance. The consideration is the $500 in return for a repaired bumper.

A large number of civil suits involve disagreements over contracts.

Property law Many kinds of legal disputes arise over using, owning, buying, and selling property. The courts define *real property* as land and whatever is attached to or growing on it, such as houses or trees. *Personal property* includes movable things like clothes or jewelry. For many Americans, the most important property they invest in is a house. This usually involves a *mortgage*—or loan to pay for the house—as well as a deed, title, and insurance. State and federal governments have passed many laws dealing with real property. For example, the Fair Housing Act protects people against discrimination based on race, religion, color, national origin, or gender when they try to buy the home they want or to get a loan.

Family Law This branch of civil law deals with the relationships among family members. This includes:

A. Marriage, which is a civil contract entered into by both parties

B. Divorce, which legally ends the marriage and leaves both parties free to marry

C. Parent-child relationships, including custody issues, such as who a child lives with after a divorce

Torts or Civil Wrongs A *tort* is any wrongful act, except breaking a contract, for which the injured party has the right to sue for damages in civil court. For example, a person may sue a person who broke his or her window. Also, the wronged party may sometimes ask for additional money as a way to punish the person who did the damage. Torts fall into the following major categories:

A. Intentional tort, which involves a deliberate act that results in harm to a person or property

B. Negligence, when someone is injured because another person does something a prudent person would not have done or fails to do something a reasonable person would have done

Name _____ Date _____ Class _____

STUDY GUIDE (continued) Chapter 15, Section 2

1. What are the four basic kinds of civil law?

_____

_____

_____

◉ Steps in a Civil Case *(page 433)*

Civil cases are called lawsuits. The *plaintiff* in a lawsuit is the person who brings the complaint. The *defendant* is the person being sued. The plaintiff in a civil suit usually seeks damages, or an award of money from the defendant. If the court decides in favor of the plaintiff, the defendant must pay the damages to the plaintiff. Usually the defendant must also pay court costs. If the court decides in favor of the defendant, the plaintiff must pay all the court costs and receives nothing from the defendant.

In some lawsuits involving equity, the plaintiff may ask the court to issue an *injunction.* This is a court order that forbids the defendant to take or continue a certain action. For example, a group of plaintiffs may take a company to court because the company plans to build a factory that will pollute the air in their neighborhood. A judge might issue an injunction to stop a company from building the factory. Lawsuits can be time consuming because they involve the following steps:

Hiring a lawyer To start a lawsuit, a person almost always needs a lawyer.

Filing the Complaint The plaintiff sets forth the charges against the defendant in a *complaint.* This is a legal document filed with the court that has jurisdiction over the problem. Then the defendant receives a *summons.* This is an official notice of the lawsuit that includes the date, time, and place of the first court appearance. The defendant's lawyer may file a motion to dismiss, or end, the case. If the court denies this motion, the defendant must file an *answer,* or formal response to the charges in the complaint. Failure to answer means victory by default for the plaintiff. The defendant may also respond by filing a counterclaim. This is a lawsuit against the plaintiff in which the defendant says that the plaintiff also did something wrong.

Pretrial discovery occurs when both sides prepare for the trial by checking facts and gathering evidence to support their case. This process can take from months to years in complicated cases.

Resolution Without Trial Ninety percent of all civil lawsuits are settled before trial in one of the following ways:

A. Either party in the lawsuit may propose a settlement at any time.

B. Judges may encourage people to settle by calling a pretrial conference where the parties talk things over.

C. The court may require the parties to settle their dispute outside of court through mediation. During mediation each side is given the opportunity to explain its side of the dispute and must listen to the other side. A professional arbitrator conducts the mediation. His or her decision is usually binding on all parties.

Trial If all else fails, lawsuits go to trial. This may take months or years because courts are so crowded. Civil trials may be heard by a judge only or by a jury of 6 to 12 people. Both sides present and summarize their cases. Then the judge or the jury gives a verdict.

Copyright © Glencoe/McGraw-Hill, a division of The McGraw-Hill Companies, Inc.

STUDY GUIDE (continued)   Chapter 15, Section 2

The Award When the plaintiff wins, the court awards damages, an injunction, or both. The loser may appeal or refuse to pay damages. If the defendant refuses to pay, the plaintiff must get a court order to take money out of the defendant's paycheck or to seize and sell the defendant's belongings.

2. What are the first three major steps in a civil case?

_____

_____

_____

◉ Small Claims Court *(page 434)*

The small claims court is an alternative to a lengthy trial process. Cases are usually heard by a judge and involve claims ranging up to $5,000. Most of these courts have simple forms to complete in order to file a complaint. No lawyers are required. The evidence may include testimony from witnesses or their ***affidavits.*** These are written statements to prove statements of fact that have been signed by the witness under oath before a magistrate or notary. The judge's decision is legally binding. However, winning is no guarantee of collecting. If the defendant refuses to pay, the plaintiff obtains a written order from the court and then turns the order over to the police or sheriff to collect the damages.

3. Why would a plaintiff use a small claims court rather than file a civil lawsuit?

_____

_____

STUDY GUIDE  Chapter 15, Section 3

For use with textbook pages 437–443.

CRIMINAL LAW

CONTENT VOCABULARY

criminal law Rules governing crimes and their punishment *(page 437)*

criminal justice system System of state and federal courts, police, and prisons that enforce criminal law *(page 437)*

petty offense A minor crime, usually punished by a ticket rather than being arrested *(page 437)*

misdemeanor A minor crime that is usually punished by a fine or jail sentence of less than one year *(page 438)*

felony A major crime *(page 438)*

arrest warrant An order signed by a judge naming the individual to be arrested for a specific crime *(page 438)*

grand jury A group that hears charges against a suspect and decides whether there is sufficient evidence to bring the person to trial *(page 439)*

indictment A formal charge by a grand jury *(page 440)*

information A sworn statement by the prosecution that there is sufficient evidence for a trial *(page 440)*

plea bargaining The process in which a defendant pleads guilty to a lesser crime than the one with which the defendant was originally charged *(page 440)*

jury A group of citizens that hears evidence during a trial and gives a verdict *(page 442)*

verdict Decision *(page 443)*

hung jury A jury that is unable to reach a decision *(page 443)*

sentence The punishment to be imposed on an offender after a guilty verdict *(page 443)*

DRAWING FROM EXPERIENCE

Recall a time when someone purposely hurt you. Would you describe your injury as major or minor? This is the way crimes are described under the criminal justice system.

This section focuses on types of crimes and the steps in criminal cases.

READING STRATEGIES

Use the graphic organizer below to help you take notes as you read the summaries that follow. Think about how different crimes are classified.

Petty Offenses	Misdemeanors	Felonies

STUDY GUIDE (continued)   Chapter 15, Section 3

READ TO LEARN

◉ Introduction (page 437)

In *criminal law* cases, the government charges someone with a crime and is always the prosecution. The defendant is the person accused of the crime. A crime is an act that breaks a criminal law and does injury or harm to people or to society in general. Not doing something can also be considered a crime. For example, a doctor who suspects a young patient is being abused and fails to report the abuse is guilty of a crime.

The *criminal justice system* includes the state and federal courts, judges, lawyers, police, and prisons that have the responsibility for enforcing criminal law. There is a separate juvenile system for dealing with people under the age of 18.

◉ Types of Crime (page 437)

Crimes fall into the following classifications:

Petty Offenses These are minor crimes such as parking illegally, littering, disturbing the peace, minor trespassing, and speeding. People who commit a petty offense often receive a ticket rather than being arrested.

Misdemeanors These are crimes such as vandalism, simple assault, stealing inexpensive items, writing bad checks for small amounts, or being drunk and disorderly. A person found guilty of a misdemeanor may be fined or jailed for a year or less.

Felonies These are serious crimes such as burglary, kidnapping, arson, rape, fraud, forgery, manslaughter, or murder. They are punishable by imprisonment for one year or more. The punishment could even be death if the crime is murder. People convicted of felonies may also lose certain civil rights such as the right to vote or serve on a jury. Sometimes misdemeanors may be treated as felonies. For example, drunk driving is often a misdemeanor. If a person has been arrested for drunk driving and has been convicted of the same offense before, the person may be charged with a felony.

   1. What are the three classifications of crimes?

_____

_____

_____

◉ Steps in Criminal Cases (page 438)

Nearly every criminal case follows these steps:

Investigation and Arrest Police begin an investigation to gather enough evidence to persuade a judge to give them a warrant to arrest someone. An *arrest warrant* must list the suspect's name and the crime. Police may arrest someone without a warrant if they catch the person in the act of committing the crime or if they have a reasonable suspicion that a person has broken the law. The arrested person is taken to a police station where the charges are recorded or "booked."

STUDY GUIDE (continued)   Chapter 15, Section 3

Initial Appearance The defendant is brought before a judge to be charged with a crime. If the crime is a misdemeanor, the defendant may plead guilty and the judge will decide on a penalty. If the defendant pleads not guilty, a date is set for a trial. The defendant usually is not asked to enter a plea if the crime is a felony. Instead, the judges sets a date for a preliminary hearing. A suspect may be released if the judge thinks the person is a good risk to return to court for trial. Or the judge may require bail. This is a sum of money the accused leaves with the court until he or she returns for trial. Bail is denied if the defendant is likely to flee.

Preliminary Hearing or Grand Jury In federal courts and many state courts, cases will go to a **grand jury.** This is a group of citizens who review the prosecution's accusations. The jury determines if there is enough evidence to put the accused on trial. If the jury finds enough evidence, it "hands up" an **indictment.** This is a formal criminal charge.

A preliminary hearing may be used instead of a grand jury. In the hearing, the prosecution presents its case to the judge. The defendant's lawyer may also present certain kinds of evidence. The case moves to the next stage if the judge decides there is "probable cause" to believe that the defendant committed the crime. If the judge decides the government does not have enough evidence, the charges are dropped.

In misdemeanor cases and many felony cases, courts use an information rather than a grand jury indictment. An **information** is a sworn statement by the prosecution that there is enough evidence to go to trial.

Plea Bargaining Most criminal cases end with a guilty plea because of **plea bargaining.** In this process, the prosecutor, defense lawyer, and police work out an agreement through which the defendant pleads guilty to a lesser crime. In return, the government does not prosecute the more serious crime with which the defendant was first charged. Supporters of plea bargaining claim that it saves the state the cost of a trial where guilt is obvious. Critics argue that plea bargaining lets criminals get off lightly.

Arraignment and Pleas At the arraignment, the judge reads the formal charge against the defendant in an open courtroom. The defendant then offers one of the following pleas:

A. Not guilty

B. Not guilty by reason of insanity

C. Guilty

D. No contest (in some states). By pleading no contest, the defendant indirectly admits guilt. However this does not go on the record as a guilty plea.

If the defendant pleads guilty or no contest, the judge decides a punishment and the defendant may be sent to prison immediately. If the plea is not guilty, the trial date is set.

The Trial A defendant accused of a felony may choose between a bench trial—one heard only by a judge—and a jury trial. A **jury** is a group of citizens who hears evidence during a trial to decide guilt or innocence. The prosecuting and defense lawyers choose jurors from residents within the court's jurisdiction. After jurors have been selected, the prosecution presents its case. Witnesses are called, and evidence is presented. Next, the defense has its turn and calls witnesses. Then the lawyers for both sides present closing arguments that summarize the cases and respond to the opposition's case.

The Decision The jury members go to a jury room to decide if the defendant is guilty or not guilty. To decide that a person is guilty, the jury must find the evidence convincing "beyond a reasonable doubt." In nearly all criminal cases, every member of the jury must agree on the *verdict,* or decision. If a jury is unable to reach a decision, it is called a *hung jury* and is dismissed. The trial ends in a mistrial. A new trial with a new jury may be scheduled at a later date.

Sentencing When the verdict is "not guilty," the defendant is released. If the verdict is "guilty," the judge usually determines the *sentence.* This is the offender's punishment. Sentences are often certain periods of time in prison. However, a sentence may include payment of a fine or a number of hours to be spent serving the community. In a few states jurors have some say in the sentencing, especially in cases in which the death penalty is a possible sentence. People found guilty of misdemeanors and felonies have the right to appeal their cases to a higher court.

During the 1990s many citizens became frustrated with lenient sentences given for serious crimes and the number of repeat offenders. In 1993 many states passed a "three-strikes law" requiring individuals convicted of three serious offenses to be sentenced to 25 years to life in prison. While these laws are controversial, supporters note they have caused a dramatic drop in serious crime offenses.

2. What happens at the initial appearance?

_____

_____

STUDY GUIDE  Chapter 15, Section 4

For use with textbook pages 436–443.

THE RIGHTS OF THE ACCUSED

CONTENT VOCABULARY

exclusionary rule A law stating that any illegally obtained evidence cannot be used in a federal court *(page 399)*

counsel An attorney *(page 401)*

self-incrimination Testifying against oneself *(page 402)*

double jeopardy Retrial of a person who was acquitted in a previous trial for the same crime *(page 404)*

DRAWING FROM EXPERIENCE

Have you ever been accused of something you did not do? The American system of justice tries to protect people who are unjustly accused.

This section focuses on the rights of the accused.

READING STRATEGIES

Use the table below to help you take notes and list the rights of the accused and a brief description at the right.

Right of the Accused	Description

STUDY GUIDE (continued)   Chapter 15, Section 4

READ TO LEARN

◉ Introduction (page 436)

Justice in a democracy means protecting the innocent as well as punishing the guilty. Thus the Constitution guards the rights of the accused as well as the rights of society.

◉ Searches and Seizures (page 436)

Getting evidence to accuse people of crimes often requires searching people or their homes, cars, or offices. The Fourth Amendment guards against unreasonable searches and seizures. Courts decide what is unreasonable on a case-by-case basis. Today police generally need a warrant to search for evidence, but in many situations, police may conduct a search without one. For example, police may arrest and search anyone who commits a crime in their presence.

In *Weeks* v. *The United States* (1914), the Supreme Court established the **exclusionary rule**—that illegally obtained evidence cannot be used in a federal court. Critics ask whether criminals should go free just because police made a mistake in collecting evidence. In *United States* v. *Leon* (1984), the Court relaxed the exclusionary rule—as long as the police act in good faith when requesting a warrant, their evidence may be used even if the warrant proves defective. The Court also ruled in 1984 that improperly obtained evidence can be used at a trial if the evidence would have been eventually discovered anyway. Other related cases are:

California* v. *Acevedo (1991) The Court established the precedent that police are free to search an automobile if they have probable cause to believe unlawful substances are hidden there.

New Jersey* v. *T.L.O. (1985) The Supreme Court ruled that school officials do not need warrants or probable cause to search students or their property.

Katz* v. *United States (1967) The Court overruled an earlier decision by prohibiting wiretapping without a warrant. Since then Congress has passed two laws that practically prohibit all kinds of electronic eavesdropping without a warrant, even wiretapping and bugging for national security reasons.

Hudson v. Michigan (2006) So long as there is a valid warrant, evidence can be used even if the police entered a home without announcing their presence.

1. When may police conduct a search without a warrant?

_____

_____

◉ Guarantee of Counsel (page 439)

The Sixth Amendment guarantees a defendant the right to **counsel,** or an attorney. Generally, the federal courts provided counsels. For years, people could be tried in state courts without a lawyer. In *Gideon* v. *Wainright* (1963), the Court ruled that every accused person had the right to an attorney. Clarence Gideon and hundreds of other Florida prisoners were retried and found innocent. The Court has since extended the *Gideon* decision. Any time a punishment of six months or more in prison is possible, the accused has a right to a lawyer at public expense from the time of arrest through the appeals process.

2. How did the *Gideon* decision extend the guarantee to counsel in the Sixth Amendment?

_____

STUDY GUIDE (continued)   Chapter 15, Section 4

◉ Self-incrimination *(page 440)*

The Fifth Amendment says that no one can be forced to testify against himself or herself. The courts have interpreted this amendment's protection against *self-incrimination* to cover witnesses before congressional committees and grand juries as well as defendants in criminal cases. The Fifth Amendment also protects defendants against forced confessions. The Supreme Court under Chief Justice Earl Warren expanded protection against self-incrimination in the following cases:

A. *Escobedo* v. *Illinois (1964)* The Court ruled that a confession or other incriminating statement that an accused person makes without access to a lawyer may not be used in trial.

B. *Miranda* v. *Arizona (1966)* The Court decided that suspects must be clearly informed of their rights before police question them. Their statements may not be used in court if they are not so informed.

In several cases after 1966, the Court relaxed its *Miranda* and *Escobedo* rules. However, in *Dickerson* v. *United States* (2000), the Court strengthened *Miranda.* The justices insisted that whether or not Miranda warnings were given was the standard for admitting self-incriminating statements as evidence at a trial.

3. In what two cases did the Supreme Court expand the protection of the Fifth Amendment?

_____

_____

◉ Double Jeopardy *(page 441)*

The Fifth Amendment also protects against *double jeopardy.* This means a person may not be tried twice for the same crime. In 1989 the Supreme Court ruled that a civil penalty could not be imposed after a criminal penalty for the same crime. However, in 1997 the Court also ruled that people who paid civil fines for violating regulations could also face criminal charges. Also, if a crime violates both state and federal laws, the case can be tried at both levels. When a single act involves more than one crime, a person may be tried separately for each offense.

4. For what kinds of crimes can a person be tried twice?

_____

_____

◉ Debating the Death Penalty *(page 442)*

The Eighth Amendment forbids cruel and unusual punishments. The Court rarely uses this provision. However, there is a debate over how this protection applies to the death penalty. In *Gregg* v. *Georgia* (1976), the Supreme Court ruled that the death penalty does not make up cruel and unusual punishment when imposed under adequate guidelines. These guidelines refer to trials and appeals that attempt to do away with arbitrary decisions and racial prejudice in imposing the death penalty.

5. When is the death penalty a cruel and unusual punishment?

_____

_____

STUDY GUIDE  Chapter 16, Section 1

For use with textbook pages 453–457.

DEVELOPMENT OF PARTIES

CONTENT VOCABULARY

political party A group of individuals with broad common interests who organize to nominate candidates for office, win elections, conduct government, and determine public policy *(page 453)*

theocracy A government dominated by religion *(page 454)*

ideologies Sets of basic beliefs about life, culture, government, and society *(page 454)*

coalition government One formed by several parties who combine forces to obtain a majority *(page 454)*

third party Any political party other than one of the two major parties *(page 455)*

single-member district Electoral district in which only one candidate is elected to each office *(page 457)*

proportional representation A system in which several officials are elected to represent the same area in proportion to the votes each party's candidate receives *(page 457)*

DRAWING FROM EXPERIENCE

Suppose you wanted to change the cafeteria menu. Would you go alone to make suggestions to the principal? Or would you go with a group of students who agree with you? If you think like members of a political party, you know there is strength in numbers.

This section focuses on how political parties came about.

READING STRATEGIES

Use the graphic organizer below to list the different kinds of third parties, their goals, and party examples.

Types of Third Parties	Description of Party Goals	Party Example

STUDY GUIDE (continued)   Chapter 16, Section 1

READ TO LEARN

◉ Introduction *(page 453)*

The voice of an individual citizen can easily be lost in a nation as large as the United States.

◉ Parties and Party Systems *(page 453)*

A political party is a group of people with broad common interests. They organize to win elections, control government, and shape government policies. The roles parties play differ in the following systems:

One-Party Systems The party is the government in a one-party system. One-party systems are usually found in nations with authoritarian governments. Such parties often come to power through force. For example, a revolution in 1917 brought the Communist Party to power in Russia. One-party systems also exist in non-Communist countries. In Iran, for example, religious leaders run the government. A government dominated by religion is called a *theocracy.*

Multiparty Systems This is the most common system in nations that allow more than one political party. The parties often represent widely different *ideologies.* These are basic beliefs about government. One party rarely gets enough support to control the government. Several parties often combine to obtain a majority and form a *coalition government.* Coalitions often break down when disputes arise. As a result, multiparty systems are politically unstable.

Two-Party Systems Only about a dozen nations have a system in which only two parties compete for power. Two major parties dominate the government even though minor parties also exist. The major parties in the United States are the Republican Party and the Democratic Party.

   1. Why are governments unstable in nations with multiparty systems?

_____

_____

◉ Rise of American Parties *(page 454)*

President George Washington warned against the harmful effects of parties. However, by the end of his second term, the United States had two major parties—the Federalists and the Democratic-Republicans.

The Federalists' power quickly declined after 1796. The Democratic-Republicans dominated politics into the 1820s. However, by 1828 the Democratic-Republicans began splitting into two parties—the Democrats and the Whigs, or National Republicans. By the 1850s the debate over slavery created divisions within both of the two parties. The Democrats split into northern and southern factions, or parts. Many Whigs joined the new Republican Party, which opposed the spread of slavery. The Republican Party remained the majority party from the Civil War until the 1930s.

In 1932 the Democratic Party won the White House and took control of Congress. The Democratic Party was the majority party for most of the next 60 years, controlling both houses of Congress in all but 6 years. Republicans took control of the White House in 1968 with the election of Richard Nixon. Republicans controlled the White House for 6 of the next 9 presidencies. In 1995 under President Clinton, a Democratic president worked with a Republican Congress for the first time since the 1940s.

╭──╮
STUDY GUIDE (continued)   Chapter 16, Section 1
╰──╯

2. What did George Washington think about political parties?

_____

_____

◉ The Role of Minor Parties *(page 455)*

A third party is any party other than one of the two major parties. Third parties are also called minor parties because they rarely win major elections. Third parties believe that neither major party is meeting certain needs. Minor parties generally fall into the following categories:

A. The single-issue party focuses on one major social, economic, or moral issue. For example, in the 1840s the Liberty Party and the Free Soil Party formed to take stronger stands than the major parties took against slavery.

B. The ideological party focuses on overall change in society. Ideological parties such as the Socialist Labor Party and the Communist Party USA demand government ownership of factories, transportation, resources, farmland, and other means of production and distribution. The Libertarian Party calls for reduced government and increased personal freedom.

C. The splinter party splits away from one of the major parties because of some disagreement. For example, in 1912 former president Theodore Roosevelt led a group out of the Republican Party to form the Progressive, or Bull Moose, Party.

Minor parties have influenced the outcome of national elections. The Bull Moose Party drew so many Republicans away from President William Howard Taft in 1912 that Democratic candidate Woodrow Wilson was elected. Some believe Ross Perot's independent candidacy may have helped Bill Clinton win in 1992.

The names of Republicans and Democrats are automatically on the ballot in many states. But third-party candidates must get a large number of voter signatures in a short time in order to get on the ballot. Nearly all elected officials in the United States are elected by *single-member districts.* Only one candidate will win no matter how many candidates compete in a district. So the winner will almost always be a Republican or a Democrat. On the other hand, many nations use *proportional representation.* In this system, several officials are elected to represent voters in an area. Offices are filled in proportion to the votes that each party's candidates receive. Such a system encourages minor-party candidates.

3. Why are third parties called "minor" parties?

_____

_____

STUDY GUIDE  Chapter 16, Section 2

For use with textbook pages 458–462.

PARTY ORGANIZATION

CONTENT VOCABULARY

independent A voter who does not support any particular party *(page 458)*

precinct A voting district *(page 459)*

precinct captain A volunteer who organizes party workers to distribute information about the party and its candidates and to get the voters to the polls *(page 459)*

ward A large district comprised of several adjoining precincts *(page 459)*

state central committee A group usually composed of representatives from the party's county organizations *(page 460)*

national convention A gathering of local and state party members chosen to nominate presidential and vice-presidential candidates *(page 460)*

national committee Representatives from 50 state party organizations who run a political party *(page 460)*

patronage The practice of granting favors to reward party loyalty *(page 462)*

DRAWING FROM EXPERIENCE

Have you ever belonged to the Boy Scouts? Scouts are organized on the local, state, national, and international levels. America's political parties are organized on several levels as well.

This section focuses on how political parties are organized and on what they do.

READING STRATEGIES

Use the graphic organizer below to show the important functions that political parties perform.

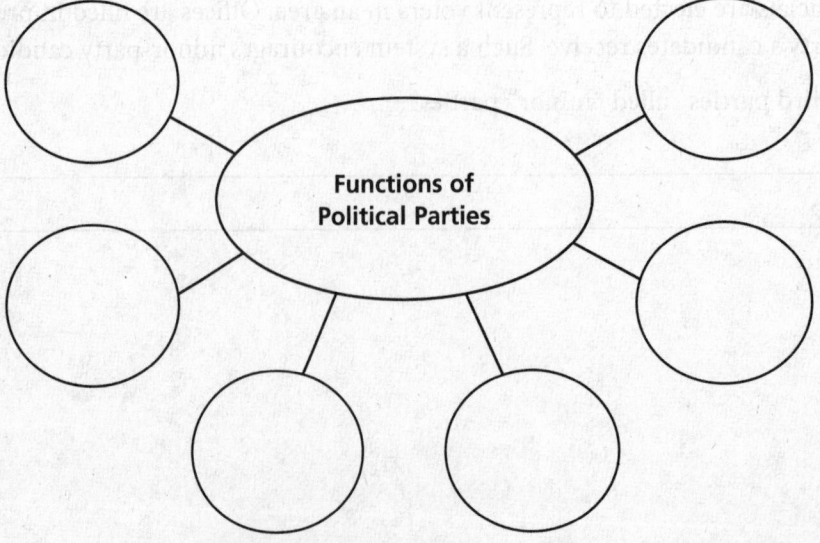

180

STUDY GUIDE (continued)   Chapter 16, Section 2

READra_TO LEARN

◉ Introduction (page 458)

Both major parties have small paid staffs in permanent party offices at the local, state, and federal levels. Parties also use volunteers to carry out a wide range of tasks. Volunteers collect campaign contributions, promote the candidates, send out campaign literature, call on voters, and watch at the polls on election day. Parties also seek the help of various professionals. Examples are media experts to prepare campaign materials and pollsters to research public opinion.

◉ Membership and Organization (page 458)

Democrats and Republicans are organized into 50 state parties and thousands of local parties that operate independently of the national party. Local, state, and national parties choose their own leaders and raise their own funds. In many states, citizens declare their party preference when they register to vote or when they vote in certain kinds of elections. A voter may declare that he or she is *independent.* In other words, the voter does not support any particular party. People who belong to a party generally support most of its ideas and candidates. Party membership involves no duties or obligations beyond voting. Some citizens, however, may contribute money to a party or do volunteer work for the party or its candidates on the following levels:

Local Party Organization The basic local unit is a *precinct.* This is a voting district ranging in size from just a few voters to more than 1,000. All voters cast their ballots at the same polling place. The *precinct captain* volunteers to organize party workers. They distribute information about the party and its candidates and get voters to the polls.

Several neighboring precincts make up a *ward.* Party members in each ward select a person to represent the ward at the next level of party organization—the party's county committee. The county committee chooses a chairperson to handle the county party's daily affairs. The party county chairperson is often the key figure in determining which candidate receives the party's support. If the state's governor or senator is from the same party, they may ask the party county chairperson for advice when appointing judges or other officials.

State Party Organization In each state the most important part of a party is the *state central committee.* This usually is composed of representatives from the party's county organization. The state central committee chooses the party state chairperson. A main job of the state central committee is to help elect the party's candidates for state government offices.

National Party Organization The national party organization is made up of the national convention and the national committee. The *national convention* is a gathering of party members and local and state party officials. It meets every four years to nominate the party's presidential and vice-presidential candidates. Between conventions the party's *national committee* runs the party. The committee is a large group made up mostly of representatives from the 50 state party organizations. The national committee elects a party national chairperson. He or she manages the daily operations of the national party. Both the Democrats and Republicans also have independent campaign committees for Congress. These committees help senators and representatives with their reelections.

STUDY GUIDE (continued)   Chapter 16, Section 2

1. Why is the party county chairperson a powerful figure in county politics?

_____

_____

◉ Political Party Functions (page 460)

Political parties are the only American institutions that do the following important tasks:

Recruiting Candidates This is the main job of political parties. Political parties are often election, rather than issue, oriented. This helps the Republicans and Democrats maintain their status as major parties.

Educating the Public Each party publishes its position on important issues, such as inflation and pollution. Some people do not know much about the issues or a candidate's background. Political parties simplify elections by helping such people decide how to vote. Voters know generally how a candidate stands on an issue just because he or she is a Democrat or a Republican.

Operating the Government Members of Congress and the state legislatures support their party's positions when considering legislation. The party also links a president or governor and the legislature. He or she works through party leaders in the legislature to promote programs.

Dispensing Patronage Political parties also give out ***patronage*** to their members. This is doing favors to reward party loyalty. The favors often include jobs, contracts, and appointments to government jobs.

The Loyal Opposition The party out of power in the legislative or executive branch assumes the role of "watchdog" over government. It observes the party in power, criticizes it, and offers solutions to political problems. This makes the party in power more aware of the will of the people.

Reduction of Conflict A party encourages groups to compromise and work together. An outcome of this process is that parties encourage government to use policies with mass appeal. Also, thanks to parties, the transfer of power takes place peacefully when one party loses control of the government. The losing party knows that someday it will return to power.

2. How do political parties help operate the government?

_____

_____

_____

_____

STUDY GUIDE  Chapter 16, Section 3

For use with textbook pages 464–470.

NOMINATING CANDIDATES

CONTENT VOCABULARY

caucus A private meeting of party leaders to choose candidates for office *(page 464)*

nominating convention An official public meeting of a party to choose candidates for office *(page 464)*

boss A powerful party leader *(page 465)*

direct primary An election in which party members select people to run in the general election *(page 465)*

closed primary An election in which only the members of a political party can vote *(page 465)*

open primary An election in which all voters may participate *(page 465)*

plurality The largest number of votes in an election *(page 465)*

runoff primary A second primary election between the two candidates who received the most votes in the first primary *(page 465)*

ticket The candidates for president and vice president *(page 466)*

platform A statement of a political party's principles, beliefs, and positions on vital issues *(page 469)*

planks Sections of a political party platform *(page 469)*

DRAWING FROM EXPERIENCE

How do students at your school choose candidates for student government? They probably use a petition method. This is only one way political parties use to choose candidates.

This section focuses on how parties choose political candidates.

READING STRATEGIES

Use the graphic organizer below to list the ways by which candidates are selected to run for office.

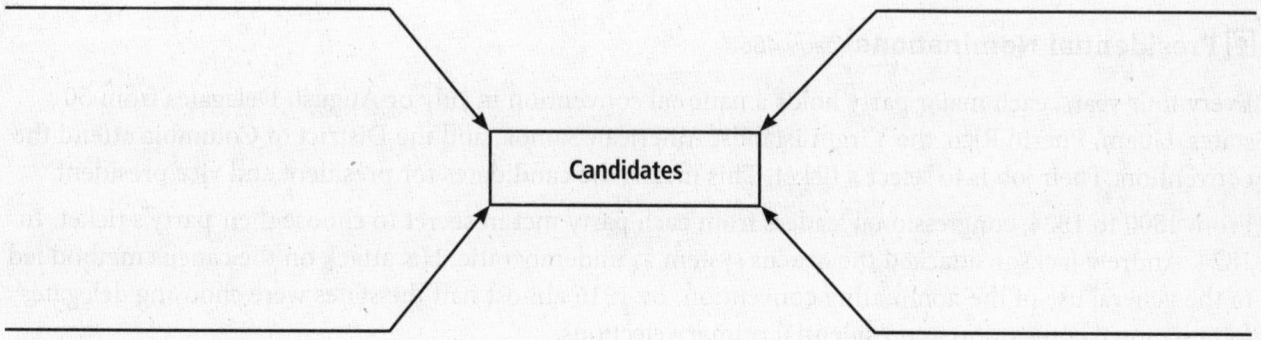

Candidates

STUDY GUIDE (continued)   Chapter 16, Section 3

READ TO LEARN

◉ Introduction (page 464)

Choosing candidates is often a difficult task for parties. The parties need to find appealing candidates and spend money to win elections.

◉ Selecting Candidates (page 464)

Individuals are nominated for public office in the following ways:

Caucuses Early in our nation's history, nearly all candidates were chosen in *caucuses.* These are private meetings of party leaders. Party rules require openness in the modern caucus process. Only 19 states now use caucuses.

Nominating Conventions The *nominating convention* is an official public meeting of a party to choose candidates for office. The convention system was supposed to be more democratic than caucuses. But powerful party leaders called bosses often chose delegates and controlled conventions. Public reaction to bosses in the 1900s led to primary elections as the preferred method of selection at state and local levels.

Primary Elections The *direct primary* is the method most often used today to select candidates. A direct primary is an election in which party members select people to run in a general election. Most states hold a *closed primary.* This means only members of a political party can vote. So only Democrats pick Democratic candidates, and only Republicans pick Republican candidates. In an *open primary,* all voters may participate. In most states a primary candidate needs only a *plurality,* or more votes than the other candidate, to win. In a few states, however, if no candidate receives a majority—more than half the votes cast—a *runoff primary* is held. The runoff is a second primary election between the two candidates who received the most votes in the first primary. In many states, party caucuses and nominating conventions take place alongside primaries.

Petition Under the petition method, a person announces his or her candidacy and files petitions that a certain number of voters have signed in order to be placed on the ballot. Some states require that all candidates submit petitions.

   1. Why did primary elections become popular in the 1900s?

_____

_____

◉ Presidential Nominations (page 466)

Every four years, each major party holds a national convention in July or August. Delegates from 50 states, Guam, Puerto Rico, the Virgin Islands, American Samoa, and the District of Columbia attend the convention. Their job is to select a ticket. This means the candidates for president and vice president.

From 1800 to 1824, congressional leaders from each party met in secret to choose their party's ticket. In 1824, Andrew Jackson attacked the caucus system as undemocratic. His attack on the caucus method led to the general use of the nominating convention. By 1916 almost half the states were choosing delegates for a national convention in presidential primary elections.

Today presidential primaries operate under a wide variety of state laws. However, the following descriptions are generally true:

A. Primaries may be a delegate selection process or a presidential preference poll, or both.

B. Either the candidate who wins the primary gets all the state's convention delegates, or each candidate gets delegates based on how many popular votes he or she receives in the primary.

C. Delegates selected on the basis of the popular vote may be required to support a certain candidate at the national convention, or they may be uncommitted.

Today only a few of the states with presidential primaries hold "beauty contests." These are preference polls in which voters indicate which candidate they prefer. Caucuses later choose the actual delegates.

Critics say that primaries are spread over too long a time in the election year. They also say that primaries seem to make the image of the candidates more important than the issues. Also, relatively few people vote in primaries. So the winner may not be as popular as the victory would indicate. Some states have joined forces to create regional primaries. For example, 6 Southern states held their 2000 Democratic presidential primaries on March 14. Candidates who failed to do well in this "Super Tuesday" election lost almost all chance of becoming the party's nominee.

2. What is a "beauty contest"?

_____

_____

◉ The National Convention (page 468)

While candidates compete in primaries, the national committee staff is preparing for the convention. It chooses the city and dates. Then the committee tells each state party organization how many votes it will have at the convention.

When delegates arrive at the convention, many are already pledged to candidates. Others are not. Candidates try to get uncommitted delegates to support them. The party chairperson calls the opening session to order. An important party member gives the keynote speech, intended to unite the party for the coming campaign. The delegates then approve the convention's four standing committees:

The rules committee proposes rules for running the convention and sets the convention's order of business.

The credentials committee must approve the delegations from each state. Candidates who trail in delegates sometimes challenge the credentials of their opponents' delegates. Two rival groups of delegates may even appear at a convention, each claiming to be a state's official delegation. It is up to the credentials committee to decide which delegates should be seated.

The committee on permanent organization selects the permanent chairperson and other officials for the convention.

The platform committee writes the party's *platform.* This is a statement of the party's principles, beliefs, and positions on important issues. It spells out how the party intends to deal with these issues. Individual parts of the platform, or *planks,* often divide the delegates. All the candidates try to get their viewpoints into the platform.

STUDY GUIDE (continued)   Chapter 16, Section 3

After each committee's reports are approved, it is time to select the party's candidate. The nominating speech for each candidate sets off a parade around the convention hall. After all the nominating speeches and seconding speeches, the balloting starts. The chairperson of each state delegation calls out the delegates' votes. The candidate who receives a majority of the votes becomes the party's nominee. If no candidate receives a majority, then further votes are taken until one candidate wins a majority.

The vice-presidential nomination usually takes place on the last day of the convention. A vice-presidential candidate is usually chosen to balance the ticket. This means he or she has a personal, political, and geographical background different from the presidential nominees. This balance is supposed to make the ticket appeal to as many voters as possible.

The presidential and vice-presidential nominees appear before the delegates and make acceptance speeches. The speeches are supposed to bring the party together, to attack the opposition party, to sound a theme for the upcoming campaign, and to appeal to a national television audience. The convention then adjourns.

3. Name a national convention's four standing committees.

_____

_____

_____

_____

STUDY GUIDE  Chapter 17, Section 1

For use with textbook pages 475–479.

ELECTION CAMPAIGNS

CONTENT VOCABULARY

campaign manager The person responsible for the overall strategy and planning of a campaign *(page 476)*

image Mental picture *(page 476)*

political action committee An organization formed to collect money and provide financial support for political candidates *(page 478)*

soft money Money raised by a political party for general purposes, not designated for a candidate *(page 479)*

DRAWING FROM EXPERIENCE

Do candidates for class president at your school give away campaign buttons? Or pencils embossed with their name? Even at the high school level, campaigning can be expensive.

This section focuses on how presidential candidates get and use their campaign funds.

READING STRATEGIES

Use the graphic organizer below to help you take notes. List the ways the Federal Election Campaign Act of 1971 changed campaign finance rules.

Sources of Campaign Funds Before 1971	Sources of Campaign Funds After 1971

STUDY GUIDE (continued)   Chapter 17, Section 1

READAD TO LEARN

⦿ **Introduction** *(page 475)*

Running for president is expensive. The reward for the winner, however, is the most powerful position in government.

⦿ **Electing the President** *(page 475)*

Candidates for president begin organizing their campaign about a year before the election. Primary races in the spring narrow the field of candidates. The national conventions follow in late summer. The campaigns end on Election Day. This is the first Tuesday after the first Monday of November.

Usually, a candidate must win at least 270 of the 538 available electoral votes to be elected president. The candidate who wins the greatest number of popular votes in any state usually receives all of that state's electoral votes. The larger a state's population, the more electoral votes it has. A candidate who won the electoral votes of 11 of the largest states would have the 270 votes. Because a candidate needs to win as many states as possible, he or she must appeal to a broad range of voters across the nation. This need for broad appeal works against candidates who run on a single issue, those who appeal only to a certain region, and third-party candidates.

A *campaign manager* heads the campaign organization. He or she plans and carries out overall strategy. In the national office, other workers handle relations with television, radio, and newspapers; manage finances, advertising, and campaign materials; and conduct opinion polls. On the state level, the state party chairperson runs the campaign. Local party officials and field workers contact voters, hold local rallies, and distribute campaign literature.

The most important communication tool for a presidential candidate is television. The *image*, or mental picture, that voters have of a candidate is extremely important. Candidates also use television for political commercials, and to take part in debates. Debates often affect voters who are undecided. Candidates at all levels are making increasing use of the Internet. The Internet is a key fundraising tool. Candidates also have campaign Web sites that provide information about the candidate's background and voting record, as well as updates on the candidate's activities.

1. Why do candidates campaign more in states with large electoral votes?

_____

_____

⦿ **Financing Campaigns** *(page 477)*

Running for political office is very expensive. Money can give candidates the chance to broadcast their views to voters. However, candidates may also need to give special favors to contributors rather than represent all voters.

Today, campaign financing is heavily regulated. The Federal Election Campaign Act (FECA) of 1977 and its amendments provide the framework governing campaign financing by:

A. Requiring public disclosure of each candidate's spending

B. Providing federal funding for presidential elections

C. Prohibiting labor unions and business organizations from making direct contributions

D. Limiting how much individuals and groups can contribute

The Federal Election Commission (FEC) keeps records on all campaign contributions over $100. The FEC's records are open to public inspection. However, in 1976 the Supreme Court ruled that limiting the total cost of a campaign was unconstitutional. Therefore, some candidates spend huge sums on their own campaigns.

Presidential candidates have the choice of accepting federal funding for their campaigns. If they do accept, they are limited in how much they can spend. Presidential candidates of third parties qualify for federal funding if their party received at least five percent of the vote in the previous presidential election.

However, the bulk of campaign funding comes from private sources, including individual citizens, party organizations, corporations, and various special interest groups. Under FECA, individual donations to a candidate are limited to $1,000. *Political action committees*, or PACs, are organizations established by interest groups to provide financial support to favored candidates or parties. PACs are also limited by FECA in how much they may donate. However, one loophole is *soft-money* donations. These are contributions given directly to a political party for general purposes but not for particular candidates. Another loophole is *issue advocacy advertising*. These advertisements, paid for by interest groups, urge voters to support a particular position on issues such as gun control or health care. While they do not ask people to vote for or against a candidate, they often contain a candidate's name or image. FECA places no limits on soft-money donations or issue advocacy advertising.

The Bipartisan Campaign Reform Act, passed in 2003, attempts to place new controls on campaign spending. This legislation bans unlimited soft-money donations to national political parties. It also prohibits interest groups from running issue ads aimed at a candidate for a certain period before an election. This law was challenged as unconstitutional, but the Supreme Court upheld most parts of the law in December 2003.

The FEC has also applied campaign finance regulations to the Internet. For example, the FEC has ruled that candidates and parties must follow established reporting procedures to receive electronic contributions.

2. How did the Bipartisan Campaign Reform Act limit the use of soft money?

_____

_____

STUDY GUIDE  Chapter 17, Section 2

For use with textbook pages 481–484.

EXPANDING VOTING RIGHTS

CONTENT VOCABULARY

suffrage The right to vote *(page 482)*

grandfather clause An exception in a law for a certain group based on previous conditions *(page 482)*

poll tax Money paid in order to vote *(page 483)*

DRAWING FROM EXPERIENCE

Suppose most students in your math class had to pass a two-page exam to go on to the next level. But all 6-foot-tall students had to pass a three-page exam. African Americans once faced a similar kind of discrimination at the polls.

This section focuses on the laws and amendments that extended voting rights to many groups.

READING STRATEGIES

Use the graphic organizer below to help you take notes on the results of the Voting Rights Acts.

Effects of the Voting Rights Acts

‡‡

STUDY GUIDE (continued)   Chapter 17, Section 2

‡‡

READ TO LEARN

◉ Introduction (page 481)

Suffrage, or the right to vote, is the foundation of American democracy. Today almost all United States citizens 18 years or older may vote. However, during various periods in American history, law, custom, and sometimes even violence stopped certain groups from voting.

◉ Early Limitations on Voting (page 481)

Before the American Revolution, women and African Americans could not vote. Neither could white males who did not own property or were not rich enough to pay taxes. Some colonies even excluded people who were not members of the dominant religion. Only about 5 to 6 percent of the adult population could vote. Many believed that voting was best left to wealthy, educated, white, property-owning males. During the first half of the 1800s, state legislatures gradually dropped property requirements and religious restrictions for voting. By the mid-1800s all white adult males could vote.

1. Which voting restrictions were dropped between the American Revolution and the mid-1800s?

_____

_____

◉ Woman Suffrage (page 482)

Women began fighting for the right to vote in the mid-1800s. By 1914 they had won the right to vote in 11 western states. Nationwide suffrage for women took effect with the passage of the Nineteenth Amendment in 1920.

2. What change occurred in woman suffrage between 1914 and 1920?

_____

_____

◉ African American Suffrage (page 482)

When the Constitution went into effect in 1789, no enslaved African Americans were allowed to vote. Free African Americans were allowed to vote in only a few states.

The Fifteenth Amendment was ratified in 1870. It said that no state could stop a person from voting because the person was of a certain race, color, or had once been a slave. For the first time, the national government set rules for voting.

Southern states tried to discourage voting by African Americans despite the Fifteenth Amendment. For example, the states included a *grandfather clause* in their constitutions. This clause provided that only voters whose grandfathers had voted before 1867 could vote without paying a poll tax or passing a reading test. This clause made voting expensive and difficult for most African Americans because their grandfathers had been enslaved and so did not vote. The Supreme Court declared the grandfather clause unconstitutional in 1915.

STUDY GUIDE (continued)   Chapter 17, Section 2

Some Southern states used literacy tests to keep African Americans from voting. White voters were judged literate if they could write their names. African Americans were often expected to do much more. For example, they were frequently asked to explain a complicated part of the state or national constitution. The Voting Rights Acts of 1965 and 1970 and later additions to these laws outlawed literacy tests.

A *poll tax* was an amount of money that a citizen had to pay before he or she could vote. The poll tax had to be paid for the current year as well as for previous unpaid years. It was a financial burden for poor citizens. Also, it had to be paid before Election Day. Voters who lost their receipts could not vote. Thousands of African Americans in states with poll taxes were unable to vote. The Twenty-fourth Amendment outlawed poll taxes in national elections in 1964. The Supreme Court ruled them unconstitutional in state elections in 1966.

The Voting Rights Act of 1965 gave the federal government the power to register voters in any district where less than 50 percent of adult African American voters were on the voting lists. Later voting rights laws of 1970, 1975, and 1982 were passed. The voting rights laws provided for:

A. banning unfair division of election districts, which lessened the influence of African American voters;

B. the appointment of poll watchers to ensure that the votes of all qualified voters were counted;

C. doing away with literacy tests;

D. ballots printed in Spanish for Spanish-speaking communities; and

E. the same right for other minority language groups such as Native Americans, Asian Americans, and Aleuts.

The Voting Rights Act resulted in a dramatic increase in African American voter registration. In 1960 only 29 percent of all African American adults in the South were registered. By 2000, however, the figure was 64 percent. Also, more than 1,000 African Americans were elected to political office within a few years after the Voting Rights Act of 1965 was passed.

Voting reform continues today. The Help America Vote Act of 2002 established new federal voting requirements for states. The goal of these requirements is to make the voting process more consistent and inclusive.

3. How did poll taxes prevent African Americans from voting?

_____

_____

◉ **Twenty-sixth Amendment** *(page 484)*

For many years the minimum voting age in most states was 21. In 1971 the passage of the Twenty-sixth Amendment gave more than 10 million citizens between the ages of 18 and 21 the right to vote.

4. Why was the Twenty-sixth Amendment important?

_____

_____

STUDY GUIDE  Chapter 17

For use with textbook pages 486–491.

VOTER'S HANDBOOK

CONTENT VOCABULARY

canvass The vote count by the official body that tabulates election returns and certifies the winner *(page 487)*

register To enroll one's name with the appropriate local government in order to participate in elections *(page 487)*

polling place The location in a precinct where people vote *(page 488)*

precinct A voting district *(page 488)*

office-group ballot One that lists the candidates together by the office for which they are running *(page 488)*

ticket-splitting Voting for candidates from different parties for different offices *(page 488)*

party-column ballot One that lists each party's candidates in a column under the party's name *(page 489)*

canvassing board The official body that counts votes and certifies the winner *(page 490)*

absentee ballot One that allows a person to vote without going to the polls on Election Day *(page 491)*

DRAWING FROM EXPERIENCE

Either you are old enough to vote or you soon will be. Do you know how to register and go to the polls? This section focuses on preparing you to vote.

READING STRATEGIES

Use the graphic organizer below to help you take notes as you read the summaries that follow. Think about the different sources of information about candidates.

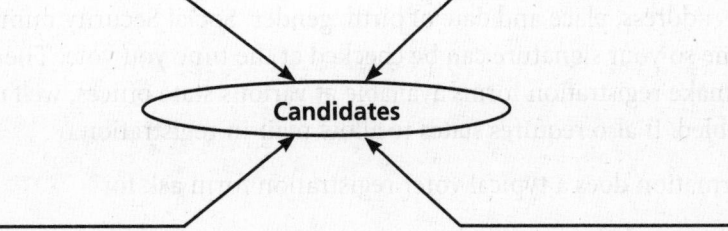

Candidates

STUDY GUIDE (continued) Chapter 17

READ TO LEARN

◉ **Introduction** (page 486)

Voting allows citizens to influence and control government.

◉ **Qualifications to Vote** (page 487)

You are qualified to vote if you are:

A. a citizen of the United States,

B. at least 18 years old, and

C. not a convicted felon or legally insane.

Most states also require that you be a resident of the state for a certain length of time and that you register, or enroll, with the local government. A series of constitutional amendments, federal laws, and Supreme Court decisions have forced states to conduct elections without discrimination because of race, creed, color, or gender. However, the registration of voters and regulation of elections are mainly in state hands.

Many elections have been decided by one or just a few votes. For example, Milton R. Young, a Republican, ran for the Senate in North Dakota. He led the challenger by a small margin out of 236,000 votes cast. His victory was confirmed by the official *canvass*. This is the final vote count that decides the winner. In the 2000 election, George W. Bush won the presidency by a margin of only 537 votes!

1. What are three qualifications to vote?

_____

_____

_____

◉ **Voting Procedures** (page 487)

Americans must *register,* or enroll with the appropriate local government, in order to vote. Registration became common in the late 1800s as a way to stop fraud. For example, in Denver in 1900, one man confessed to voting 125 times on Election Day.

Registration requirements are set by state law and differ from state to state. Registration forms typically ask for your name, address, place and date of birth, gender, Social Security number, and party. You must also sign your name so your signature can be checked at the time you vote. The National Registration Act requires states to make registration forms available at various state offices, welfare offices, and agencies that serve the disabled. It also requires states to allow mail-in registration.

2. What information does a typical voter registration form ask for?

_____

_____

STUDY GUIDE (continued)   Chapter 17

◉ Voting procedures (page 488)

You vote at a **polling place** in your home **precinct**. A precinct is a voting district.

At the polling place on Election Day, follow these steps:

A. Look over the sample ballot posted on the wall near the entry.

B. Go to the clerk or election judge's table and sign your name and address on an application form.

C. Listen as the clerk reads your name aloud and passes your application to a challenger, a local election official representing a political party.

D. Wait as the challenger compares your signature with your voter registration form. If they match, the challenger initials your form and returns it to you.

E. Give your form to one of the judges and enter the booth to vote.

Your right to vote can be challenged if your registration or identification is in question.

An **office-group ballot** lists the candidates of all the parties together by the office for which they are running. Their political party is listed beside their name. Many believe this form encourages **ticket-splitting.** This is voting for candidates from different parties for different offices. The **party-column ballot** lists each party's candidates in a column under the party's name. By putting one mark in an oval or a square at the top of the column, you can vote a straight ticket for all the party's candidates. You may also vote for each office individually by marking one box in each column.

Besides newer touch-screen systems, the two other most common types of voting machines are the:

Punch-card Machine Insert your punch card in the voting machine. It is then lined up with the names of the candidates. To vote, use the stylus provided to punch holes in the ballot.

Lever Machine Pull the large lever to one side to close the curtain around you. To vote, pull down the small levers by the names of the candidates you prefer. Then pull the large lever again to record your vote and to reset the machine.

The law entitles you to a secret ballot. This is modeled after the Australian ballot developed in 1856. It listed all the candidates, was given out at polls on Election Day, was marked in secret, and was counted by government officials.

A **canvassing board** counts the votes. It is an official board that is usually made up of members from both parties. These boards put all the returns together and send them to the state canvassing authority. Within a few days, the state canvassing authority certifies the election of the winner.

The best way to prepare to vote is to stay informed about candidates and public issues. You can get this information from newspaper, radio, and television. You might also try the following sources of information:

A. A *Voters' Information Bulletin* published by the local League of Women Voters

B. Literature put out by each political party

C. Ratings of members of Congress by interest groups such as the American Conservative Union or the AFL-CIO Committee on Political Education

STUDY GUIDE (continued)   Chapter 17

To help you decide which candidate to choose, ask these questions:

A. Does the candidate stand for things I think are important?

B. Is the candidate reliable and honest?

C. Does the candidate have relevant past experience?

D. Will the candidate be effective in office?

E. Does the candidate have a real chance of winning?

3. How does an office-group ballot differ from a party-column ballot?

_____

_____

_____

◉ Special Circumstances *(page 490)*

Special procedures and protections have been developed to help all eligible Americans vote. Over the years, early voting guidelines have significantly weakened. In many states, voters no longer need a special reason or excuse to vote early. Early voting can occur in two ways: in-person voting and absentee voting.

Early voting in-person has become a trend in many states. States hope to reduce the pressure on precincts on Election Day by allowing voters to cast their ballots early.

An **absentee ballot** allows you to vote without going to the polls on Election Day. You must obtain the ballot within a certain time before Election Day, fill it out, and return it to the proper election official. Check with local election officials for the deadlines to obtain and return an absentee ballot. In many states, rules have been adjusted so that no excuse is needed.

Any voter who needs help in voting because of a disability is entitled to receive it. Some states allow you to choose the person to help you. Other states require that only officials at the polling place can help. Election officials may not disclose any information about how the disabled person they helped voted.

Under the Voting Rights Act of 1975, ballots and related election materials must be printed in the language of voting minorities as well as in English. This provision applies only in areas where illiteracy in English is high or recent voter turnout was unusually low. For example, in Hawaii, election materials have been put in Cantonese, Ilocano, and Japanese as well as English.

4. In what ways can a voter cast his or her vote?

_____

_____

STUDY GUIDE  Chapter 17, Section 3

For use with textbook pages 492–497.

INFLUENCES ON VOTERS

CONTENT VOCABULARY

cross-pressured voter One who is caught between conflicting elements in his or her own life *(page 493)*

straight party ticket One where a voter has selected candidates of his or her party only *(page 493)*

propaganda The use of ideas, information, or rumors to influence opinion *(page 495)*

DRAWING FROM EXPERIENCE

Is a teenager or a senior citizen more likely to enjoy the music that you enjoy? Probably, the person closer to your own age enjoys the same kind of music. Age often influences voters' tastes in candidates, too.

This section focuses on factors that influence voters' decisions.

READING STRATEGIES

Use the table below to help you identify the factors in voters' backgrounds that influence their vote.

Background Influences

STUDY GUIDE (continued)   Chapter 17, Section 3

READ TO LEARN

⦿ Introduction (page 492)

The biggest decision a voter makes is whether to vote on Election Day. However, many factors influence voters' decisions about how to vote.

⦿ Personal Background of Voters (page 492)

Voters' personal backgrounds affect their decisions. For example, a person's age may influence his or her vote. A 68-year-old citizen would probably favor a candidate who promised an increase in Social Security benefits. A 23-year-old voter, on the other hand, might resent having more money taken from his or her paycheck to support increased Social Security benefits. So the younger voter might vote against the same candidate. Other background factors include education, religion, and racial or ethnic background. A person's background does not always forecast how he or she will vote. A *cross-pressured voter* is one who is caught between conflicting elements in his or her life, such as religion, income, and peer group. For example, Catholics are more inclined to vote Democratic than Republican. Yet, a Catholic may also be a wealthy businessperson. Most wealthy businesspeople vote Republican. So this particular Catholic may choose to vote Republican.

   1. List four factors from a person's background that may influence his or her vote.

_____

_____

_____

⦿ Loyalty to Political Parties (page 493)

Strong party voters usually vote a *straight-party ticket.* They select the candidates of their party only. Weak party voters are more likely to switch their votes to the rival party's candidates from time to time. Weak party voters are more influenced by issues than by party loyalty.

Independent voters think of themselves as neither Republicans nor Democrats. The number of independent voters has increased over the years. Experts believe that the number of weak party voters and independents will increase. Presidential candidates will no longer be able to rely on party loyalty for victory.

   2. Why do weak party voters vote for the rival party's candidates from time to time?

_____

_____

⦿ Issues in Election Campaigns (page 494)

Today's voters are more informed about issues than voters of earlier years because:

A. Television has brought the issues into almost every home.

B. Voters are better educated than voters of the past.

C. Current issues seem to have a greater direct impact on people's lives. These issues include Social Security, health care, taxes, education, affirmative action, abortion, gun rights, and the environment.

STUDY GUIDE (continued) Chapter 17, Section 3

3. What were four important issues in recent election campaigns?

_____

_____

_____

_____

◉ The Candidate's Image *(page 495)*

The way the voters see the issues is just as important as the issues themselves. For example, voters may believe that the administration is doing a good job with the economy. They may then reward the president with their votes. If voters believe the administration is doing a poor job with the economy, they might vote for the other candidate to punish the president. Also, most Americans want a president who appears to be someone they can trust as a national leader. A candidate, then, must give the impression of having the qualities voters expect in a president.

4. How do many voters react if they believe a president who is seeking reelection is doing a poor job?

_____

_____

◉ Propaganda *(page 495)*

Propaganda involves using ideas, information, or rumors to influence opinion. It uses information in a way that supports a predetermined purpose. Campaign managers often use these propaganda techniques:

A. calling a candidate just "plain folks";

B. making "glittering generalities"—broad statements with little substance;

C. urging voters to jump on the candidate's "bandwagon" because everyone else is;

D. "transferring" patriotic images to the candidate;

E. using movie or music stars to endorse, or give "testimonials," for a candidate;

F. labeling the opposite side or "calling names";

G. "card stacking," when each candidate quotes only the statistics that support his or her side.

Political propaganda often becomes obviously misleading. Then people question the honesty of politicians. Critics say the result can be reduced voter turnout.

5. When does propaganda negatively affect voter turnout?

_____

_____

◉ Profile of Regular Voters *(page 496)*

Important factors in predicting whether citizens will vote are:

Education The more education a voter has, the more likely he or she will vote.

Age Middle-aged citizens have the highest voting turnout of all age groups.

Income The higher the person's income, the more regularly the person votes.

6. Describe the type of citizen who votes most regularly.

_____

◉ Profile of Nonvoters *(page 496)*

Many Americans do not vote because they do not meet the basic requirements of citizenship, residency, and registration in their state. One problem with meeting residency and registration requirements is that Americans move often. Most states require that citizens reside in the state for 30 days before they can vote. Also, new residents may forget to register or find registration offices are open at inconvenient times.

The percentage of Americans voting in presidential elections declined from 1960 to 2000. Even fewer Americans voted in congressional elections. Fewer still voted in state and local elections.

In 2004, however, voter participation jumped sharply as President George W. Bush narrowly defeated Massachusetts senator John Kerry to win reelection. Despite the rise in voter turnout, there were still millions of eligible voters who did not participate in the election. Voter turnout continued to be high in the 2008 election when Illinois senator Barack Obama defeated Arizona senator John McCain.

Political experts have suggested the following ways to increase voter turnout:

A. Shift Election Day from Tuesday to Sunday, when citizens are free to vote without taking time off from work.

B. Allow voters to register on Election Day.

C. Establish national registration so that voters' registration follows them to a new state when they move.

7. Why is meeting residency and registration requirements a problem for many Americans?

_____

_____

_____

STUDY GUIDE  Chapter 18, Section 1

For use with textbook pages 503–507.

INTEREST GROUP ORGANIZATION

DRAWING FROM EXPERIENCE

Have you ever belonged to a fan club? Members of a fan club have a common interest in a celebrity. Interest groups are also organized around common interests.

This section focuses on the different interest groups that try to influence American government.

READING STRATEGIES

Use the graphic organizer below to categorize several interest groups.

Business Interest Groups	Labor Interest Groups	Agricultural Interest Groups

STUDY GUIDE (continued)   Chapter 18, Section 1

READyd TO LEARN

◉ Introduction (page 503)

An *interest group* is a group of people who share common goals and organize to influence government. Americans have organized to pressure all levels of government. These groups spend much time and money trying to influence officeholders to support laws that the groups believe will be good for them.

◉ Power of Interest Groups (page 503)

Political parties and interest groups differ in the following ways:

A. Political parties nominate candidates for office and try to win elections. Interest groups may support candidates who favor their ideas, but they do not nominate candidates for office.

B. Interest groups are concerned with only a few issues and do not try to gain members with different point of view, as parties do.

C. Most interest groups are organized on the basis of common values rather than on geographic location, as parties are.

Citizens communicate their needs and wants to government leaders through interest groups. Members of an interest group swing into action when lawmakers begin to address the important concerns of the group.

An interest group has a stronger bargaining position with government leaders by representing more than one person. On the state and national levels, an interest group draws from the money and knowledge of its many members. As a result, it can have an influence far beyond the power of any individual member.

1. What is the purpose of interest groups?

_____

_____

◉ Leadership and Membership (page 505)

Leaders of interest groups play the following roles:

A. They strengthen the political power of the group by unifying its members.

B. They inform members of the group's activities through newsletters, mailings, and telephone calls.

C. They act as speakers for their group and try to improve its image in the media.

D. They plan the group's strategy.

E. They raise money to run the organization.

F. They oversee financial decisions of the group.

People join interest groups for the following reasons:

A. A group may help promote an individual's self-interests. For example, a labor union works for higher wages for its members.

B. Many citizens believe in certain ideas or political principles that they wish to see passed into law. For example, Sierra Club members work to conserve natural resources.

C. Some people just like the company of other people with similar backgrounds or goals.

STUDY GUIDE (continued)   Chapter 18, Section 1

Many people do not belong to any interest group. People at low income levels are less likely than people from upper income levels to join such groups. So those who might benefit most by joining a group often do not join.

2. For what three reasons do many people join interest groups?

_____

_____

_____

◉ Business and Labor Groups (page 505)

Many interest groups are concerned with economic issues. They try to convince lawmakers of policies that the groups feel will strengthen the economy.

Business-related interest groups include:

the *National Association of Manufacturers* (NAM), which works to lower individual and corporate taxes and to limit government regulation of businesses;

the *United States Chamber of Commerce,* which speaks for smaller businesses; and

the *Business Roundtable,* which is made up of executives from about 150 of the country's largest and most powerful corporations.

The largest and most powerful labor organization is the AFL-CIO. Among the many unions in the AFL-CIO are the United Auto Workers (UAW), United Mine Workers (UMW), and the International Brotherhood of Teamsters. A separate group called the Committee on Political Education (COPE) raises funds, conducts voter registration drives, and supports political candidates for the AFL-CIO.

3. What is the role of COPE?

_____

_____

◉ Agricultural Groups (page 505)

America's almost 6 million farmers are represented by the following groups:

the *American Farm Bureau Federation,* which speaks for large farmers;

the *National Farmers' Union* (NFU), which represents smaller farmers and favors high price supports for crops and livestock; and

the *Patrons of Husbandry,* or the Grange, the oldest of the farm groups.

Commodity associations represent groups such as dairy farmers and potato growers. Several congressional subcommittees are organized around commodities.

4. Why do commodity associations have influence on Congress?

_____

_____

STUDY GUIDE (continued)   Chapter 18, Section 1

◉ Other Interest Groups *(page 506)*

Other interest groups range from professional and environmental associations to governmental and public-interest groups.

The American Bar association and the American Medical Association are two examples of interest groups that include members of specific professions. These two groups influence the licensing and training of lawyers and doctors.

The goals of several hundred environmental interest groups range from conserving natural resources to protecting endangered wildlife. Key environmental groups are the Sierra Club, the National Wildlife Federation, Friends of the Earth, the American Farm Bureau, and the Paragon Foundation.

Public-interest groups claim to work for the interests of all Americans. For example, Ralph Nader's Public Citizen, Inc., devotes itself to consumer and public safety issues.

Organizations and leaders within American government may also act as interest groups. Two examples are the National Council of Legislators and the National Governors' Association. State and local governmental officials in these groups try to influence members of Congress and the executive branch.

Thousands of other interest groups have been formed for other reasons. Even foreign governments and foreign nations seek to influence government in the United States. Foreign-interest groups may seek military aid, economic aid, or a favorable trade agreement. They may make political donations in an effort to sway political decisions.

5. What are two goals of environmental interest groups?

_____

_____

STUDY GUIDE  Chapter 18, Section 2

For use with textbook pages 508–513.

AFFECTING PUBLIC POLICY

CONTENT VOCABULARY

lobbying Direct contact made by a lobbyist in order to persuade government officials to support the policies their interest group favors *(page 508)*

lobbyist An interest group representative *(page 508)*

DRAWING FROM EXPERIENCE

Have you ever seen students try to influence a teacher to get better grades? Did they beg and plead? Did they give the teacher gifts and compliments? Or did they try to give convincing reasons? Lobbyists use similar ways to influence public officials.

This section focuses on how interest groups try to affect public policy.

READING STRATEGIES

Use the graphic organizer below to list the ways by which lobbyists provide information to members of Congress and government officials.

Information from Lobbyists

READ TO LEARN

◉ Introduction *(page 508)*

To influence public policy, interest groups use the following methods:

A. Representatives of groups directly contact government officials.

B. Groups use television, radio, magazine, and newspaper ads to create public support for their policies.

C. They may resort to court action or seek a constitutional amendment to achieve their goals.

◉ The Work of Lobbyists *(page 508)*

Representatives of interest groups often approach senators and representatives in the outer room or lobby of the capitol. So the process is called lobbying. The people who do this work are called lobbyists. Lobbying is one of the most widely used methods of interest groups.

Congress defines a lobbyist as anyone who is hired by a client, makes more than one contact on behalf of the client, and spends more than 20 percent of his or her time serving the client. Lobbyists must register and file reports with the Clerk of the House and the Secretary of the Senate. These reports tell the issues the

STUDY GUIDE (continued) Chapter 18, Section 2

lobbyist addressed, the agencies contacted, and about how much the client pays the lobbyist. Many lobbyists were once members of Congress or the executive branch. Many are lawyers or public relations experts.

Lobbyists provide policy makers with information and statistics that support an interest group's position. They are limited in the gifts they can give lawmakers. Lobbyists also testify before congressional committees.

Lobbyists and interest groups may also help to write bills. Many interest groups have research staffs that help members of Congress draft proposed laws.

1. What kinds of work experience do lobbyists generally have?

_____

_____

◉ Interest Groups Seek Support (page 510)

Interest groups use the following methods to seek support:

Media Campaigns Ads on television, newspapers, magazines, and radio inform the public and create support for groups' views.

Letter Writing Members write letters or e-mails to government officials to show broad support for or against a public policy.

Factors that limit the effectiveness of interest groups are:

A. Groups compete for power and influence, keeping any single group from controlling lawmakers and other public officials.

B. The larger the group, the more diverse the members. Diversity means that a large group may be unable to agree on broad policy goals. So smaller groups have been more effective in shaping policy.

C. Most groups struggle to pay even small staffs. However, interest groups' contributions to political campaigns have been a great concern in recent years.

2. How do interest groups seek support?

_____

_____

◉ The Rise of Political Action Committees (page 511)

Interest groups provide a large amount of the funds used in candidates' election campaigns. Most of these funds come from political action committees (PACs). In 1974 new laws prevented corporations and labor unions from contributing directly to federal candidates. However, the laws permitted their political action committees to do so.

According to law, PACs must:

A. register with the government 6 months before an election,

B. raise money from at least 50 contributors,

C. give to at least 5 candidates in a federal election,

D. follow strict accounting rules, and

E. give no more than $5,000 directly to each candidate.

The government does not limit the amount of money a PAC can give a candidate's campaign as long as the PAC does not work directly with the candidate.

The Federal Election Commission (FEC) issues regulations and opinions that control PAC activities. Its decisions have encouraged the growth of PACs among businesses. The Supreme Court also encouraged PAC growth. It ruled that national, state, and local committee support of federal candidates was a form of free speech. There could be no spending limit. Afterward, spending for federal campaigns soared.

3. How does the law limit a PAC's contributions to candidates?

_____

_____

◉ PACs and the Groups They Serve (page 512)

PACs can be divided into the following groups:

Affiliated PACs These are tied to corporations, labor unions, trade groups, and health organizations. They raise funds through voluntary contributions from business executives, union officials, workers, and stockholders. An example of an affiliated PAC is the Realtors' Political Action Committee.

Independent PACs Groups interested in a particular cause such as free trade may set up PACs that are not connected to any existing interest group. An example of such a PAC is Americans for Free International Trade. Independent or nonconnected PACs raise money largely through direct-mail appeals to people across the nation.

4. How does an affiliated PAC differ from an independent PAC?

_____

_____

◉ Strategies for Influence (page 513)

Political action committees generally influence public policy in the following ways:

A. Interest groups promise campaign support for legislators who favor their policies. They also threaten to withhold support. Groups know that a campaign contribution does not guarantee a lawmaker will vote their way. However, campaign contributions at least assure access to officials they help to elect.

B. PACs generally support incumbents, or those government officials already in office. Incumbents in both the House and Senate have a good chance of winning reelection. Lawmakers disagree about the amount of influence that PAC support has on their decisions.

5. What do interest groups, including PACs, get from lawmakers in return for campaign contributions?

_____

_____

STUDY GUIDE  Chapter 18, Section 3

For use with textbook pages 514–517.

SHAPING PUBLIC OPINION

CONTENT VOCABULARY

public opinion The ideas and attitudes a significant number of Americans hold about issues *(page 514)*

peer group An individual's close friends, religious group, clubs, or work groups *(page 515)*

mass media Means of communication, such as television, newspapers, movies, books, and the Internet, that reach large audiences *(page 515)*

political culture A set of shared values and beliefs about a nation and its government *(page 516)*

DRAWING FROM EXPERIENCE

Do your friends ever discuss baseball players? Their opinions probably help shape your attitudes toward certain players. In a similar way, public opinion helps shape government attitudes toward issues.

This section focuses on the factors that shape public opinion.

READING STRATEGIES

Use the Venn diagram below to list the views of liberals, conservatives, and moderates. Then label the diagram.

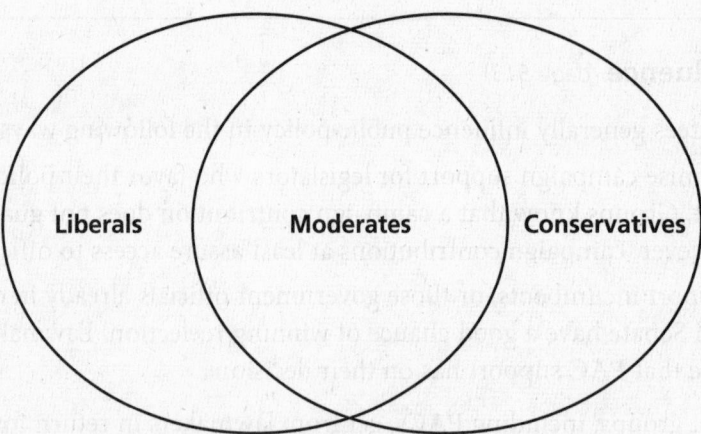

STUDY GUIDE (continued)   Chapter 18, Section 3

READ TO LEARN

◉ **Introduction** (page 514)

The media in the United States reflect and direct what the American people are thinking about.

◉ **The Nature of Public Opinion** (page 514)

Public opinion includes the ideas and attitudes many Americans hold about government and political issues. It is characterized by the following three factors:

Diversity Different people hold different opinions on almost every issue because of the diversity of the American people.

Communication Officials need to weigh public opinion when making decisions. Interest groups communicate the opinions of many individuals to the officials. Officials also rely on opinion polls and private letters and E-mails to know what people are thinking.

Significant Numbers Enough people must hold a particular opinion to make government officials listen to them. For example, President Lyndon Johnson did not run for reelection in 1968 because so many people opposed the way he conducted the Vietnam War.

   1. What three factors characterize public opinion?

_____

_____

_____

◉ **Political Socialization** (page 515)

Individuals learn their political beliefs and attitudes from the following sources:

Family and Home Children learn many of their early political beliefs from their parents. In most cases, the political party of the parents becomes the political party of their children.

Schools All students learn about their nation, its history, and its political system. School clubs and school rules also teach democratic values.

Peer Groups A person's *peer groups* influence and shape opinions. Peer groups include close friends, religious groups, clubs, and work groups.

Social Characteristics Economic and social status is part of political socialization, or shaping. For example, being African American or white affects individual political opinions.

The Mass Media The *mass media,* especially television, provide political information and images that influence political attitudes. Movies, recordings, novels, and television also affect opinions. For example, showing police as heroes or as criminals can shape opinions about authority.

Other Influences Government leaders influence people's opinions. For example, members of Congress often go back to their home states and talk to their constituents. Many legislators send newsletters to voters. They also appear on television programs and give newspaper interviews on issues. Interest groups as well as churches and other religious organizations also try to shape public opinion.

Some people are socialized to believe that they cannot change the "system." Others are socialized to believe their actions can lead to changes important to them.

STUDY GUIDE (continued) Chapter 18, Section 3

2. How do the mass media help socialize people?

_____

_____

⊙ Political Culture *(page 516)*

Every nation has a *political culture.* This is a set of basic values and beliefs about a nation and its government that most people share. For example, a belief in individual freedom is part of the American political culture. The American political culture helps shape public opinion in the United States in the following ways:

A. The political culture sets limits within which citizens develop and express their opinions. For example, Americans may disagree over how much the federal government should regulate airlines. However, few Americans argue that the government should not regulate airlines at all, and few believe that it should take over and run the industry.

B. A nation's political culture also influences how its citizens interpret what they see and hear. For example, a Russian might interpret a line outside a store as a sign of a food shortage. An American would likely think the store was holding a sale.

3. In what two ways does political culture shape public opinion?

_____

_____

⊙ Ideology and Public Policy *(page 517)*

An ideology is a set of beliefs about life, culture, government, and society. It provides the framework for looking at government and public policy. American political values tend to fall into the following ideological patterns:

Liberal A liberal believes the national government should be active in promoting health, education, justice, and equal opportunity. Liberals are willing to give up some economic freedom in order to increase economic equality. In social matters, however, liberals believe the government should not restrict individual freedoms.

Conservative A conservative believes government should be limited, except in supporting traditional moral values and promoting freedom of opportunity. Conservatives oppose government limits on businesses and individuals. They believe free markets ensure the best economies.

Moderate and Libertarian Moderate beliefs fall between liberal and conservative views. A libertarian supports both economic and social freedoms—free markets and unrestricted speech.

4. What are four patterns of American political values?

_____

_____

_____

Name _____ Date _____ Class _____

For use with textbook pages 519–522.

Measuring PUBLIC OPINION

CONTENT VOCABULARY

biased sample In polling, a group that does not accurately represent the larger population *(page 520)*

universe In polling, the group of people that are to be studied *(page 520)*

representative sample A small group of people, typical of the universe, that a pollster questions *(page 520)*

random sampling A polling technique in which everyone in the universe has an equal chance of being selected *(page 521)*

sampling error A measurement of how much the sample results may differ from the sample universe *(page 521)*

cluster sample A polling method that groups people by geographical divisions *(page 521)*

DRAWING FROM EXPERIENCE

Have you ever responded to a question on a radio talk show by calling the station? You may have participated in a straw poll. This is just one way of measuring public opinion.

This section focuses on traditional and scientific ways of measuring public opinion.

READING STRATEGIES

Use the graphic organizer below to help you take notes about the disadvantages of using mail and phone polls.

Disadvantages of Mail Polls	Disadvantages of Phone Polls

STUDY GUIDE (continued) Chapter 18, Section 4

READE TO LEARN

⊙ Introduction (page 519)

Officials have always wanted to know what Americans are thinking between elections. The methods they have used to measure public opinion have changed and multiplied over the years.

⊙ Nonscientific Methods (page 519)

In the past, elected officials read newspapers, met with leaders of interest groups, and talked with voters to assess public opinion.

Political party organizations were once a reliable source of information about voters. Local and state party leaders were in close touch with voters. In the early 1900s political reforms curbed abuses by party organizations but weakened their ability to provide reliable information.

Interest groups make sure public officials know the opinions of their members. Yet interest groups represent a minority concerned with certain issues. They are not a good measure of broader public opinion.

The mass media speak to a broad audience that helps determine the media's content. Politicians watch newspaper headlines, magazine cover stories, and talk shows to know what the public is thinking. However, the media give a distorted view because they focus on news that has visual appeal or shock value.

Letter writing is a time-honored form of expressing opinions in a democracy. Interest groups stage massive letter-writing campaigns using computerized mailings to generate thousands of letters on an issue. However, officials often give more attention to personal letters from individuals.

Electronic Access E-mail, fax, telephone, and telegrams to members of Congress and the White House allow citizens to react almost immediately to events and government decisions.

Straw polls are unscientific attempts by newspapers, radio, and television stations to measure public opinion. Newspapers may print ballots in the paper and ask readers to mail in their vote. Television and radio hosts ask questions and give the audience telephone numbers to call in *yes* or *no* answers. Members of Congress often send voters questionnaires. However, straw polls always have a *biased sample.* This means that the people who respond to them are self-selected, or choose to respond.

  1. Which methods of measuring public opinion were not available before 1900?

  _____

  _____

⊙ Scientific Polling (page 520)

Almost every politician uses scientific polls to measure public opinion. This involves three basic steps:

A. Selecting a sample of the group to be questioned

B. Presenting carefully worded questions to the individuals in the sample

C. Interpreting the results

The group of people to be studied is called the *universe.* For example, a universe might be all the women in the United States. Pollsters question only a *representative sample,* or a small group of people typical of the universe. A small group such as 1,200 to 1,500 adults is representative because pollsters use *random sampling.* This means everyone in the universe has an equal chance of being selected.

STUDY GUIDE (continued)   Chapter 18, Section 4

A *sampling error* is a measure of how much the sample results may differ from the sample universe. Sampling error decreases as the sample size becomes larger. A national poll of 1,500 people has an error of plus or minus 3 percent. So if a poll says that 65 percent of Americans favor tougher pollution laws, with a 3 percent sampling error, between 62 and 68 percent of the entire population favor such laws.

Pollsters use various ways of drawing random samples. A *cluster sample* organizes people by geographical divisions. For example, the clusters may be counties. Sometimes pollsters adjust or weight the results of a poll. For example, if pollsters found that not enough people over 65 had been interviewed, they would give extra weight to the opinions of people over 65.

The way a question is phrased can greatly influence people's responses and thus poll results. For example, in a 1971 Gallup Poll, most people favored bringing "home all American troops from Vietnam before the end of the year." Then the question was reworded to read "withdraw all U.S. troops by the end of the year regardless of what happens there after U.S. troops leave." Less than half agreed with this proposal.

Recent public opinion polls have been conducted by mail or telephone. However, few people return the mail questionnaires, and pollsters cannot control people's careless or confusing replies. In telephone polling, pollsters use a method called "random digit dialing" to select a representative sample. They select an area code and the first three local digits. Then a computer randomly dials the last four digits. Sometimes pollsters fail to reach people, and some people are confused or inattentive.

Major polling organizations have learned how to take polls that are usually reliable within a few percentage points. However, polling is never completely accurate. One problem is that pollsters cannot be sure that the people they are interviewing are being honest. Serious problems with polling occurred during the 2000 presidential election, when flawed data gathered during exit polling resulted in extreme confusion about whether Al Gore or George W. Bush had won the state of Florida.

2. What does a poll mean when it says that 70 percent of Americans favor a law, with a 3 percent sampling error?

_____

_____

◉ Public Opinion and Democracy (page 522)

The Framers of the Constitution tried to meet two goals in forming a representative democracy. They wanted to provide for popular rule. They also wanted to protect government from the whims of public opinion. Research shows that the government is responsive to public opinion. However, public opinion is not the only influence on public policy. Interest groups, political parties, the mass media, other institutions of government, and the ideas of activists and public officials also help shape public policy.

3. What factors besides public opinion help shape public policy?

_____

_____

STUDY GUIDE  Chapter 19, Section 1

For use with textbook pages 527–534.

How MEDIA IMPACT GOVERNMENT

CONTENT VOCABULARY

mass media Means of communication, such as television, newspapers, movies, and the Internet, that influence large audiences *(page 527)*

news release A ready-made story government officials prepare for members of the press *(page 528)*

news briefing A meeting during which a government official makes an announcement or explains a policy, decision, or action *(page 528)*

leak The release of secret information by anonymous government officials to media *(page 529)*

media event A visually interesting event designed to reinforce a politician's position on some issue *(page 529)*

front-runner The early leader in an election *(page 530)*

spot advertising The brief, frequent, positive descriptions of a candidate or a candidate's major themes broadcast on television or radio *(page 531)*

DRAWING FROM EXPERIENCE

Have you ever been influenced about political candidates by print or broadcast media?

This section focuses on how media impacts the government.

READING STRATEGIES

Create an outline to help you take notes about the ways by which the media affect government.

◉ How Media Impact Government

I. The President and the Media

   A. News releases and briefings

   B.

   C.

   D.

II. Media and Presidential Campaigns

READ TO LEARN

◉ Introduction *(page 527)*

The **mass media** include all the means for communicating information to the general public. This includes print media, such as newspapers and magazines; broadcast media, such as radio and television; and the Internet. They play a crucial role in government as "the means by which the people receive that

STUDY GUIDE (continued)   Chapter 19, Section 1

free flow of information and ideas essential to intelligent self-government." Politicians use the mass media to help meet goals such as getting reelected. Politicians also want the media to pass on their messages just as the politicians present them.

◉ The President and the Media *(page 528)*

The mass media offer presidents the best way to sell their ideas and policies to the public. Franklin D. Roosevelt was the first president to master the broadcast media. One journalist called Roosevelt the "first great American radio voice." The era of television politics began with the presidential debates of 1960. All presidents since then have paid great attention to their television image.

To control the flow of information about the president, White House staff use the following tools:

News releases are ready-made stories prepared for members of the press. They can be printed or broadcast word for word, or used as background information.

News briefings are announcements where a governmental official explains a policy, decision, or action. Briefings give reporters the chance to ask officials about news releases.

Press conferences involve reporters from the news media questioning a high-level government official.

Backgrounders are important pieces of information that the president or other top official gives reporters. The reporters may then use a backgrounder in a story, but they cannot reveal where the information came from. Backgrounders give government officials the chance to test new ideas or to send unofficial messages.

A *leak* is the release to the media of secret information by an unnamed government official. These officials may be seeking support for a policy others in the government do not like. Or low-level officials may leak information to expose corruption or to get top officials to pay attention to a problem.

A *media event* is a visually interesting happening used to support a politician's position on some issue. A president who takes a strong stand against pollution, for example, makes a stronger statement by standing in front of a state-of-the-art manufacturing plant than in the Oval Office.

1. What is the difference between a news release and a leak?

_____

_____

◉ Media and Presidential Campaigns *(page 529)*

Television influences who runs for office, how candidates are nominated, how election campaigns are constructed, and how political parties approach the election process. It influences the types of candidates who run for office in the following ways:

A. Candidates who run for major offices must project a pleasant appearance and performance on camera.

B. Television has made it much easier for people who are political unknowns to become serious candidates for major offices.

C. Television has encouraged celebrities from other fields to enter politics. Such people have instant name recognition and do not need to work their way up through their party's local and state organizations.

STUDY GUIDE (continued)   Chapter 19, Section 1

The mass media give horse-race coverage of elections, especially primaries. Early presidential primaries are important to a candidate's chances. The media declare a candidate the *front runner*, even when he or she wins by a very small margin. Then only the front runners can attract the millions in loans and contributions needed to succeed in the nominating process. Conventions are also affected by television. They are now huge made-for-television events.

Andrew Jackson began the era of stump speeches and parades in presidential campaigns. Around 1900, candidates began using advertisements in newspapers, magazines, and mass mailings. In 1924 candidates began radio campaigning. Television campaigning began with Dwight D. Eisenhower in 1952. Television campaigns use *spot advertising*, the same method companies use to sell products. Spot advertisements give positive descriptions of a candidate and the candidate's message or present negative images of the opposing candidate.

Television campaigns cost huge amounts of money. Candidates must rely on extensive fundraising efforts in order to pay for them. Television has also weakened the role of political parties as the key link between politicians and voters in national politics. Voters can get information about a candidate without depending on the party organization. Candidates can appeal directly to the people, bypassing party leadership. Finally, candidates must also approach additional donors outside the party to raise the money necessary to successfully win an election.

2. How has television influenced the types of candidates who run for president?

_____

_____

◉ Congress and the Media (page 532)

The mass media tend to report on the most controversial aspects of Congress:

Confirmation Hearings The Senate usually holds hearings to review presidential appointments to high government posts. These can attract wide media coverage. In addition, the media often conduct their own investigations of people nominated for high office. Sometimes the media will uncover damaging information about an appointee. For instance, President George H.W. Bush nominated former senator John Tower to the Cabinet. The media accused Tower of alcoholism and marital problems. As a result, the Senate rejected Tower.

Oversight Activities Congress has the power to review how the executive branch does its job. This power is handled through hearings. The media cover the hearings when lawmakers uncover a major scandal, such as the Iran-*contra* affair in 1987. Millions watched the investigation of the use of money from arms sales to Iran to support rebels called *contras* in Nicaragua.

Personal Business Even powerful lawmakers do not escape the attention of the media. For example, under media scrutiny in 1994, future Speaker of the House Newt Gingrich returned to the publisher a large cash advance on a book he was writing.

In the 1970s, congressional leaders were losing in the struggle for more media coverage than the president, especially on television. Today the floor work of the House and Senate are broadcast to lawmakers' offices and to cable viewers across the nation via C-SPAN, or Cable-Satellite Public Affairs Network. Also, both the House and Senate have recording studios where lawmakers can prepare radio and television messages to mail to hometown stations for local news programs.

STUDY GUIDE (continued) Chapter 19, Section 1

3. In what aspects of Congress are the media most interested?

_____

_____

◉ The Court and the Media *(page 534)*

Major newspapers and television and radio networks assign reporters to cover the Supreme Court. However, the judicial branch gets less coverage than the other branches for the following reasons:

A. As appointed officials, Supreme Court justices and other judges do not need publicity and rarely appear on radio or television. They fear that publicity may interfere with their ability to decide cases fairly.

B. The Court handles complex cases that interest only a small number of people.

4. Why do justices and judges seldom appear on radio and television?

_____

_____

◉ Setting the Public Agenda *(page 534)*

The public agenda is a list of problems in society that leaders and citizens agree need government action. Examples of these problems are aid to the homeless, long-term health care for children and the elderly, and high crime rates. The media's role in setting the public agenda is to bring these issues to the attention of the public and the government.

The media, especially television, make decisions about which issues to cover based in part on competition with other media networks. To try to attract the largest possible audience, network news organizations will prioritize the stories that they believe will influence the largest number of viewers. The fact that the media cover some issues more than others affects how people rank an issue's importance.

The media, along with a person's family and socioeconomic views, also play a role in teaching children and adults their basic attitudes and values toward politics. For example, the media, especially television, sends messages about war, crime, and environmental problems. Media can also reassure people that all is going well or give them a sense of distrust and cynicism about their world. For example, studies have shown that people who rely on television as their main source of news have more negative feelings about government and the political system than people who use other sources of information.

5. How do media set the public agenda?

_____

_____

STUDY GUIDE  Chapter 19, Section 2

For use with textbook pages 536–541.

Ⓡ EGULATING PRINT AND BROADCAST MEDIA

CONTENT VOCABULARY

prior restraint Government censorship of information before it is published or broadcast *(page 537)*

libel False written or published statements intended to damage a person's reputation *(page 537)*

shield law A law that gives reporters some means of protection against being forced to disclose confidential information or sources in state courts *(page 537)*

fairness doctrine A rule requiring broadcasters to provide opportunities for the expression of opposing views on issues of public importance *(page 538)*

DRAWING FROM EXPERIENCE

Have you ever said something inappropriate or false about someone in class or at home? Media can be held accountable by the government just like you might be held accountable by parents or a teacher for false statements.

This section explains the ways in which media is regulated by the government.

READING STRATEGIES

Use the table below to list the ways in which the Federal Communications Commission regulates broadcast media.

Regulating Broadcast Media

READ TO LEARN

◉ Introduction *(page 534)*

Government regulations try to provide order, fairness, and access to the media.

◉ Protecting the Media *(page 536)*

The First Amendment guarantees freedom of the press. In the United States, this means that the print media are free from **prior restraint**. This is government censorship of information before it is published. Editors and reporters have freedom to decide what goes in or stays out of their publications.

STUDY GUIDE (continued) Chapter 19, Section 2

Freedom of the press is not absolute. It does not allow false statements intended to damage a person's reputation. To publish such statements is called *libel*. However, there is no law against criticizing public officials.

1. What does freedom of the press mean in the United States?

_____

_____

◉ The Right to Gather Information *(page 537)*

Freedom to publish whatever they want means little if the media cannot collect information on government actions and decisions. Generally, the Supreme Court has rejected the idea that the media have special rights to government information. The lower courts, however, have decided for the media in 60 percent of *right-to-access* cases. Still, authorities do not have to give the media special right of access, for example, to crime scenes or disaster sites, if the general public is excluded.

Reporters often use secret informants when investigating news. If the courts, the police, or legislators force reporters to name their sources, these sources may vanish. On the other hand, criminals may go unpunished if reporters do not give police information about them. More than half the states have passed *shield laws* to protect reporters from having to reveal their sources. No national shield law exists, but the Privacy Protection Act of 1980 prevents all levels of government from searching for and seizing source documentation, except in special circumstances.

2. How do shield laws protect reporters and the media?

_____

_____

◉ Regulating Broadcast Media *(page 537)*

The mass media, like other money-making businesses, are subject to some government regulation. The federal government has more power to regulate broadcast media than print media because broadcast media must share public airwaves.

The Federal Communications Commission (FCC) is the government agency with authority to regulate interstate and international communications by radio, television, telephone, telegraph, cable, and satellite. The FCC grants licenses to all radio and television stations in the country. The FCC cannot censor broadcasts. However, it can fine stations that violate rules and threaten not to renew a station's license. Over the years, the extent of FCC regulation has varied to reflect changes in technology, court rulings, and ideas about the role of government. One change was the *fairness doctrine*, a rule that required broadcasters to provide airtime to both sides of a controversial issue. Some broadcasters claimed the fairness doctrine was actually censorship. It caused stations to avoid reporting on any type of controversy. In 1987 the FCC dropped the fairness doctrine.

Owners can influence the messages their media present. Shortly after its creation in 1934, the FCC began creating a complex series of rules aimed at keeping media ownership from being concentrated in the hands of a few people or large companies. Supporters of ownership limits argued that the limits allowed citizens to be exposed to a wide array of ideas, and promoted competition. However, by the mid-1990s,

STUDY GUIDE (continued)   Chapter 19, Section 2

new technologies had changed telecommunications. For example, phone lines could carry the same signals as cable television, and both phone and cable companies could offer Internet services. Broadcast owners began to pressure Congress to review its policy towards media communications.

In 1996, Congress passed the Telecommunications Act. This law ended or greatly relaxed many of the FCC's limits on media ownership. Congress also required the FCC to review media ownership rules every two years. A key objective of the Act was to increase competition and loosen media monopolies. However, the Act appears to have actually led to an even greater concentration of media ownership. Media companies can now merge to create powerful new communications giants, so that a few companies now dominate key markets. The Telecommunications Act of 1996 also prohibited obscene or harassing conversation on any telecommunications facility, and amended the federal criminal code to apply current obscenity laws to Internet users. However, in 1997 this part of the Act was struck down by the Supreme Court as an undue limitation on free speech.

3. Which issue addressed by the Telecommunications Act do you think is most important? Explain.

_____

_____

◉ Media and National Security *(page 541)*

The government tries to control information affecting national security by classifying it as secret and by limiting press coverage of military actions. Government restriction on media coverage of military actions has varied. During the Vietnam War, there were few limits on the press. Reporters were allowed to roam combat zones freely and report their stories on daily television news. During the 1991 Persian Gulf War, the Defense Department limited media access to a small group of reporters. Most reporters had to depend on official briefings. In the 2003 Iraq War, the Pentagon allowed 500 "embedded" journalists to accompany troops into battle. However, the reporters could not announce their exact location or the direction they were traveling.

4. How did most reporters get information about the Persian Gulf War?

_____

_____

STUDY GUIDE  Chapter 19, Section 3

For use with textbook pages 543–549.

THE INTERNET AND DEMOCRACY

CONTENT VOCABULARY

partisan Web sites offering information and ideas that support only one point of view on an issue *(page 544)*

electronic mailing list E-mail updates that provide subscribers with current information on a topic *(page 545)*

action alert A message from an interest group that calls upon each of its members to immediately respond to a specific lawmaker or other official *(page 546)*

electronic petition A message asking recipients to electronically "sign" their name to a request to an official to show him or her how a large number of people feel about an issue *(page 546)*

DRAWING FROM EXPERIENCE

How can you find information quickly for a report or help with homework? The federal government provides a great deal of information on Web sites that allow citizens to participate in government.

This section explores the relationship between the Internet and democracy.

READING STRATEGIES

Use the graphic organizer below to analyze the impact of the Internet on citizen participation.

READ TO LEARN

● Introduction *(page 543)*

The Internet is a vast web of computer networks linked all over the world. It is rapidly becoming a new type of global electronic mass media with a major impact on American government and politics.

● Key Features of the Internet *(page 543)*

The Internet offers several unique benefits for politics and government:

A. *Widespread* Web traffic has been growing by 100 percent per year. Many of these new users are also new voters.

B. *Interactivity* Communication among many people at once allows political activists to mobilize people with similar interests and views.

C. *Global Scope* The Internet represents a diverse range of opinions. However, its global nature often makes it difficult to determine which national law should govern Internet activities.

STUDY GUIDE (continued)   Chapter 19, Section 3

1. What benefits does the interactive nature of the Internet offer for politics and government?

_____

_____

◉ Gathering Information (page 544)

The Internet is a useful tool for Americans to access information on political issues and government at all levels.

A. *Political Web sites* are devoted to political issues. Major newspapers and newsmagazines often have *archives*, or files, of older stories. Thousands of Web sites are devoted to politics and government. These are sponsored by Congress, political parties, universities, or interest groups such as the Sierra Club and the National Rifle Association. Many Web sites are *partisan*, meaning that they offer information and ideas that support only their point of view on issues.

B. *Tracking Legislation* The Internet also allows citizens to track legislation. One example is THOMAS, a Web site that lets you search for all versions of House and Senate bills by either bill number or key word. Reports filed by committees within the House and Senate are available on the database. It is also a useful place to find contact information on members of Congress and other offices within the legislative branch.

C. *Electronic mailing lists* are automated E-mail notifications that provide subscribers with current information on a topic, such as gun control or copyright laws, upon which their list focuses. The national offices of the Democratic and Republican parties also operate several mailing lists that provide information about issues, candidates, press briefings, and upcoming events.

D. *E-Government* Governments at all levels provide services and information over the Internet. For example, local and state government websites can be used to register to vote or to obtain hunting or fishing licenses. However, some of these sites are poorly organized and difficult to access. In 2002 Congress passed the *E-Government Act*. This law established the Office of Electronic Government to help federal agencies provide better online service to the public.

2. In what ways does the Internet make government more accessible to individual citizens?

_____

_____

◉ Impact on Citizen Participation (page 546)

The Internet is also becoming a powerful tool for citizen activism in the following ways:

A. *Communicating with officials* E-mail has become a popular way for citizens to tell legislators and other government officials what they think. For example, Congress receives about 12 E-mail messages every second. Many Web sites offer interactive message boards and E-mail directories that make it easy to contact government officials.

B. *Action alerts and petitions* An *action alert* is a message from an interest group that calls upon its members to immediately respond by telephone, fax, or E-mail to a lawmaker or other official. For example, an action alert might ask you to contact a lawmaker to tell them you support or oppose and bill on gun control. *Electronic petitions* ask recipients to "sign" their name electronically to a request going to an official. The goal is to show lawmakers that a large number of people agree on how an issue should be decided.

C. *Grassroots Web sites* Individual citizens often set up their own Web sites in support of candidates. This allows people to become involved with elections and government without leaving home. However, independent Web sites can also present misleading information about candidates. It can also be difficult to tell the difference between official and unofficial Web sites.

D. *Volunteering* Election candidate Web sites often give information on how to sign up for volunteer jobs, such as working on a telephone bank. "Cybervolunteering" involves volunteer activities that can only be done on the Internet, such as putting a "banner ad" supporting a candidate or issue on your own personal Web site. 2004 Democratic presidential candidate Howard Dean used his campaign Web site to recruit over 500,000 volunteers and raise several million dollars in campaign funds.

E. *Political Blogs* Blogs provide a new way to participate in politics. Individuals and interest groups can create a blog, a kind of online personal journal, and publish material on the Web for millions to read and comment on. While bloggers sometimes highlight information missed by the major media, they also publish inaccurate information or even lies.

F. *Electronic Voting* The growth of the Internet has led a number of states to conduct studies on the effects of online voting in primary and general elections. Proponents claim that online voting will make voting easier and more efficient, while critics are concerned about sabotage or vote stealing by hackers. The first use of online voting was in Arizona's 2000 Democratic primary. Voter turnout doubled that of the previous primary, and 40% of votes were cast online. However, critics claim that online voting discriminates against underprivileged and minority voters who may not have online access.

3. What are some ways in which the Internet allows citizens to become more active in government?

_____

_____

◉ **Challenges for Public Policy** *(page 548)*

The rise of the Internet creates a need for new laws to deal with the impact of the new technology on politics, businesses, and people's daily lives.

A. *Offensive Content* The Supreme Court ruled in *Reno* v. *American Civil Liberties Union* (1997) that the First Amendment guarantees freedom of expression on the Internet. Since then, the Supreme Court has blocked several attempts by Congress to protect children from online pornography while upholding free speech rights. In 2000 Congress passed the Children's Internet Protection Act. This law requires public libraries that accept federal funds to install anti-pornography filters on computers used by the public. In 2003 the Supreme Court ruled that this law does not violate the First Amendment rights of library users, because Congress can attach conditions to federal funding.

B. *Taxing E-Commerce* The growth of E-commerce, or the sale of goods and services online, has raised questions about taxation. Because state sales tax laws are so cumbersome, the Supreme Court has blocked attempts by state governments to require online retailers to collect sales taxes. While state governments worry that they will lose billions of dollars by not taxing online goods, online retailers, technology companies, and Congress remain resistant.

4. Does the Children's Internet Protection Act violate the First Amendment? Explain.

_____

_____

STUDY GUIDE  Chapter 20, Section 1

For use with textbook pages 555–559.

RAISING MONEY

CONTENT VOCABULARY

taxes The money that people and businesses pay to support the activities of the government *(page 555)*

taxable income The total income of an individual minus certain deductions and personal exemptions *(page 555)*

dependent One who depends primarily on another person for basic needs such as food and shelter *(page 556)*

withholding The money an employer withholds from workers' wages as payment of anticipated income tax *(page 556)*

securities Financial instruments, including bonds, notes, and certificates, that are sold as a means of borrowing money with a promise to repay the buyer with interest after a specific time period *(page 559)*

national debt The total amount of money the government owes at any given time *(page 559)*

DRAWING FROM EXPERIENCE

Where do you get spending money? Allowance? Part-time wages? The federal government has its sources of money, too.

This section focuses on how the federal government raises money.

READING STRATEGIES

Use the graphic organizer below to list the types of taxes the federal government uses for revenue.

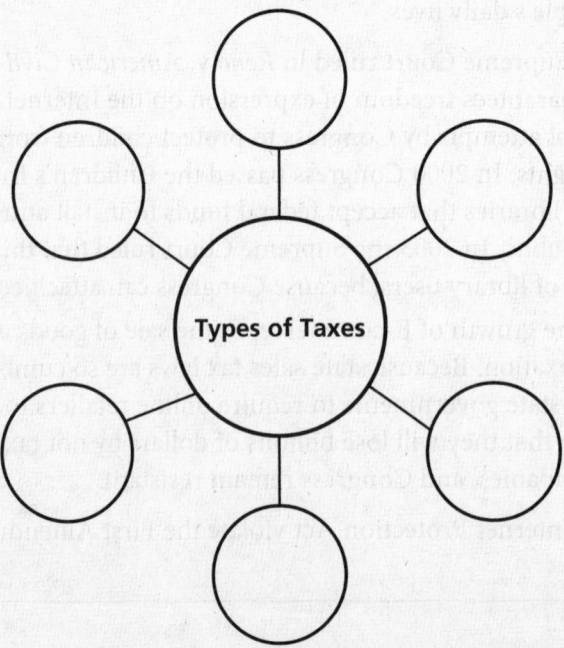

Types of Taxes

╔══╗
║ **STUDY GUIDE** (continued)   **Chapter 20, Section 1** ║
╚══╝

READ TO LEARN

◉ Introduction (page 555)

The two major sources of the money the federal government takes in are taxes and borrowing.

◉ Taxes as a Source of Revenue (page 555)

Taxes are payments by individuals and businesses to support the activities of government. The individual income tax is the federal government's biggest single source of income. The federal income tax is taken from a person's *taxable income.* This is the total income of an individual minus certain deductions and personal exemptions. People may choose to take deductions for contributions to charity and other expenses.

Exemptions are based on the number of dependents a wage earner has. A *dependent* is someone who depends primarily on another person for such things as food, clothing, and shelter. The U.S. income tax is a progressive tax. This means it is based on a taxpayer's ability to pay. The more a taxpayer makes, the higher the tax rate.

The deadline for filing taxes each year is April 15. Employers withhold a certain amount from each paycheck. This *withholding* pays the income tax ahead of the filing date. The Internal Revenue Service (IRS) collects these taxes from employers. They also audit, or check more closely, a certain percentage of returns each year.

Corporations also pay income taxes. Their payments equal about 10 percent of the government's total revenues.

The government also collects money to pay for Social Security, Medicare, and unemployment compensation programs. This money is called social insurance taxes. Employers deduct them from each worker's paycheck and send the total to the federal government. Social insurance taxes are regressive taxes because people with lower incomes usually pay a larger portion of their income for these taxes than do people with higher incomes.

Excise taxes are paid on the manufacture, transportation, sale, or consumption of goods and services. Some excise taxes are called luxury taxes because they are placed on goods such as cigarettes and liquor, which are not considered necessities.

Taxes placed on goods coming into the United States are called custom duties, tariffs, or import duties. A high custom duty is called a protective tariff. These raise the price of foreign goods and make them less desirable to American buyers than American-made goods.

The federal government also collects estate taxes. These are collected on large amounts of property and money left by a person who dies. A gift tax is collected on gifts of money from a living person. The estate tax became controversial. The tax law passed by Congress and President Bush in 2001 gradually phases out the federal estate tax over the next several years.

1. List the kinds of taxes that supply money to the federal government.

_____

_____

STUDY GUIDE (continued) Chapter 20, Section 1

◉ Taxes and the Economy (page 557)

The tax system is very complex. It contains provisions that benefit certain groups. These are called tax loopholes. However, in the 1980s the tax system was even more complicated. Then Congress passed the Tax Reform Act of 1986. It reduced or ended many tax deductions, tax credits, and tax shelters, which often favored the wealthy. It also reduced the number of tax brackets or rates.

In 2003 President Bush signed the Job and Growth Act, a $1.35 trillion tax cut. This legislation, aimed at stimulating the economy, increased the child tax credit and gave millions of taxpayers an average tax reduction of over $1,000.

2. How did the Tax Reform Act of 1986 affect the tax system?

_____

_____

◉ Borrowing for Revenue (page 559)

The government borrows money by selling federal securities to individuals, corporations, and others. Government securities include bonds, notes, and certificates. They are popular with investors because they are safe and sometimes the interest they earn is not taxed. Small investors favor savings bonds.

When government spending is more than its income, it must borrow money. Government borrowing over time created the ***national debt.*** The size of the national debt affects the economy and the federal budget.

3. Why are government securities popular investments?

_____

_____

STUDY GUIDE  Chapter 20, Section 2

For use with textbook pages 560–564.

ⓟREPARING THE FEDERAL BUDGET

CONTENT VOCABULARY

fiscal year A 12-month accounting period *(page 560)*

uncontrollables Government expenditures required by law and resulting from previous budgetary commitments *(page 561)*

entitlement A required government expenditure that continues from one year to the next *(page 561)*

incrementalism The term used to explain that the total budget changes little from year to year *(page 564)*

DRAWING FROM EXPERIENCE

Does your family have a budget? A family budget usually allots money each month for expenses such as food and entertainment. Even more than a family, a government needs a budget to plan its expenses.

This section focuses on how the federal budget is prepared.

READING STRATEGIES

Use the graphic organizer below to help you take notes and list entitlements provided by the government.

Entitlements

STUDY GUIDE (continued) Chapter 20, Section 2

READO TO LEARN

◉ Introduction (page 560)

The federal budget helps the government predict and control revenue and spending for each fiscal year. This is a 12-month accounting period from October 1 of one year to September 30 of the next year. The executive branch draws up the proposed budget under the president's leadership. Congress uses the president's budget to prepare a tax and spending plan to send back to the president.

◉ The President's Budget (page 560)

The president is responsible for directing the preparation of the budget and making major decisions about national budget priorities. The actual day-to-day preparation of the budget is in the hands of the Office of Management and Budget (OMB).

Budget making begins in the spring and goes through the following steps:

A. The Director of the OMB takes the first set of figures to the president. The secretary of the treasury and the Council of Economic Advisers (CEA) help the president decide how well the budget fits the president's economic goals and policy.

B. The White House sends its decisions on the budget to the agencies and departments in the executive branch with guidelines to help each of them prepare their own final budgets.

C. The executive departments and agencies cut and add to bring each agency's budget in line with the president's decisions.

D. During the fall, the OMB submits a complete budget document to the president for final review and approval.

E. The administration rushes the president's budget to the printer. The president sends the formal budget to Congress with an annual budget message.

About 70 percent of the budget is made up of uncontrollables. These are expenditures required by law. Many of the uncontrollables are called entitlements. These are benefits which individuals have an established legal right to receive. Entitlements include Social Security, pensions for retired government employees, Medicare, Medicaid, and veterans' benefits. Another largely uncontrollable item is the interest that must be paid on the national debt.

   1. Where does the president send his decisions on the first set of budget figures? Why?

_____

_____

◉ Congressional Budget Action (page 562)

The president draws up budget proposals, but no money may be spent until Congress approves it. Congress changes the president's budget as it sees fit. Chief lawmakers and the president often make compromises before the budget is passed.

The Congressional Budget Office (CBO) evaluates the overall federal budget for Congress. Experts on the committee report to Congress and balance out the OMB in the executive branch.

By the mid-1980s, the size of the national debt worried economists. So Congress passed the Gramm-Rudman-Hollings Act. This law tried to force Congress to reduce budget deficits. However, the budget deficit continued to grow because the president and Congress disagreed about spending priorities.

In 1990 Congress passed the Budgetary Enforcement Act. It divided the budget into three categories: domestic policy, defense, and international affairs. Spending that exceeded the budgeted limit in any of these three areas would come out of next year's funding for that area. Economic hard times in 1991 derailed the deficit-cutting plans. Then in 1993, tax income increased. Some members of Congress called for a balanced budget. Other members of Congress and President Clinton were satisfied that the annual deficit was falling.

The budget-making process in Congress generally follows these steps:

A. House and Senate Budget Committees review the major features of the president's budget proposals. On April 15 they prepare a concurrent resolution. This resolution sets forth the total federal spending and tax plan for the coming fiscal year.

B. Reconciliation occurs between April 15 and June 15. House and Senate committees use this time to reconcile, or fit, the spending and taxing plans with existing plans. They create a reconciliation bill that both the House and Senate must approve.

C. The House then passes an appropriation bill. This officially sets aside money for all expenditures approved in the reconciliation process. This bill is supposed to be finished by June 30 but is often delayed.

D. On October 15 the OMB issues an official report and may make cuts in the budget to fit deficit-reduction targets.

2. What happens in the preparation of the budget between April 15 and June 15?

_____

_____

◉ Incremental Budget Making *(page 564)*

Analysts call the budget-making process ***incrementalism.*** This means that the total budget changes only a little from one year to the next. So the best predictor of this year's budget is last year's budget. Federal agencies usually can assume they will get the same amount of funding as last year. Also, most budget debates focus on small increases or decreases for an agency, not completely doing away with agencies.

3. How does incrementalism in the budget affect the work of federal agencies?

_____

_____

STUDY GUIDE  Chapter 20, Section 3

For use with textbook pages 566–570.

Ⓜ ANAGING THE ECONOMY

CONTENT VOCABULARY

fiscal policy A government's use of spending and taxation to influence the economy *(page 567)*

monetary policy A government's control of the supply of money and credit to influence the economy *(page 567)*

gross domestic product (GDP) The sum of all goods and services produced in a nation in a year *(page 568)*

discount rate The interest rate the Federal Reserve System charges member banks for loans *(page 569)*

reserve requirement The percentage of money member banks must keep in Federal Reserve Banks as a reserve against their deposits *(page 569)*

open market operations The method the Federal Reserve System uses to affect the economy by buying or selling government securities on the open market *(page 570)*

DRAWING FROM EXPERIENCE

What would happen if the students and teachers at your school stopped spending money at nearby stores? Do you think store owners would feel the effect? If the government stopped spending money, the national economy would certainly feel the effects.

This section focuses on how the government manages the economy.

READING STRATEGIES

Use an outline to help you take notes about how the federal government manages the economy.

◉ **Managing the Economy**

 I. Where the Money Goes

  A.

  B.

  C.

 II. Fiscal and Monetary Policy

  A.

  B.

STUDY GUIDE (continued) Chapter 20, Section 3

READ TO LEARN

◉ Introduction *(page 566)*

Officials in both the executive and legislative branches try to promote a healthy economy.

◉ Where the Money Goes *(page 566)*

In addition to paying interest on the national debt, the federal government spends its money in the following major areas:

Direct Benefit Payments Almost half of every dollar goes for Social Security, social-welfare, and health-care programs. The biggest entitlement program is Social Security.

National Defense Since 1991 the federal government has gradually reduced the share of the budget that goes to defense. In 1996, defense spending represented about 17 percent of the budget, down from 22 percent in 1992. However, by 2003 the defense budget had increased by $81 billion from its 2000 figure.

Discretionary Spending A large part of tax revenues are spent on the environment, transportation, criminal justice, and other areas. Much of this money is in the form of grants to states and localities. They use the federal money for road repair, public housing, police training, school lunch programs, flood insurance, and more.

1. How is almost 50 percent of every tax dollar spent?

_____

_____

◉ Fiscal and Monetary Policy *(page 567)*

Most Americans expect the government to play an important part in money matters. To influence the economy, the government uses the following methods:

Fiscal policy uses government spending and taxes to influence the economy.

Monetary policy controls the supply of money and credit to influence the economy.

The federal budget shapes how much money the government will spend and how much it will collect through taxes and borrowing. The government may spend more money than it takes in to put more people back to work and increase economic activity. Or it may lower taxes to give consumers and investors more purchasing power. As a result, the United States had a budget deficit for many years because people thought it would benefit the economy. By the early 1980s, however, economists worried about the effects of debt on the nation's future. However, some economists said that the deficit as a percentage of the *gross domestic product* (GDP) was more important than the deficit alone. They pointed out that the deficit represented only about 5 percent of the GDP. However, by 2003, interest payments on the debt equaled nearly half of that spent for defense.

Today, the federal government tries to control the economy through its monetary policy. This involves controlling the supply of money and credit—the cost of borrowing money. The government controls the money supply through the Federal Reserve System.

2. Decribe two ways the government tries to control the economy today.

_____

_____

◉ The Federal Reserve System (page 568)

The Federal Reserve System, known as the "Fed," is the central banking system of the United States. When banks need money, they go to the Fed. The United States is divided into 12 Federal Reserve Districts. Each district has one main Federal Reserve Bank. In addition, most Federal Reserve Banks have branch banks within their districts. About four out of every ten banks in the United States are members of the Federal Reserve. They control the largest share of total deposits in the nation.

A seven-member board directs the entire Federal Reserve System. The president appoints the members, and the Senate approves them. Then the president selects one member to chair the board. Afterward, the president and Congress have little control over the board. Its members make economic decisions without fear of political pressure.

The board has two major responsibilities:

A. It supervises the Federal Reserve Banks.

B. It determines the general money and credit policies of the United States.

The Fed uses the following tools to control the nation's banks:

A. The Fed can lower or raise the *discount rate.* This is the rate the Fed charges member banks for loans. Low discount rates encourage banks to borrow money from the Fed to make loans to customers. High discount rates mean banks will borrow less.

B. The Fed may raise or lower the *reserve requirement* for member banks. Member banks must keep a certain percentage of their money in Federal Reserve Banks as a reserve against their deposits. If the Fed raises the reserve requirements, the banks must leave more money with the Fed. Thus, they have less money to lend. When the Fed lowers the reserve requirement, member banks have more money to lend.

C. The Fed can put money into the economy by buying government bonds and other securities on the open market. These *open-market operations* help expand the economy. The Fed may also sell government securities. This causes the economy to slow down.

The president and Congress largely control taxing and spending. They have little control over the Fed. The Fed's policies may help or hinder programs of the president or of Congress. Some people would like to make the Fed less independent. Others say that the nation needs a group outside politics to watch over monetary policy.

3. What are the major responsibilities of the Federal Reserve Board?

_____

_____

STUDY GUIDE  Chapter 21, Section 1

For use with textbook pages 575–583.

BUSINESS AND LABOR POLICY

CONTENT VOCABULARY

mixed economy A system in which the government regulates private enterprise *(page 575)*

laissez-faire The philosophy that government should keep its hands off the economy *(page 577)*

trust A form of business consolidation in which several corporations combine their stock and allow a board of trustees to operate a giant enterprise *(page 578)*

monopoly A business that controls so much of an industry that little or no competition exists *(page 578)*

interlocking directorate The same people serving on the boards of directors of competing companies *(page 578)*

oligopoly A situation where only a few firms dominate a particular industry *(page 579)*

securities Financial instruments, including bonds, notes, and certificates, that are sold as a means of borrowing money with a promise to repay the buyer with interest after a specific period *(page 581)*

collective bargaining The practice of negotiating labor contracts *(page 581)*

injunction An order that will stop a particular action or enforce a rule or regulation *(page 582)*

DRAWING FROM EXPERIENCE

Could you find a job at age 13? Probably not. For most jobs, the law limits child workers to those 14 or over. However, this was not always so.

This section focuses on government regulation of business and labor.

READING STRATEGIES

Use the time line below to help you take notes about when government started regulating business.

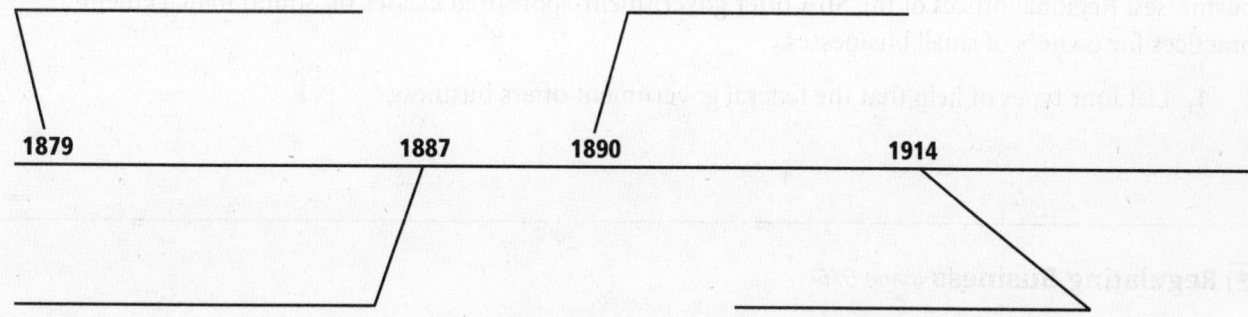

1879   1887   1890   1914

STUDY GUIDE (continued) Chapter 21, Section 1

READ TO LEARN

◉ Introduction (page 575)

The American economic system is a *mixed economy.* This means that the government both supports and regulates private business.

◉ Promoting and Protecting Business (page 575)

After the War of 1812, the British flooded American markets with cheap British goods. They were trying to destroy America's new industries. The United States government responded by passing higher tariffs.

Today the federal government stresses lower tariffs and free trade for many items. Consumers benefit from the lower cost of many imported goods. However, tariffs are still used to protect some American industries from foreign competition. The government also restricts some products through quotas, or limits on the number that may be imported.

Today the federal government provides subsidies, or aid, to business in the following ways:

A. Tax incentives allow businesses to deduct certain expenses from their annual tax returns.

B. Government loans, or credit subsidies, provide funds for business at low interest rates.

C. Free services, such as weather information, census reports, and other valuable information are provided to businesses across the nation.

D. The government provides direct cash payments to businesses whose products or services are considered important to the general public.

The sole purpose of the Department of Commerce is the promotion of business. Its main jobs are to provide:

A. Information services

B. Financial assistance

C. Development services

The Bureau of the Census, a part of the Department of Commerce, supplies important economic data to businesses.

The Small Business Administration (SBA) offers credit help, free advice, and information to small businesses. Regional offices of the SBA offer government-sponsored classes on sound management practices for owners of small businesses.

1. List four types of help that the federal government offers business.

_____

_____

◉ Regulating Business (page 576)

Federal regulation of economic activity comes from the Constitution. It grants Congress the power to "lay and collect taxes" and to "regulate commerce . . . among the several states." Today commerce among states covers production and transportation of goods, communications, mining, and the sale of stocks and bonds. Regulations now include laws that prohibit, promote, protect, assist, and establish standards for many areas of interstate commerce.

Until the late 1800s, the government took a *laissez-faire,* or hands off, approach to business. However, many abuses came with the rapid industrialization of the late 1800s. Americans questioned the fairness of a system that allowed railroads to charge higher rates for farmers than for manufacturers. Americans began to demand government regulation of business. Congress responded by passing the Interstate Commerce Act in 1887. This act established the Interstate Commerce Commission (ICC) and placed limits on freight rates that railroad companies charged.

Congress later passed the following measures to control corporations that threatened to destroy competition:

The Sherman Antitrust Act In a *trust* several corporations combine their stock and allow a board of trustees to run the corporations as one giant company. The trustees could set production quotas, fix prices, and control the market, thereby creating a *monopoly.* A monopoly is a business that controls so much of a product, service, or industry that little or no competition exists. John D. Rockefeller established such a trust in the Standard Oil Trust. In 1879 it controlled 90 percent of the oil refined in the United States. In 1890 Congress passed the Sherman Antitrust Act to halt monopolies. In 1906 the federal government charged the Standard Oil Company with violating the act. The company was split into a number of smaller companies.

The Clayton Antitrust Act This act, passed in 1914, banned charging high prices in an area where little competition existed. The act also outlawed *interlocking directorates.* This is an organization where the same people serve on boards of directors of competing companies.

Congress established the Federal Trade Commission to enforce the Clayton Act. The commission may:

A. define unfair competitive practices,

B. issue orders to halt these practices,

C. examine corporate purchases of stock,

D. investigate trade practices,

E. enforce laws that prohibit false advertising,

F. require truthful labels on textiles and furs,

G. regulate the packaging and labeling of certain consumer goods,

H. require the full disclosure of the lending practice of finance companies and retailers who have installment plans, and

I. check consumer credit agencies.

Today economic power belongs to oligopolies. An *oligopoly* exists when a few firms dominate a particular industry. About 50 multibillion-dollar companies during the 1990s controlled about one-third of the manufacturing capacity in the United States.

   2. What laws did Congress pass to control monopolies and to encourage competition?

_____

_____

STUDY GUIDE (continued)   Chapter 21, Section 1

◉ Consumer Protection *(page 579)*

Congress has passed other laws protecting consumers and ensuring fair product standards. It also established independent regulatory agencies that protect consumers or regulate certain economic activities.

Before 1900 some food companies mislabeled foods and sold tainted meat. Books such as *The Jungle* and magazine articles about conditions in food processing plants angered the public. As a result, Congress passed the Pure Food and Drug Act in 1906. This law made selling contaminated, unhealthful, or falsely labeled foods or drugs illegal. The 1906 Meat Inspection Act provided for the federal inspection of all meatpacking companies that sold meat across state lines. The Food and Drug Administration (FDA) is responsible for protecting the public from poorly processed and improperly labeled foods and drugs.

The Federal Trade Commission (FTC) protects consumers from misleading and false advertising. An example of an FTC regulation is that all manufacturers must clearly list the contents of packaged products on their labels.

Congress created the Consumer Product Safety Commission (CPSC) in 1972. The CPSC investigates injuries caused by merchandise such as lawn mowers, kitchen appliances, toys, and sports equipment. It established standards of safety for each type of product. If a product fails to meet these standards, the CPSC can order it off the market.

The Securities and Exchange Commission (SEC) regulates the trading of *securities*, or stocks and bonds. The SEC regulates the nation's securities issued by public utility companies. It also requires all corporations that issue public stock to file regular reports on their financial status, which are made available to investors. To further protect investors, the Sarbanes-Oxley Act of 2002 requires the chief officers of investment companies to personally sign SEC reports and to pay penalties if accounting fraud is later discovered.

3. What is the responsibility of the FDA?

_____

_____

◉ Government and Labor *(page 581)*

Large corporations multiplied in the late 1800s. As a result, federal laws were created to regulate the relationship between employers and employees. For many years, the government favored businesses over labor unions. The government's attitude toward labor changed in 1914. The Clayton Antitrust Act included a provision that labor unions were not to be treated as "conspiracies in restraint of trade."

In 1937 the Supreme Court upheld a minimum wage set by the state of Washington. Today laws set minimum wages and maximum working hours and prohibit child labor. In addition, the Department of Labor, established in 1913, provides employment offices and job-training programs, collects data, and offers unemployment insurance.

In the 1930s, 1940s, and 1950s, Congress passed the following labor-related laws:

The Norris-LaGuardia Act of 1932 gave workers the right to join unions and to strike. It outlawed contracts which forced workers to sign away their right to join a union. The act also restricted the use of federal court *injunctions.* These are court orders to stop an action from taking place. These were often used to force striking unions back to work.

The Wagner Act of 1935 guaranteed the right of all workers to organize and bargain collectively. According to the act, employers could not refuse to bargain collectively with recognized unions, interfere in union organization, or fire or otherwise punish a worker because of union activities. The Wagner Act established the National Labor Relations Board (NLRB). The board supervised the elections of union leaders, heard labor's complaints, and issued orders to end unfair labor practices.

The Taft-Hartley Act of 1947 required unions to give 60 days' notice before calling a strike. The act also restored limited use of injunctions. The act provided that employers could sue unions for damages caused during a strike. The law outlawed the closed shop––where only members of a union could be hired––but permitted the union shop. In a union shop, workers are required to join a union soon after they are hired but not before. State right-to-work laws provide that all workplaces be open shops where workers may freely decide whether or not to join a union.

The Landrum-Griffin Act of 1959 made misusing union funds a federal crime. It also protected union members from being threatened by their leaders and included a "bill of rights" for union members.

4. Which act passed by Congress was pro-business rather than pro-labor? Explain your choice.

_____

_____

Name _____ Date _____ Class _____

For use with textbook pages 584–589.

AGRICULTURE AND ENVIRONMENT

CONTENT VOCABULARY

price supports The program under which the Congress buys farmers' crops if the market price falls below the support price *(page 586)*

acreage allotment The program under which the government pays supports for farmers' crops grown on an assigned number of acres *(page 586)*

marketing quotas A limit set among farmers to market only an assigned portion of an overproduced crop *(page 586)*

DRAWING FROM EXPERIENCE

Where does your food come from? Most is raised on American farms, often with government help.

This section focuses on government regulation of agriculture and the environment.

READING STRATEGIES

Use the graphic organizer below to show the three major ways by which the Department of Agriculture helps farmers.

```
──────────────────────→  ┌──────────────┐  ←──────────────────────
                         │              │
                         │   Farmers    │
                         │              │
                         └──────────────┘
                                ↑
                              ╱
```

STUDY GUIDE (continued)   Chapter 21, Section 2

READ TO LEARN

◉ Introduction (page 584)

The federal government has always encouraged American agriculture, or farming. The total number of farms has decreased in the United States. However, farm output per hour increases almost every year. In 1900, for example, one farmer could feed about seven people. Today the average farmer can feed about 80 people.

◉ Farmers and Government (page 584)

Governments at the federal, state, and local levels support and help farmers. For example, the federal government created the Department of Agriculture to improve and modernize farming methods. During the Great Depression, President Roosevelt's New Deal helped farmers by limiting the production of products that were in oversupply to raise their prices. Under the Agricultural Adjustment Act of 1933, the government also paid farmers for not producing their usual amounts of corn, wheat, hogs, and other commodities. The act also provided loans to help farmers pay their expenses and keep their land.

1. How did the New Deal help farmers during the Great Depression?

_____

_____

◉ Aid for Farmers Today (page 586)

Today the Department of Agriculture provides the following services:

Marketing Farmers' Produce The Agricultural Marketing Service of the Department of Agriculture advises farmers on the demand for crops, current prices, and transportation methods. It also researches where and when to sell farmers' products. The Foreign Agricultural Service promotes the sale of American farm goods in foreign markets.

Stabilizing Farm Prices The government has tried several ways to stop farm prices from falling below a certain level. Today the Commodity Credit Corporation (CCC) handles the following price-stabilizing programs:

A. Congress establishes price supports for a particular product.

B. The government assigns farmers acreage allotments of a certain number of acres and pays support prices for only the crops grown on the assigned acres.

C. Farmers agree to marketing quotas and market only an assigned portion of their overproduced crop.

Promoting Conservation The Forest Service, a Department of Agriculture agency, has restored millions of acres of forests for outdoor recreation, timber, and wildlife habitat. The Soil Conservation Service, another agency, works with farmers to manage conservation problems.

2. In what three ways does the Department of Agriculture try to stabilize farm prices?

_____

_____

◉ Protecting the Environment (page 586)

The 1970 Clean Air Act established the Environmental Protection Agency (EPA) with the power to enforce air quality standards. The 1990 Clean Air Act ordered reductions in emissions of carbon monoxide, carbon dioxide, and smog. The 1992 Kyoto Protocol attempted to set global greenhouse emissions standards. However, in 2001 the United States refused to implement the agreement, calling it an inefficient solution that would damage the economy.

The Water Quality Improvement Act of 1970 banned the discharge of harmful amounts of oil and other dangerous materials into waterways. The law applied to such pollution sources as ships, onshore refineries, and offshore oil drilling platforms. It also controlled the drainage of pesticides into the Great Lakes. The Water Pollution Act of 1972 set the goal of completely stopping the discharge of pollutants into the nation's waterways. All polluters—cities, farmers, and industries—dumping wastes into waterways needed a permit.

The EPA issued hundreds of regulations to enforce environmental laws. State and local leaders began to complain about unfunded mandates. These are programs that the federal government orders but does not pay for. So in the 1990s Congress passed new laws that limited the requirements that the federal government could make for state and local governments without providing funds to pay for them.

3. How did the Water Pollution Act of 1972 improve on the Water Quality Improvement Act of 1970?

_____

_____

◉ Energy and the Environment (page 588)

By the early 1960s, many American rivers and lakes were fouled by sewage and chemical wastes. Smog engulfed major cities. Oil spills polluted beaches. The heavy use of pesticides endangered wildlife. Then in 1973 Americans were in the midst of an energy crisis. The federal government responded with a new energy policy to meet future energy crises. People saw that there were built-in costs and conflicts. For example, preserving clean air might require them to drive cars with pollution-control devices. These made cars more costly to buy and drive. Oil companies wanted to drill more offshore oil, but environmentalists believed that such drilling was too risky for sea life. Recently, environmental groups have worked to prevent the George W. Bush administration from drilling for oil in a wildlife refuge off the coast of Alaska.

4. How did solutions for energy shortages in the 1970s conflict with environmental goals?

_____

_____

STUDY GUIDE  Chapter 21, Section 3

For use with textbook pages 590–595.

ⒽEALTH AND PUBLIC ASSISTANCE

CONTENT VOCABULARY

social insurance Government programs designed to help elderly, ill, and unemployed citizens *(page 590)*

public assistance Government programs that distribute money to poor people *(page 590)*

unemployment insurance Programs in which federal and state governments cooperate to provide help for people who are out of work *(page 591)*

DRAWING FROM EXPERIENCE

Do you ever worry about whether the medicine you take is safe? Government regulation is partly responsible for the confidence Americans feel when taking drugs.

This section focuses on how the government promotes health and helps the aged, disabled, and poor.

READING STRATEGIES

Use the graphic organizer below to help you list and describe the programs the government uses to protect public health.

Government Program/Agency	Description

STUDY GUIDE (continued) Chapter 21, Section 3

READ TO LEARN

◉ Introduction (page 590)

Until the 1930s, ill health, old age, poverty, and disability were private matters. The Great Depression changed public attitudes, and the government began programs to care for the sick and the poor.

◉ The Depression's Impact (page 590)

As the Depression worsened, private charities and local and state governments could not take care of the problems of the increasing number of poor people. So Congress passed the Social Security Act in 1935. This act included government-supported social insurance, public assistance, and health-care programs. Today the United Sates still has social insurance and public assistance programs. *Social insurance* helps the elderly, ill, and unemployed. *Public assistance* programs distribute public money to the poor.

1. How does social insurance differ from public assistance?

_____

_____

◉ Social Insurance Programs (page 591)

The government's social insurance system has three main parts:

A. Social Security, or Old Age, Survivors, and Disability Insurance (OASDI)

B. Medicare, or health-insurance programs

C. Unemployment insurance.

More than 90 percent of American workers take part in Social Security. Employers and employees contribute equally, while self-employed persons pay their own Social Security tax. Retirees, survivors, disabled persons, and Medicare recipients are eligible for benefits.

In 1965 Congress added Medicare to the Social Security program. More than 30 million senior citizens take part in Medicare. The basic Medicare plan pays much of an eligible person's total hospital bills.

The 1935 Social Security Act set up *unemployment insurance* for people who are out of work. Federal and state governments work together. Employers pay a tax to the federal government to fund the program. When workers are laid off, they may apply for benefits from a state employment office.

2. What are the main parts of the government's social insurance system?

_____

_____

◉ Public Assistance Programs (page 592)

The major public assistance programs are:

A. Supplemental Security Income (SSI)

B. Food stamps

C. Medicaid

D. The Job Opportunity and Basic Skills program (JOBS)

```
••••••••••••••••••••••••••••••••••••••••••••••••••••••••••••••••••••••••••••••••
```
STUDY GUIDE (continued)   Chapter 21, Section 3
```
••••••••••••••••••••••••••••••••••••••••••••••••••••••••••••••••••••••••••••••••
```

In 1974 Congress brought all state programs for the aged, blind, and the disabled under Supplemental Security Income. The federal government makes a monthly payment to anyone who is 65 or older, who is blind or disabled, or who has little or no regular income.

Congress passed a food stamp system in 1964. The purposes of the food stamp program is to increase the food-buying power of low-income families and help dispose of America's surplus agricultural production.

Congress established the Medicaid program in 1965 as part of the Social Security system. Medicaid helps pay hospital, doctor, and other medical bills for persons with low incomes.

Aid to Families with Dependent Children was designed during the Depression. It helped families in which the main wage earner died, was disabled, or left the family. The public eventually became frustrated over the welfare system because of reports of welfare fraud and the cycle of dependence that developed among many welfare recipients. Congress responded to demands for reform in the Family Support Act of 1988. It required states, by 1990, to have welfare-to-work programs to help people get off welfare. In 1996 a major national bill ended Aid to Families with Dependent Children (AFDC), a cash welfare program. The goal of the new program was to make welfare aid a temporary solution for needy families, rather than a long-term one.

3. What are the major public assistance programs today?

_____

_____

◉ Promoting Public Health (page 594)

Congress established the United States Public Health Service in 1798. Ever since, the federal government has been interested in public health. Today the largest percentage of federal spending on health goes for the Medicare and Medicaid programs. Other programs designed to promote health include the following:

The Department of Defense provides hospital and other medical care for active and retired American military personnel and their families.

The Veterans' Administration operates medical, dental, and hospital care programs for needy veterans.

The Public Health Service operates research, grant, and action programs designed to promote the health of all citizens.

The Centers for Disease Control (CDC) work to control diseases such as AIDS, diphtheria, measles, and many different strains of flu.

The Food and Drug Administration (FDA) tests samples of food and drug products in its laboratories. The agency has the power to ban or withdraw from distribution drugs it finds unsafe or ineffective.

4. How does the Food and Drug Administration promote public health?

_____

_____

Name _____ Date _____ Class _____

STUDY GUIDE  Chapter 21, Section 4

For use with textbook pages 597–602.

EDUCATION, HOUSING, AND TRANSPORTATION

CONTENT VOCABULARY

urban renewal Programs under which cities apply for federal aid to clear slum areas and rebuild *(page 600)*

public housing Government-subsidized housing for low-income families *(page 600)*

mass transit Systems such as subways and light rail that are used to transport a large number of people *(page 602)*

DRAWING FROM EXPERIENCE

Who pays for your textbooks? In many public schools, the federal government foots the bill for books. Funds to school districts are just one way the government supports education.

This section focuses on the federal government's role in education, housing, and transportation.

READING STRATEGIES

Use the graphic organizer below to list the different federal programs that promote education, housing, and transportation.

Education	Housing	Transportation

STUDY GUIDE (continued)   Chapter 21, Section 4

READ TO LEARN

◉ Introduction (page 597)

One of the main powers the Constitution reserved for the states was providing for public education.

◉ Public Education Programs (page 597)

In most states, elementary and high school education remains a local responsibility under state guidelines. However, the federal government plays an ever-increasing role. It contributes direct aid to local public schools and distributes additional funds through the states.

In 1965 Congress passed the first general aid-to-education law—the Elementary and Secondary Education Act. This act and later amendments provided federal aid to most of the nation's school districts. The federal government provides even more support to higher educational institutions, such as colleges and technical schools.

In 1862 Congress passed the Morrill Act. The law granted states more than 13 million acres of public land to help pay for colleges that taught "agriculture and the mechanical arts." More recently, Congress has passed various G.I. Bills of Rights that provide funds for college education for veterans.

In the 1980s opponents of federal aid to education argued that it was a state and local concern. However, declines in students' scores made education a top concern during both the Bush and Clinton administrations. In 2002 President George W. Bush signed the No Child Left Behind Act. This legislation provides federal money to state educational programs, but only if the state demonstrates steady improvement.

   1. How has the federal government provided support for higher education?

   _____

   _____

◉ Housing and Urban Programs (page 599)

The Department of Housing and Urban Development (HUD) administers federal housing projects for cities. HUD's best-known program is The Federal Housing Administration (FHA). The FHA guarantees banks and other private lenders against losses on loans they make to people who wish to buy or build homes. HUD also offers rent assistance to low-income families.

The federal government supports *urban renewal* projects to stop the decline of neighborhoods and to help the rebuilding of central cities. The goal of urban renewal is to restore slum areas and make cities more attractive places to live. Critics charge that urban renewal neglects new low-income housing. It forces lower-income people from their homes to make way for commercial centers and houses for the wealthy. Supporters point to the Housing and Community Development Act of 1974. This law requires cities to demonstrate that they are actually serving the needy when using urban renewal money to redevelop areas.

Since 1937 the federal government has given aid to local governments to build and run *public housing* projects for low-income families. Public housing is largely concentrated in major cities. Local authorities have mismanaged some public housing projects. Many have turned into high-rise slums and centers of crime. In 1973 President Nixon stopped federal aid for public housing. However, in 1976 Congress resumed aid for public housing projects on a limited scale. In 1994 the federal government gave local

STUDY GUIDE (continued) Chapter 21, Section 4

and state officials more control over housing policies. HUD aims to close the gap between minority and white homeownership by placing over 5 million more minority families in homes by 2010.

2. Why do critics disapprove of urban renewal?

_____

_____

◉ Transportation Programs (page 601)

In 1966 Congress created the Department of Transportation (DOT) to coordinate national transportation policies and programs. Important services are provided by these DOT agencies:

A. The Federal Aviation Administration works to ensure safety in aviation, or flying.

B. The Federal Highway Administration oversees federal roads.

C. The Federal Railroad Administration promotes and regulates the nation's railroad transportation.

D. The National Highway Traffic Administration enforces laws to protect drivers and to promote highway safety.

E. The Federal Transit Administration, formerly the Urban Mass Transit Administration, administers federal grants to support alternatives to the car, such as subways, commuter railroads, and bus systems.

The Federal Road Act of 1916 provided annual grants to the states for road building. It required each state to match this aid dollar-for-dollar. These grants are the basis of today's federal highway programs. States also receive billions of dollars to build and improve the Interstate Highway System under the Federal Highway Act of 1956. The system includes more than 45,000 miles of superhighways connecting the nation's major cities. The money for federal highway grants comes from the Highway Trust Fund. This is a special account that receives federal excise taxes on gasoline, tires, truck parts, and related items.

3. How is the Interstate Highway System paid for?

_____

_____

STUDY GUIDE  Chapter 22, Section 1

For use with textbook pages 607–613.

DEVELOPMENT OF FOREIGN POLICY

CONTENT VOCABULARY

foreign policy The strategies and goals that guide a nation's relations with other countries *(page 607)*

national security Protection of a nation's borders and territories against invasion or control by foreign powers *(page 607)*

isolationism The avoidance of involvement in world affairs *(page 608)*

internationalism Involvement in world affairs *(page 608)*

containment The policy designed to keep the Soviet Union from expanding its power *(page 610)*

DRAWING FROM EXPERIENCE

How is your life affected when the United States goes to war? Do you have family or friends in the military? What are your feelings on preemptive war?

This section focuses on the development of the United States's foreign policy.

READING STRATEGIES

Use the time line below to trace the transition of U.S. foreign policy from isolationism to internationalism.

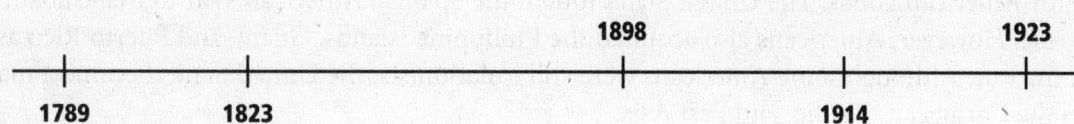

READ TO LEARN

◉ Introduction *(page 607)*

The United States faces a rapidly changing world marked by new challenges.

◉ Goals of Foreign Policy *(page 607)*

Foreign policy consists of the strategies and goals that guide a nation's relations with other countries and groups. The nation's long-range goals include:

National Security The protection of a nation's borders and territories is called *national security.* This goal is basic, since no nation can achieve aims such as improving its educational system if it is under attack.

STUDY GUIDE (continued)   Chapter 22, Section 1

Free and Open Trade A nation's important economic interests must also be protected. American factories and farms need foreign markets in which to sell their goods. Generally, the United States supports trade that is free from both export and import restrictions.

World Peace American leaders work for world peace because they believe it helps the nation avoid being drawn into conflict and aids national security. The United States has helped other nations settle disputes and supplied economic aid in part to prevent uprisings and revolutions. However, the rise of terrorist groups and terrorist attacks have presented a great challenge to the goal of world peace.

Democratic Governments The United States aids democratic nations and helps others to create democratic political systems.

Concern for Humanity The United States provides food, medical supplies, and technical help to victims of natural disaster and starvation. This aid keeps political stability when countries are in crisis.

   1. Why does the United States support free trade?

   _____

   _____

◉ Development of U.S. Foreign Policy *(page 608)*

Until the late 1800s, American foreign policy was based on *isolationism.* This means avoiding involvement in world affairs. During the twentieth century, most presidents shifted towards *internationalism.* This policy holds that involvement in world affairs is necessary for national security.

President George Washington believed that the United States should not become involved in the politics and wars of Europe. In 1823 President James Monroe announced the Monroe Doctrine, which extended the meaning of isolationism. The United States committed itself to protect the American continents, not just the United States, from European powers.

In the 1890s many leaders believed the United States needed to build a colonial empire to create more markets for American goods. The United States fought the Spanish American War to free Cuba from Spanish rule. However, Americans also acquired the Philippine Islands, Guam, and Puerto Rico as a result of the war. Although some Americans were still isolationists, the United States became a major power in the Caribbean, Pacific, and East Asia.

American troops went overseas to fight a European war for the first time during World War I. After the war, Americans returned for a time to isolationism. However, the Japanese attack on Pearl Harbor in 1941 brought the United States into World War II. Ever since World War II, the United States has based its foreign policy on internationalism.

◉ The Cold War *(page 609)*

After the war, the United States and the Soviet Union emerged as world powers. The communist leaders of the Soviet Union took control over Eastern Europe, and communism spread to China. The United States wanted to stop the spread of communism. So a rivalry known as the Cold War grew between the United States and the Soviet Union. This was a war of ideologies and words rather than weapons.

President Harry S. Truman adopted a policy called *containment.* Under this policy, the United States responded to any action of the Soviet Union with a countermove. Americans also tried to halt the spread of communism by giving aid to nations they said were threatened by totalitarian regimes such as the Soviet Union. The Marshall Plan provided badly needed economic aid for war-torn Western European nations and strengthened them to resist communism. The Cold War also led to a costly arms race between the United States and the Soviet Union, including an increase in nuclear weapons.

Containment drew the United States into two wars. In the Korean War, the United States aided pro-American South Korea when Communists from North Korea invaded. In the Vietnam War, U.S. troops fought with the South Vietnamese government against communist North Vietnam.

By the late 1980s, decades of competition with the United States had taken their toll, and the Soviet Union began to collapse. In 1989 the Berlin Wall that divided West Germany from Communist East Germany fell. Other Eastern European countries overthrew their Communist leaders. By 1992 the Soviet Union itself had split into Russia and 14 other separate nations.

◉ The Post-Cold War Era *(page 611)*

The end of the Cold War left the United States as the world's single superpower. However, the United States still had international concerns. In 1990, Iraqi leader Saddam Hussein invaded Kuwait, threatening Middle Eastern oil supplies. President George H.W. Bush sent troops to the region to defeat Iraq in the Persian Gulf War. However, throughout the 1990s tensions in the Middle East remained high. At the same time, President Clinton also sent American troops to Somalia, Haiti, and the former Yugoslavia.

◉ The War on Terror *(page 612)*

The September 11, 2001, terrorist attacks brought about a change in American foreign policy. President George W. Bush announced a war on terrorism and a new policy of preemption, meaning the United States would attack first if the nation was threatened with weapons of mass destruction. Supporters argued preemption was necessary in a world of suicide bombers and outlaw nations.

President Bush put preemption into practice. With the help of Great Britain and several other nations, the United States invaded Iraq in March 2003. The coalition forces quickly defeated the Iraqi army and removed Saddam Hussein from power. The victory did not end the fighting. Insurgents, or rebels, launched a guerrilla war against the American troops and the new Iraqi police forces. Some insurgents had supported Saddam Hussein while others were affiliated with al-Qaeda. One strong divide among Iraqis was between the Shia and Sunni Muslims—rival Muslim groups. In 2006, a civil war erupted between Shia and Sunni groups, causing even more casualties.

From 2003 to 2008, American troops fought the insurgents. Billions of dollars in aid were spent to rebuild Iraq's infrastructure and economy. Iraqis voted for a new constitution and held their first free multiparty elections in 50 years. But the fighting continued. By 2007, President Bush decided on a new strategy involving a surge of additional troops to Iraq. By mid-2008, violence in Iraq had dropped dramatically and Iraqi Sunni and Shia groups had begun working together. Whether or not the situation would remain stable remained unclear.

2. Which "hot" wars were the result of the American policy of containment?

_____

Copyright © Glencoe/McGraw-Hill, a division of The McGraw-Hill Companies, Inc.

STUDY GUIDE 📖 Chapter 22, Section 2

For use with textbook pages 614–620.

Ⓢ HARED FOREIGN POLICY POWERS

CONTENT VOCABULARY

ambassador An official of the government who represents the nation in diplomatic matters *(page 615)*

treaty A formal agreement between the governments of two or more countries *(page 615)*

executive agreement An agreement made between the president and another head of state *(page 619)*

bipartisan Consisting of members of both major political parties *(page 620)*

DRAWING FROM EXPERIENCE

Who pays the bills in your family? In many families, paying the bills is a shared responsibility. In United States government, making foreign policy is also a shared responsibility.

This section focuses on foreign policy powers that the president and Congress share.

READING STRATEGIES

Use the graphic organizer below to list the ways in which Congress can influence foreign policy.

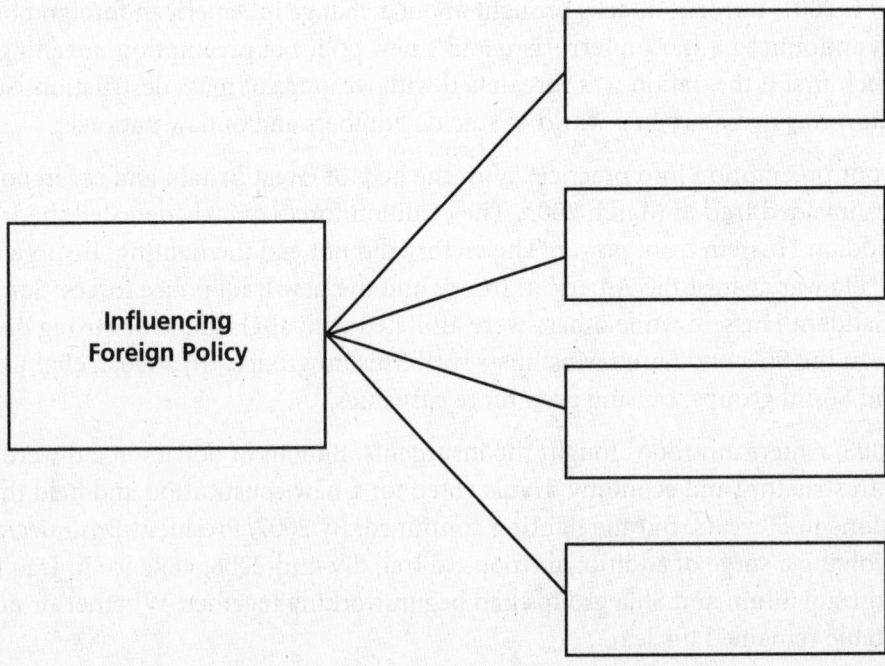

READ TO LEARN

◉ Introduction (page 614)

The Framers of the Constitution tried to divide powers over foreign policy between the president and Congress. However, over the years the president has taken on more responsibility in foreign policy.

◉ Presidential Powers and Responsibilities (page 614)

The president gets his power to make foreign policy from:

A. The Constitution

B. The position as the head of a superpower.

    1. What gives the president power to make foreign policy?

_____

_____

_____

◉ Commander in Chief (page 615)

The Constitution names the president commander in chief of the nation's military forces. This means the president may send troops, ships, and planes anywhere around the world without congressional approval.

The Constitution also gives the president the following powers as head of state:

Appointing ambassadors These are officials of the United States government who represent the nation in diplomatic matters abroad.

Receiving ambassadors The president gives formal recognition to governments when receiving their ambassadors or other diplomats. This is important because it qualifies a country to receive economic and other forms of aid.

Treaty making A *treaty* is a formal agreement between the governments of two or more nations.

    2. What powers related to foreign policy does the Constitution give the president?

_____

_____

_____

◉ Foreign Policy Advisers (page 616)

The president usually asks for advice from cabinet members, the White House staff, or officials in special agencies before making foreign policy decisions.

Foreign affairs are the full-time concern of the secretary of state and the secretary of defense. The secretary of state supervises all the diplomatic activities of the United States government. The secretary of defense oversees the military activities of the American government. He or she gives the president advice on the nation's military forces, weapons, and bases.

STUDY GUIDE (continued)   Chapter 22, Section 2

The national security adviser, or head of the National Security Council, plays a major role in foreign affairs. Former advisor Dr. Condoleezza Rice was the first woman to be appointed for this office.

The Central Intelligence Agency (CIA) gathers and coordinates information about governments, economies, and armed forces of other countries. The CIA gathers information from spies but also from news media coverage and official publications in foreign countries.

Each president has taken a different approach to foreign policy. For example, President Eisenhower relied heavily on his secretary of state for advice, and President Kennedy put together a team of foreign affairs experts who worked in the basement of the White House. However, it is the president who determines foreign policy.

3. For which two cabinet officers are foreign affairs a full-time concern?

_____

_____

◉ Powers of Congress *(page 617)*

The Constitution gives Congress the power to declare war and to appropriate money. The Senate must ratify treaties and confirm diplomatic appointments. Although the president may send troops anywhere, only Congress can declare war.

The United States has been officially at war with a foreign government in five cases when both houses of Congress adopted a war resolution by a majority vote. At other times, presidents have asked Congress to pass a joint resolution to use American troops. For example, President Johnson asked Congress for authority to use troops in Vietnam in 1964. Dismayed by the results, Congress tried to check the president's power to use troops for combat by passing the War Powers Act of 1973. This act declared that the president could not send troops into combat for more than 60 days without the consent of Congress.

Congress must appropriate the money to equip American armed forces and to build new weapons. Congress must also authorize funds for defense and foreign aid each year. If Congress disapproves of a president's committing troops to a limited war, it can refuse to provide funds to maintain the force.

Treaties do not take effect until two-thirds of the Senate votes to ratify them. Increasingly presidents have turned to *executive agreements* for making commitments to foreign government. These are pacts between the president and the head of a foreign government that have the legal status of treaties but do not require Senate approval.

Under United States law the president may grant most-favored nation (MFN) status to trading partners. Such agreements lower tariff rates on all exports from the nation to the United States. Congress may overturn the president's decision to grant MFN status by a two-thirds majority vote.

The Senate must also confirm presidential appointments to diplomatic posts. However, the Senate usually accepts the president's appointments.

4. How do presidents try to sidestep the problem of winning Senate approval for a treaty?

_____

_____

STUDY GUIDE (continued)   Chapter 22, Section 2

◉ The President Versus Congress *(page 619)*

In times of war and crisis, the president's foreign policy has enjoyed bipartisan, or two-party, congressional support. During the Vietnam War, however, bipartisan support began to unravel when Congress and the public became deeply divided about the war. The president enjoys the following advantages over Congress in conducting foreign affairs:

A. Only the president—or a chosen spokesperson such as the secretary of state—can represent the nation in dealings with other governments.

B. The president controls agencies such as the Department of State that help formulate and carry out foreign policy on a daily basis.

C. The president can take quick action. The House and Senate, on the other hand, must discuss, vote, and take into consideration the opinions of many members.

D. The president can bypass the Senate when making agreements with other nations.

   5. Why can the president act more quickly than Congress in foreign affairs?

   _____

   _____

◉ Influence of Public Opinion *(page 620)*

Public opinion often influences the foreign policy decisions of the president and Congress. For example, mass protests in the 1960s influenced President Johnson's decision not to seek reelection, and demonstrations in the 1970s influenced President Nixon's decision to pull troops out of Vietnam. Pressure from interest groups also affects the votes of Congress on public policy. These groups' concerns range from trade to human rights issues, and they have a great impact on laws that affect their interests.

   6. What kinds of interest groups try to influence the votes of Congress on foreign policy?

   _____

   _____

STUDY GUIDE  Chapter 22, Section 3

For use with textbook pages 621–625.

STATE AND DEFENSE DEPARTMENTS

CONTENT VOCABULARY

embassy An ambassador's official residence and offices in a foreign country *(page 623)*

consulate Office that promotes American business and safeguards its travelers in a foreign country *(page 623)*

consul A government official who heads a consulate in a foreign nation *(page 623)*

passport A document entitling a traveler to certain protections established by international treaty *(page 623)*

visa A special document, required by certain countries, that is issued by the government of the country that a person wishes to enter *(page 623)*

conscription Compulsory military service; also called the draft *(page 625)*

DRAWING FROM EXPERIENCE

A coach decides the plays in a football game. But who actually carries out the plays? The players. When it comes to foreign policy, the president is the coach and appointed officials are the players.

This section focuses on the duties of the State and Defense Departments.

READING STRATEGIES

Use the outline below to help you take notes about the State and Defense Departments. Add as many lettered points as you need.

State and Defense Departments

I. Department of State

   A.

   B.

II. Department of Defense

   A.

   B.

STUDY GUIDE (continued)   Chapter 22, Section 3

READE TO LEARN

⦿ Introduction (page 621)

The president and Congress make foreign policy. However, appointed officials in the Department of State actually carry out foreign policy. Officials in the Department of Defense look after national security.

⦿ The Department of State (page 621)

The State Department advises the president and carries out foreign policy. Its other duties include:

A. Keeping the president informed of international issues and events

B. Maintaining diplomatic relations with foreign governments

C. Negotiating treaties with foreign governments

D. Protecting the interests of Americans who are traveling or doing business abroad

Six assistant secretaries direct the Bureaus of:

A. African Affairs

B. European and Eurasian Affairs

C. East Asian and Pacific Affairs

D. Western Hemisphere Affairs

E. Near Eastern Affairs

F. South Asian Affairs

Other bureaus analyze information about specific foreign policy topics, such as educational and cultural affairs. So the work of the department is organized by regions and topics.

More than half the employees of the State Department serve in other countries. These officials belong to the Foreign Service. Foreign Service Officers (FSOs) usually spend several years abroad in a diplomatic post. They are normally assigned to an American embassy or an American consulate.

An *embassy* includes the official home and offices of the ambassador and his or her staff. The main job of an embassy is to make communications between the two governments easier. Embassy officials keep the State Department informed about the politics and foreign policies of the host government. They also keep the host government informed about American policies. An ambassador heads each American embassy. Each embassy includes specialists who resolve disputes between the host country and the United States. In the case of major disputes, governments may break off diplomatic relations by closing their embassies.

Consulates are offices in major cities of foreign nations. Their main job is to promote American business in foreign countries and to serve and safeguard American travelers. A Foreign Service Officer called a *consul* heads each consulate.

A *passport* is a document that the State Department issues to an American traveling abroad. An American citizen with a passport can expect to be granted entry into many countries. In some cases, however, a *visa* is necessary. This is a special document issued by the government of the country that a person wishes to enter. American immigration laws require almost all visitors to the United States to obtain a visa before entering the United States, but Western European countries do not require Americans to carry visas.

STUDY GUIDE (continued)   Chapter 22, Section 3

1. What is the difference between embassies and consulates?

_____

_____

◉ The Department of Defense (page 624)

The Department of Defense makes sure the armed forces are strong enough to defend American interests. Before 1947 the Departments of the War and Navy took care of the nation's defense. After World War II these departments were reorganized, and in 1949 became the Department of Defense. The president of the United States is the ultimate commander of the armed forces because the Framers of the Constitution wanted the military under civilian leaders. The top leaders of the Department of Defense must also be civilians. Congress has authority over the military because it determines how much money the Department of Defense spends each year. In addition, Congress determines how each branch of the military is organized.

The Department of Defense is the largest executive department. In a recent year, it had 800,000 civilian employees and about one million military personnel.

The major divisions within the Department of Defense are the:

A. Department of the Army

B. Department of the Navy

C. Department of the Air Force

The United States Marines are under the jurisdiction of the Navy but have their own leadership, identity, and traditions.

The president relies on the Joint Chiefs of Staff (JCS) for military advice. This group is made up of the top ranking officers of the armed forces.

The United States has staffed its armed forces through volunteers and conscription. **Conscription** is compulsory military service. The United States used conscription in the Civil War, World War I, and World War II. President Richard Nixon ended conscription, or the draft, by executive order in 1973. However, his order did not do away with the Selective Service System, which administered the draft. As a result, males between the ages of 18 and 25 could be required to serve if conscription is reinstated.

Since 1980 all males of eligible age have been required to register their names and addresses with local draft boards. Women are not eligible to be drafted. However, they may volunteer to serve in any branch of the armed services.

2. Why does the Constitution name the president commander in chief of the armed forces?

_____

_____

Name _____ Date _____ Class _____

For use with textbook pages 627–630.

FOREIGN POLICY IN ACTION

CONTENT VOCABULARY

mutual defense alliance An agreement between nations to support each other in case of an attack *(page 627)*

regional security pact A mutual defense treaty among nations of a region *(page 627)*

multilateral treaty International agreement signed by several nations *(page 629)*

bilateral treaty Agreement between two nations *(page 629)*

collective security A system by which the participating nations agree to take joint action against a nation that attacks any one of them *(page 629)*

sanction A measure such as withholding economic aid to influence a foreign government's activities *(page 630)*

DRAWING FROM EXPERIENCE

You have probably seen pictures of needy people from developing countries. The United States offers economic aid to many of these countries in an effort to help their needy people.

This section focuses on economic aid and other ways the United States puts foreign policy into action.

READING STRATEGIES

Use the graphic organizer below to help you take notes as you read the summaries that follow. List the foreign policies the government uses to ensure the nation's security.

```

  ─────────►           ◄─────────


                 ┌──────────────────┐
                 │                  │
                 │                  │
                 │                  │
                 │    National      │
                 │    Security      │
                 │                  │
                 │                  │
  ─────────►     │                  │     ◄─────────
                 │                  │
                 │                  │
                 └──────────────────┘

```

Copyright © Glencoe/McGraw-Hill, a division of The McGraw-Hill Companies, Inc.

STUDY GUIDE (continued)   Chapter 22, Section 4

READts TO LEARN

⦿ Introduction (page 627)

The United States tries to minimize dangers to national security. To do this it uses the following tools:

A. Alliances

B. Foreign aid

C. Economic sanctions

D. Military action

⦿ Alliances and Pacts (page 627)

Nations have often negotiated *mutual defense alliances* when they felt a common threat to their security. These nations usually agree to support each other in case of an attack. The United States has signed mutual defense treaties in the following regions:

A. Western Europe and the North Atlantic

B. Central and South America

C. South Pacific island nations

These treaties are called *regional security pacts.*

In 1945 the leaders of the United States and the nations of Western Europe agreed to protect each other from domination by the Soviet Union. This mutual defense treaty became the North Atlantic Treaty Organization (NATO). During the Cold War, NATO countered the military might of the Soviet Union while enabling the Western European nations to establish strong democracies. Since the end of the Cold War, NATO has expanded its mission to include crisis intervention and peacekeeping in other areas of the world, such as the former Yugoslavia. NATO has also expanded its membership to include three former Warsaw Pact nations—Poland, Hungary, and the Czech Republic. In recent years, due to increased defense spending and preoccupation with national security, many European leaders believe that the United States is less interested in cooperating with NATO than it was during the Cold War.

In 1947 the United States and its Latin American neighbors signed the Rio Pact. The purpose of the pact was for members to come to one another's aid in case of an attack. Cuba withdrew from the pact in 1960. In 1948 the United States signed a related treaty that established the Organization of American States (OAS). The OAS is primarily concerned with promoting economic development. A second goal of the OAS is to help members settle international disputes peacefully.

The ANZUS Pact was signed in 1951. It obliges Australia, New Zealand, and the United States to come to one another's aid in case of attack. However, New Zealand adopted a policy in 1984 that excludes nuclear weapons and nuclear powered ships from its ports and waters. As a result, the United States refuses to guarantee New Zealand's security.

NATO, the Rio Pact, OAS, and ANZUS are *multilateral treaties*—agreements signed by several nations. The United States has also signed many *bilateral treaties*—agreements between only two nations. For example, in 1951 the United States promised to defend the Philippines. The purpose of these treaties is to provide collective security for the United States and its allies. *Collective security* is a system by which nations agree to take joint action against a nation that attacks any one of them.

1. How did the Rio Pact and OAS differ?

_____

Foreign Aid Programs (page 629)

In addition to alliances, American leaders can also offer foreign nations:

A. Military support in the form of grants or loans to purchase American armaments

B. Economic aid

Economic aid to other countries has the following purposes:

A. To establish friendly relations with nations

B. To help the nations emerge as eventual economic partners

Today the Agency for International Development (AID), part of the State Department, gives out loans and technical help to developing nations in need of food, housing, and education for their people.

2. Why does the United States give economic aid?

_____

_____

Economic Sanctions (page 630)

American policy makers sometimes use sanctions when dealing with governments that follow policies the United States dislikes. *Sanctions* are measures such as withholding loans, arms, or economic aid to force a foreign government to stop certain activities. The United States may also restrict trade with another nation as an economic sanction. The United States used sanctions 75 times during the twentieth century. For example, it directed sanctions against Iraq in 1990.

3. When does the United States apply sanctions?

_____

_____

The Use of Military Force (page 630)

In 1938 Great Britain allowed German dictator Adolf Hitler to take over part of Czechoslovakia rather than risk war. Hitler went on to swallow the rest of the country. Eventually World War II broke out. Some people believe that limited military action in 1938 could have prevented a major war. For similar reasons, the United States has used military force to settle disputes with other nations. Since World War II, the United States has committed troops in Korea, Vietnam, Grenada, Panama, the Persian Gulf Region, Bosnia-Herzegovina, and Haiti. Beginning in 2001, President George W. Bush's war on terrorism sent American troops to Afghanistan and Iraq.

4. Why do some people believe that military force is one way to settle disputes between nations?

_____

_____

STUDY GUIDE  Chapter 23, Section 1

For use with textbook pages 637–640.

STATE CONSTITUTIONS

CONTENT VOCABULARY

initiative A method by which citizens propose a constitutional amendment or a law *(page 639)*

constitutional convention A gathering of citizens elected to consider changing or replacing a constitution *(page 639)*

constitutional commission A group of experts appointed to study a state constitution and recommend changes *(page 640)*

DRAWING FROM EXPERIENCE

Have you ever seen a copy of your state constitution? It is probably a lot longer than the United States Constitution. It probably includes several provisions that affect your daily life.

This section focuses on the importance of state constitutions.

READING STRATEGIES

Use the graphic organizer below to help you take notes as you read the summaries that follow. List the similarities and differences between the United States Constitution and state constitutions.

United States Constitution	Both	State Constitutions

READ TO LEARN

◉ **Introduction** (page 637)

Constitutional government in America began with colonial charters. This was long before the United States Constitution was written. Some states kept their old colonial charters as their state constitutions. Other states wrote new constitutions. Since 1776, 20 states have kept their original constitutions, and all the states have added many amendments.

◉ **Why Constitutions Matter** (page 637)

State constitutions are important for the following reasons:

A. They provide for the separation of powers among three branches—legislative, executive, and judicial.

B. They establish the different types of local governments, such as countries, townships, and parishes.

C. They regulate the ways state and local governments can raise and spend money.

D. They establish independent agencies, boards, and commissions that have power in areas that affect citizens' lives directly. For example, public utility commissions regulate gas and electric rates.

The state constitution is supreme above all other laws made within the state. However, it cannot disagree with or contradict the Constitution of the United States.

1. How do state constitutions directly affect citizens' daily lives?

_____

_____

◉ **Characteristics of Constitutions** (page 638)

Most state constitutions share the following basic characteristics:

Bill of Rights This is in all state constitutions. It includes all or most of the protections of the Bill of Rights in the United States Constitution. Some state constitutions include protections not in the national Constitution. An example is the worker's right to join a union.

Length The average state constitution has more than 30,000 words, over four times the length of the United States Constitution.

Detail State constitutions are filled with detail. They cover many aspects of life in the state. For example, one state constitution includes a special tax to help Civil War veterans. State constitutions are sometimes very detailed because groups and individuals have lobbied to include provisions that help them.

2. Describe the typical state constitution.

_____

_____

STUDY GUIDE (continued)   Chapter 23, Section 1

◉ Amendments and Changes (page 639)

Changing a constitution may be necessary because new conditions require new actions or policies. The amendment process has two steps.

Proposal State constitutions provide for the following methods of proposing amendments:

A. In every state the state legislature has the power to propose an amendment to the constitution. This method is the one most often used.

B. Eighteen states also allow people to propose constitutional amendments by popular initiative. An initiative is a method by which citizens propose an amendment or a law. The initiative process begins when an individual or group writes a proposed amendment. People in favor of the amendment sign a petition. The number of signatures required varies from state to state.

C. A gathering of citizens, usually elected by a popular vote, meets to consider changing or replacing the constitution in a constitutional convention.

D. Many states use a constitutional commission. This is a group of experts appointed to study the state constitution and recommend changes.

Ratification All states except Delaware require ratification of amendments by popular vote. The kind of majority needed to approve an amendment varies. When the voters rather than the legislature vote on an issue, it is called a *referendum*.

3. What four methods do state constitutions provide for proposing constitutional amendments?

_____

_____

_____

◉ Criticism and Reform (page 640)

Over the years many people have criticized state constitutions for being too long or full of needless detail. Most states require a constitutional convention to replace existing state constitutions. In a few states, a special commission may also draft a new constitution that must be reviewed by the state legislature followed by ratification by the people.

The process of calling a constitutional convention begins when the state legislature proposes the convention. If the people vote their approval, the state holds an election to choose delegates. The delegates may write a new constitution or suggest changes in the existing document. The voters then must ratify the changes or the new constitution.

The number of amendments to state constitutions have declined in the last twenty years. However, more and more state judges have begun to interpret state constitutions. Judicial review has become an important means of constitutional change in state government as well as in the national government.

4. In what two ways do states replace existing state constitutions?

_____

_____

STUDY GUIDE  Chapter 23, Section 2

For use with textbook pages 641–647.

THE THREE BRANCHES

CONTENT VOCABULARY

bicameral Two-house legislative body *(page 641)*

lieutenant governor The presiding officer of the upper house in some state legislatures *(page 642)*

plurality The largest number of votes in an election *(page 643)*

item veto The power to turn down a particular item in a bill without vetoing the entire bill *(page 645)*

civil case Legal issue usually involving a dispute between two or more private individuals or organizations *(page 646)*

criminal case Legal issue in which the state brings charges against a citizen for violating the law *(page 646)*

DRAWING FROM EXPERIENCE

Who is your state's governor? Who represents your district in the state legislature? More than the United States president and members of Congress, these people affect your daily life.

This section focuses on the three branches of state government.

READING STRATEGIES

Use the graphic organizer below to help you take notes about the different officials in the three branches of state government.

Executive	Legislative	Judicial

STUDY GUIDE (continued)   Chapter 23, Section 2

READ TO LEARN

⦿ **Introduction** *(page 641)*

The states divide power among three branches—legislative, executive, and judicial.

⦿ **The Legislative Branch** *(page 641)*

The state legislature has the power:

A. To pass laws that deal with health, crime, labor, education, transportation, and other matters

B. To tax, spend, and borrow money

C. To check the power of the governor and the bureaucracy

Almost every state has a **bicameral** legislature. This means one with two houses. Nebraska has the only unicameral, or one-chambered, state legislature in the United States.

Members of state legislatures are elected from legislative districts with roughly equal populations. Until 1964 many state voting districts were based on area rather than population. Then the Supreme Court ruled that voting districts for both houses of state legislatures had to be based on equal populations. Most states redrew voting districts to comply with the Court's "one person, one vote" ruling.

In most states a person must be a resident of the district he or she wishes to represent. A person usually must be at least 25 years old to be a senator, or serve in the upper house. A person usually must be 21 years or older to serve in the lower house. Many state legislators are lawyers. A large number of state legislators work in fields that state law directly affects, such as real estate and insurance. Most state legislators are part-time lawmakers and are not well paid. In seven states, legislatures meet every other year. They meet every year in all other states.

In the lower house, the presiding officer is called the speaker of the house. In 26 states the presiding officer of the upper house is the **lieutenant governor.** He or she serves much like the vice president of the United States, who presides over the United States Senate. Committees conduct most work in state legislatures.

Lawmaking usually follows these steps:

A. A member of either house in the state legislature may introduce a bill. However, many of the bills begin in the departments and agencies within the executive branch.

B. The presiding officer sends the bill to a committee that specializes in its subject matter. The committee discusses the bill and may hold hearings. It may rewrite or change the bill.

C. The bill is sent back to the full house with a recommendation to pass or not pass it.

D. If the bill passes one house, it must go through a similar process in the other house. Sometimes the other house changes a bill it has received. Then a conference committee from both houses resolves the differences.

E. Both houses vote on the conference committee's bill.

F. If passed, the bill goes to the governor for signature or veto.

STUDY GUIDE (continued)   Chapter 23, Section 2

1. Compare the requirements for serving as a legislator in the upper and lower houses of most states.

_____

_____

▣ The Executive Branch *(page 643)*

In most states a governor must be at least 30 years old, an American citizen, and a state resident for 5 years or more. Most governors have served in state or local government before running for governor. One-half of the recently elected governors are lawyers.

Most states follow these steps when electing governors:

A. A person gets the nomination of a major political party by winning a party primary.

B. The party nominee goes on to win the general election. In most states the candidate who wins a plurality vote is elected governor. A ***plurality*** is the largest number of votes in a election. In five states, however, a majority, or more than half the votes, is required.

Most governors serve four-year terms. Most states limit the number of terms a governor may serve. Governors' salaries range from $179,000 in New York to $65,000 in Nebraska. Eighteen states also allow ***recall***, which allows people to vote to remove state officials, including governors, from office.

The amount of control a governor has over the executive branch varies from state to state. Since 1965 more than half the states have reformed their constitutions to give governors greater executive power. Governors are usually looked upon as the leaders of the party in their state.

In all but eight states, the governor prepares the state budget. This allows the governor to push certain programs and policies. All governors can exercise military powers as commander in chief of the state National Guard. He or she calls on the guard in case of state emergencies.

Governors often play an important legislative role. A governor can propose legislation to the legislature and arouse public opinion to support these legislative proposals. Today all governors have a veto power over legislation the state legislature passes. In all but a few states the governor also possesses an ***item veto.*** This is the power to turn down a particular section or item in a bill without vetoing the entire law. Finally, the governor can call a special session of the legislature to deal with issues important to the state.

Governors appoint about one-fourth of the judges in a state. Governors also may have the power to grant pardons, shorten sentences, waive fines, and release prisoners on parole.

In most states, voters elect other executive branch officials. These include the:

A. Lieutenant governor, who presides over the state senate

B. Attorney general, or top legal officer in state government

C. Secretary of state, or official in charge of state records and official state documents

D. State treasurer, who pays the bills of state government and often serves as the state tax collector

2. How do many governors affect legislation in their state?

_____

_____

STUDY GUIDE (continued)   Chapter 23, Section 2

◉ The Judicial Branch *(page 646)*

State courts interpret and apply state and local laws. The courts deal with two general types of cases:

A. *Civil cases,* which involve disputes between two or more private individuals or organizations

B. *Criminal cases,* which the state brings against citizens for violating laws

In general, the state court systems involve three types of courts:

Minor Courts The best-known minor court is the justice court headed by a justice of the peace. The justice of the peace performs marriages, handles minor civil and criminal cases, and legalizes documents. In many cities, police courts, municipal courts, or magistrate courts handle minor legal matters. Other minor courts include:

A. Small claims court, involving civil cases about small amounts of money

B. Juvenile court, involving people under age 18

C. Domestic relations court, involving family disputes

D. Traffic court, dealing with traffic and parking violations

E. Probate court, which handles cases involving inheritance of property

General trial courts These are also known as county courts, circuit courts, courts of common pleas, superior courts, and district courts. They may hear any type of civil or criminal case. Serious cases involving crimes like murder, arson, and robbery are heard in general trial courts.

Appeals courts These hear cases that a lower court has already decided. The highest court is usually called the supreme court. The supreme court is the state court of final appeal.

State judges are selected in the following ways:

A. Some judges are elected in popular elections.

B. Others are elected by the legislature.

C. Governors appoint some judges.

D. Others are chosen through the Missouri Plan, which combines appointment by the governor and popular election.

One method of removing judges is impeachment, or accusing the judge of misconduct. Another method is having a disciplinary board or commission investigate complaints about judges. The board or commission makes a recommendation to the state supreme court, and the court may suspend or remove the judge.

3. What are the different kinds of minor courts that states have?

_____

_____

_____

STUDY GUIDE  Chapter 23, Section 3

For use with textbook pages 648–654.

STATE GOVERNMENT POLICY

CONTENT VOCABULARY

corporate charter A document that gives a corporation legal status *(page 648)*

public utility An organization that supplies necessities such as electricity, gas, or telephone service *(page 648)*

workers' compensation Payments people unable to work receive as the result of a job-related injury or ill health *(page 649)*

unemployment compensation Payments to workers who lose their jobs *(page 649)*

mandatory sentencing A system of fixed, required terms of imprisonment for certain types of crimes *(page 651)*

victim compensation A program in many states whereby the state government provides financial aid to victims of certain crimes *(page 651)*

extradition The legal procedure through which a person accused of a crime who has fled to another state is returned to the state where the crime took place *(page 652)*

parole Means by which a prisoner is allowed to serve the rest of a sentence in the community under the supervision of a parole officer *(page 653)*

shock probation Program designed to show young offenders how terrible prison life is through brief incarceration followed by supervised release *(page 652)*

shock incarceration A prison program involving shorter sentences in a highly structured environment where offenders participate in work, community service, education, and counseling *(page 652)*

house arrest A sentence which requires an offender to stay at home except for certain functions the court permits *(page 652)*

DRAWING FROM EXPERIENCE

Who decides what textbooks you use? In many states, the state government decides.

This section focuses on state governments' major areas of concern, including education.

READING STRATEGIES

Use the graphic organizer below to help you list the areas that state governments regulate and protect.

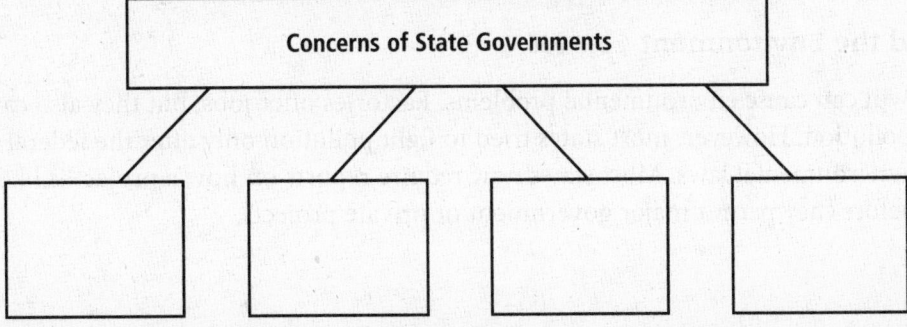

Concerns of State Governments

STUDY GUIDE (continued)   Chapter 23, Section 3

READ TO LEARN

◉ **Introduction** (page 648)

The major areas of concern for most states include:

A. Regulating business

B. Administering and controlling natural resources

C. Protecting individual rights

D. Carrying out education, health, and welfare programs

◉ **State Business Regulation** (page 648)

Every business corporation must have a charter issued by a state government. A **corporate charter** is a document that grants certain rights, powers, and privileges to a corporation.

To regulate corporations, state governments have passed laws that:

A. regulate interest rates that banks can charge;

B. set insurance companies' rates; and

C. administer licensing exams.

State laws regulating banks, insurance companies, and public utilities are especially strict. A **public utility** supplies a necessity such as electricity, gas, telephone service, or transportation. However, states have recently reduced regulations to encourage competition.

Nearly all of the states have laws regulating landlord-tenant relations. Most states also regulate health-care industries. In addition, state laws try to protect consumers from high interest on credit cards, unfair estimates for automobile repairs, unfair home-repair costs, and unreasonable mortgage rates.

Many states regulate the hours that 16- and 17-year-olds work. In most states, minors need permits to work. State governments also provide **workers' compensation.** This program provides payments to people unable to work as a result of a job-related injury or ill health. State governments also set up and regulate **unemployment compensation**—payments to workers who lose their jobs. Some states have passed laws that protect workers from being forced to join unions.

State governments also try to attract new businesses. They may offer a tax credit, or a reduction in taxes, in return for new businesses or more jobs.

1. How do states try to protect non-adult workers?

_____

_____

◉ **States and the Environment** (page 650)

Economic growth can cause environmental problems. Factories offer jobs, but they also can produce air and water pollution. However, most states tried to fight pollution only after the federal government passed strong environmental laws. Most states now require reports on how a project is likely to affect the environment before they permit major government or private projects.

Many states require industries to get permits if their wastes pollute the air or water. Often the permits cost so much that businesses find installing antipollution devices cheaper. In addition, most states have developed garbage-management programs, and they regulate the disposal of radioactive waste.

Recently, state governments have increased their efforts in conservation. This is the care and protection of land, lakes, rivers, forests, energy resources, and wildlife. State laws allow the state to plan and regulate land use. For example, states can set aside land for parks.

2. How do many states pressure businesses into installing anti-pollution devices?

_____

_____

◉ Protecting Life and Property *(page 651)*

States deal with crimes such as murder, rape, assault, burglary, and the sale and use of dangerous drugs. Several states have *mandatory sentencing.* This is fixed, required terms of imprisonment for certain kinds of crime. In most other states, a judge has more choice when imposing sentences. Most states also have *victim compensation* laws, which provide financial aid to victims of crime.

The justice system has been described as "decentralized" because criminal justice is usually a state responsibility. Decentralized justice creates some problems. For example, *extradition* is a legal procedure through which an accused person who has fled to another state is returned to the state where the crime was committed. Sometimes governors have refused to extradite people.

State police are normally limited to highway patrol units. However, in many states, state police have investigative powers. State prisons, county and municipal jails, and other houses of detention make up a state's correction system. However, judges often choose probation as a sentence. Hundreds of other prisoners are on parole. This means that a prisoner serves the rest of a sentence in the community under the supervision of a parole officer. Three-fourths of all offenders are either on probation or on parole. Many states give judges these other sentencing choices:

Shock probation This is a brief imprisonment followed by a supervised release. Shock probation is supposed to show young offenders how terrible prison life is.

Shock incarceration This involves short sentences in a highly structured environment where offenders take part in work, community service, education, and counseling.

Intensive supervision probation or parole This keeps high-risk offenders in the community under close supervision that involves home visits or even nightly curfew checks.

House arrest This choice requires an offender to stay at home with a few exceptions, such as going to work.

3. What are six sentencing choices that many state judges have?

_____

_____

_____

STUDY GUIDE (continued)   Chapter 23, Section 3

◉ Education, Health, and Welfare (page 652)

Education, health, and welfare programs make up the largest part of state spending.

Public school financing varies from state to state. For example, in Hawaii the state contributes about 90 percent of all public school funds while South Dakota contributes less than 30 percent. Local funds in South Dakota account for the largest share of school money. State governments establish local school districts and give these districts the power to administer public schools. The states regulate the taxes the districts levy and the amount of money they borrow. Some state governments also establish detailed course content, approve textbooks, and create statewide exams.

In the area of health, the states:

A. license doctors and dentists;

B. regulate the sale of drugs;

C. require vaccinations for school children;

D. support mental hospitals, mental health clinics, and institutions for the disabled;

E. provide care for mothers and their newborns;

F. treat contagious diseases and chronic illnesses and provide immunizations;

G. provide mental health care and public dental clinics;

H. control air and water quality, radiation, and hazardous waste management;

I. provide laboratory services to local health departments; and

J. pay for public health services that local authorities deliver.

Public welfare consists of government efforts to give poor people basic health and living conditions. In 1996 the federal government replaced its welfare program with lump-sum payments to the states. The states were given the power to use the money to operate their own welfare programs. State governments also administer Medicaid, set certain conditions for eligibility, and provide almost 45 percent of the total cost. Medicaid is another federal-state welfare program that provides money to states to help people who cannot afford the medical services they need. Most states also have programs that help people who do not fall into the federally mandated categories.

4. How are states involved with public education?

_____

_____

_____

_____

STUDY GUIDE  Chapter 23, Section 4

For use with textbook pages 656–658.

Financing State Government

CONTENT VOCABULARY

excise tax Tax on the manufacture, transportation, sale, or consumption of certain items such as gasoline, cigarettes, or liquor *(page 656)*

regressive tax A tax in which people with lower incomes pay a larger portion of their income *(page 657)*

progressive tax A tax based on a taxpayer's ability to pay *(page 657)*

proportional tax A tax that is assessed at the same rate for everyone *(page 657)*

intergovernmental revenue Revenue distributed by one level of government to another *(page 657)*

block grant A grant of money to a state or local government for a general purpose *(page 658)*

DRAWING FROM EXPERIENCE

Did you pay sales tax the last time you made a purchase? The sales tax is an important source of money for most state governments.

This section focuses on how state governments get the money they need.

READING STRATEGIES

Use the graphic organizer below to list the ways by which states collect revenue.

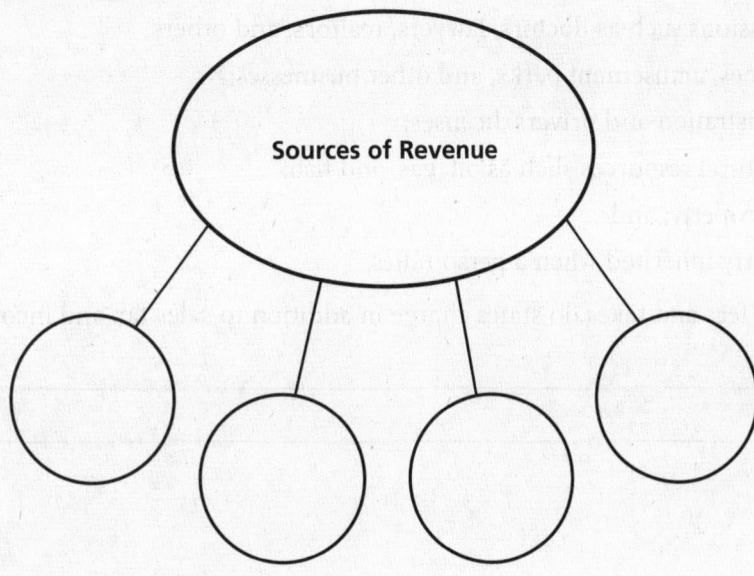

Sources of Revenue

STUDY GUIDE (continued)   Chapter 23, Section 4

READ TO LEARN

◉ Introduction (page 656)

State taxes raise nearly half of the general revenue of state governments. States also receive money from the federal government, lotteries, license fees, and borrowing.

◉ Tax Revenue (page 656)

The U.S. Constitution limits a state's power to tax in the following ways:

A. A state cannot tax goods or products that move in or out of the state or country. Only Congress can tax imports and exports.

B. A state cannot tax federal property.

C. A state cannot use taxes to deprive people of the equal protection of the law.

D. State constitutions may also limit the power of states to tax. For example, some constitutions limit certain taxes such as income tax.

States get much of their revenue from the following types of taxes:

Sales tax The general sales tax is imposed on items such as cars, clothing, household products, and other types of products. Some states do not tax food and drugs. The selective tax, or *excise tax*, is imposed on certain items such as gasoline, liquor, and cigarettes. Critics call the sales tax a *regressive tax* because the percentage of income taxed drops as incomes rise. Thus, the sales tax represents a higher percentage of the poorer person's income.

State income tax Most states have individual and corporate income taxes. When the tax rate rises as a person's income rises, it is called a *progressive tax*. However, some states assess income taxes at the same rate for everyone. This is called a *proportional tax*.

Other taxes States also levy fees or taxes for:

A. licenses for professions such as doctors, lawyers, realtors, and others;

B. licenses for bus lines, amusement parks, and other businesses;

C. motor vehicle registration and drivers' licenses;

D. the removal of natural resources such as oil, gas, and fish;

E. certain kinds of property; and

F. money and property inherited when a person dies.

1. What kinds of fees and taxes do states charge in addition to sales tax and income tax?

_____

_____

STUDY GUIDE (continued)　　Chapter 23, Section 4

◉ Other Sources of Revenue *(page 657)*

States usually borrow money to pay for large, long-term expenses like highway construction. They borrow by selling bonds. A bond is a contractual promise on the part of the state to repay a certain sum plus interest by a certain date.

Almost three-fourths of the states run public lotteries. The states spend about half the lottery earnings on prizes and 6 percent on administration.

Almost 20 percent of all state revenues come from ***intergovernmental revenue.*** This is money distributed by one level of government to another. It may be in the form of a federal grant. Grants supply funds for programs that states may not be able to afford. Grants help carry out programs and goals that the federal government considers important. Finally, grants set minimum standards in states. For example, the federal government provides grants to make sure states provide minimum public welfare programs.

Categorical grants go to states based on a formula. Different amounts go to different states depending on the states' wealth. State governments prefer ***block grants.*** These are large grants of money to be used for a general purpose, such as public health or crime control. Block grants have fewer guidelines and offer more choice over how the money may be spent than categorical grants.

A mandate is a formal order given by a higher authority. Between 1980 and 1990 the federal government increased the number of mandated programs for which states had to raise their own revenue. State and local governments complained about the unfunded or underfunded federal mandates. In 1995 Congress passed the Unfunded Mandate Reform Act (UMRA), which required Congress to estimate the cost of a mandate to the state, local, or tribal government. This helped to reduce state budgetary pressure.

2. What is the difference between categorical grants and block grants?

_____

_____

STUDY GUIDE  Chapter 24, Section 1

For use with textbook pages 663–668.

STRUCTURE OF LOCAL GOVERNMENT

CONTENT VOCABULARY

county The largest political subdivision of a state *(page 664)*

county board The governing board of most counties *(page 664)*

township A unit of local government found in some states, usually a subdivision of a county *(page 664)*

municipality An urban unit of government chartered by a state *(page 665)*

special district A unit of local government that deals with a specific function, such as education, water supply, or transportation *(page 665)*

incorporation The process of setting up a legal community under state law *(page 666)*

referendum A special election *(page 666)*

DRAWING FROM EXPERIENCE

What form of local government does your community have? If you do not already know, try to figure out the answer from the descriptions in the section.

This section focuses on the different kinds of local government.

READING STRATEGIES

Use the graphic organizer below to help you take notes about the roles of officials in the council-manager form of government. Then fill in the missing labels.

Voters
elect

↓

| | hires | → | |

elects

↓

appoints

↓

| | | | |

STUDY GUIDE (continued) Chapter 24, Section 1

READeterminate TO LEARN

⊙ **Introduction** (page 663)

Local governments take many forms, such as counties, townships, municipalities, and special districts.

⊙ **Created by the State** (page 663)

Local governments are established by the states and are dependent on state governments. The state may take control of or even abolish them. For example, a state may take control of a school district that has money problems. State constitutions may set forth the powers and duties of local governments, the forms of government they may adopt, and the kinds of taxes they can levy.

1. What do state constitutions set forth for local governments?

_____

_____

⊙ **Types of Local Government** (page 663)

The United States has the following basic types of local government:

The County is normally the largest territorial and political subdivision of a state. All states except Connecticut and Rhode Island have counties. Louisiana calls its counties parishes, and Alaska calls them burroughs. County government is important in rural areas. On the other hand, county government is unimportant in New England. County government has grown in importance in some metropolitan areas where counties have assumed the jobs that cities once handled.

A **county board** has the authority to govern most counties. Board members are almost always popularly elected. County boards usually decide on the county budget, taxes, and zoning codes. In many counties, the board has both executive and legislative powers. In other counties the board members share powers with elected officials such as the county sheriff, attorney, clerk, and school superintendent.

The Township Twenty states, mainly in New England and the Midwest, have **townships.** Counties are subdivided into townships in most states. In areas of rapid urban growth, townships have assumed some of the jobs of city government, such as providing water, sewage disposal, and police protection.

The New England Town The town meeting served as the center of government in New England towns. At the town meeting, citizens took part in making laws, decided on taxes, and appropriating money for public projects. They also elected town officials called "selectmen." Today citizens of large towns and cities elect representatives to attend town meetings in their stead. These selectmen now have the power to make decisions the citizens at town meetings once made. Some towns have also hired town managers.

The Municipality is an urban unit of government—a town, borough, city, or urban district that has legal rights granted by a state charter. Most states divide municipalities into classes according to population. Each class gets a standard type of charter.

The Special District is a unit of local government that deals with a specific area, such as education, water supply, or transportation. Special districts are the most common type of local government.

Tribal Government Some states have a separate level of government that serves its Native American population. Each tribal office has a governor and a lieutenant governor. In New Mexico, the Indian Affairs Department was established in 1953 to serve as a liaison between the tribal governments and the state government.

STUDY GUIDE (continued) Chapter 24, Section 1

2. What are the basic types of local government in the United States?

_____

_____

◉ Forms of Municipal Government *(page 666)*

A municipal government may be formed when a group of people ask the state legislature to permit their community to incorporate, or set up a legal community. The process of *incorporation* differs from state to state. Generally a community must have a population of a certain size and petitions signed by a certain number of residents requesting incorporation. A referendum, or special election, may be held to decide if people want incorporation. Once the community is incorporated, the state issues a charter. This allows the community to have its own government and gives the municipal corporation legal status. It can then enter into contracts, sue and be sued in court, purchase, own, and sell property.

Today urban areas in the United States use one of the following basic forms of municipal government:

The Mayor-Council form is the most widely used form of municipal government. Executive power belongs to an elected mayor. Legislative power belongs to an elected council. Most cities have a unicameral, or one-house, council.

The two main types of mayor-council government are the:

A. Strong mayor system, in which the mayor has powers, such as a veto, over the city council

B. Weak-mayor system, in which the mayor has little control over the budget or the hiring and firing of municipal workers

The Commission form combines executive and legislative powers in an elected commission of five to seven members. Each member is in charge of departments such as police, fire, public works, finance, and parks. The commissioners also make laws. This form of government has the following problems:

A. The absence of a powerful leader often leads to a lack of cooperation and planning.

B. Commissioners often agree to support one another's budget requests. This results in a budget that is more generous than it should be.

The Council-Manager Form An elected council of between five and nine members makes the laws. It also appoints the city manager. The manager is responsible for:

A. appointing and firing municipal workers,

B. preparing the budget, and

C. running the day-to-day affairs of the city.

The council-manager form of government often includes a mayor whom the council elects for a two-year term. Supporters of the system believe it makes it easy for voters to place the blame because the executive and legislative powers are clearly separated. Critics point out that the council-manager plan may not provide the leadership needed in large cities with ethnic and economic diversity.

3. Describe some of the problems of the commission form of government.

_____

_____

STUDY GUIDE  Chapter 24, Section 2

For use with textbook pages 669–675.

SERVING LOCALITIES

CONTENT VOCABULARY

zoning The method used by a local government to regulate the uses of land and buildings in order to shape community development *(page 669)*

mass transit Systems such as subways that are used to transport a large number of people *(page 670)*

metropolitan area A large city and its surrounding suburbs *(page 671)*

suburb A densely settled territory adjacent to a central city *(page 671)*

real property Land and whatever is attached to or growing on it *(page 674)*

personal property Movable belongings such as clothes and jewelry as well as intangible items like stocks, bonds, copyrights, and patents *(page 674)*

assessment The process of calculating the value of property to be taxed *(page 674)*

market value The amount of money an owner may expect to receive if property is sold *(page 674)*

DRAWING FROM EXPERIENCE

Who provides the clean water that comes through your tap? The answer is probably local government. This section focuses on services that local governments provide.

READING STRATEGIES

Use the graphic organizer below to help you take notes as you read the summaries that follow. Think about the results of relying on property taxes.

CAUSE	EFFECT
Wealthy and poor districts rely on property taxes to fund their schools.	

STUDY GUIDE (continued)   Chapter 24, Section 2

READ TO LEARN

◉ Introduction (page 669)

Taxes pay for most of the services local government offers.

◉ Local Government Services (page 669)

Local government provides:

Education A large share of local tax revenues go to pay for public schools. Local funding contributes to inequalities in schools because wealthier districts can afford to provide much better educational opportunities.

Zoning Local governments use *zoning* to regulate the way land and buildings are used. For example, a zoning board may rule that certain districts, or zones, be used only for homes, others only for businesses, and others only for parks.

Police and Fire Protection Police protection is the second largest expense of many American cities, after utilities. Fire protection is a local service that varies with the size of the community. In small towns volunteers usually staff the fire department. In large cities, full-time professional fire fighters provide protection.

Water Supply Small communities may contract with privately owned companies to supply water. Some local governments create special water districts to deal with the threat of water pollution and water shortages.

Sewage and Sanitation Many local governments maintain sewage treatment plants. Untreated sewage can endanger life and property. Sewage and sanitation costs have forced some small communities to contract with private companies. Landfills are no longer the only solution to waste disposal. Some local governments use garbage-processing plants to dispose of their solid wastes.

Transportation Millions of Americans rely on either the automobile or mass transit systems such as subways, trains, and buses to get to work and to shop. Local governments spend millions of dollars to maintain more than 3 million miles of streets. They also encourage people to use mass transit for the following reasons:

A. Mass transit carries more people per vehicle than automobiles.

B. Mass transit pollutes less than automobiles.

C. Mass transit uses less energy per person than automobiles.

Social Services Local governments offer the following services to people who cannot afford them:

A. Aid to people who are temporarily unemployed

B. Hospital care for people who need medical attention

C. Direct assistance to needy people in the form of cash payments

The money local governments put into social services continues to rise even though federal and state governments pay part of the cost.

Recreation and Cultural Activities Many local communities offer programs in swimming, dancing, theater, puppetry, arts and crafts, and sports. They also maintain parks, zoos, and museums. In addition, many cities have helped build stadiums, arenas, and convention centers.

STUDY GUIDE (continued)   Chapter 24, Section 2

1. Why do municipalities encourage mass transit?

_____

_____

◉ Metropolitan Communities *(page 671)*

Cities, towns, and villages are metropolitan communities. A ***metropolitan area*** is a large city and its surrounding suburbs. This area may also include small towns that lie beyond the suburbs.

Cities are densely populated areas with commercial, industrial, and residential sections. They are chartered by the state as municipal corporations.

Towns were home to most Americans in the early history of the United States. Cities grew faster than towns after 1860. However, towns experienced growth between 1970 and 1990 as cities faced problems.

Suburbs are the densely populated territory neighboring one or more central cities. Today more Americans live in suburbs than in cities or rural areas. A suburb may be called a village, town, or city, and it usually has its own form of government.

2. How has the American population shifted between the early history of the United States and today?

_____

_____

◉ Special Districts *(page 673)*

Special districts make their own policies, levy taxes, and borrow needed money. Local governments establish special districts because they are:

A. better able to respond to solving specific problems than other units of local government, and

B. not subject to the financial limitations of local budgets strained to meet the needs of a community.

The local school district is one such special district. The school board is responsible for:

A. setting school policies,

B. hiring a superintendent of schools,

C. overseeing the daily workings of schools,

D. making up the school budget,

E. deciding on new school programs and facilities,

F. approving the hiring of teachers and supervisors, and

G. deciding on the amount of local school taxes, in some cases.

3. Why would a local government with a tight budget create a special district?

_____

_____

STUDY GUIDE (continued)   Chapter 24, Section 2

⦿ Regional Arrangements (page 673)

In the 1990s local governments joined together to develop collective approaches to regional issues. Their efforts address issues from waste management to law enforcement. For example, city police departments and county sheriffs' offices in some areas share crime laboratories, keep joint records, operate joint radio bands, and share the cost of training personnel.

4. What are the advantages of regional arrangements?

_____

_____

⦿ Financing Local Government (page 673)

Taxes provide the funds to pay for local government services. Today property taxes are the most important source of revenue for local governments. Property taxes are collected on real property and personal property. **Real property** includes land and buildings. **Personal property** consists of such things as jewelry, bonds, and furniture. Figuring the value of the property to be taxed is called **assessment.** The tax assessor appraises the market value of homes and other real property in the community. The **market value** is the amount the owner may expect to receive if the property is sold. Government usually taxes property based on its assessed value, which is only a percentage of its market value. Critics charge that the property tax is unfair for the following reasons:

A. It places a heavier burden on low-income people and on retired homeowners with fixed incomes.

B. Property values are difficult to determine on a fair and equal basis.

C. Reliance on the property tax results in unequal services. A wealthy community with a large tax base can afford better services than a less wealthy community with a small tax base.

D. Some properties, such as those used by religious or charitable organizations, are tax exempt. So nonexempt property owners have to bear a heavier share of the tax.

E. Other local revenue sources include local income taxes, sales taxes, fines and fees, and government-owned businesses. Local governments also raise money for large, expensive projects such as sports stadiums or school buildings by selling municipal bonds.

Most local governments receive economic aid from state and federal governments. This aid comes in the form of grants. Most state aid consists of categorical-formula grants for specific programs. Federal aid comes in categorical grants and block grants. Local governments prefer block grants, or unrestricted aid. These grants transfer cash from the federal government to community development or social services.

5. What is the difference between a property's market value and its assessed value?

_____

_____

STUDY GUIDE  Chapter 24, Section 3

For use with textbook pages 677–682.

CHALLENGES OF URBAN GROWTH

CONTENT VOCABULARY

urban renewal Programs under which cities apply for federal aid to clear slum areas and rebuild *(page 678)*

infrastructure The basic facilities of a city, such as paved streets and sidewalks, water pipes, sewers, bridges, and public buildings *(page 680)*

revitalization Investments in new facilities in an effort to promote economic growth *(page 681)*

gentrification The phenomenon of new people moving into old neighborhoods, forcing out those who live there and changing the essential character of the neighborhood *(page 681)*

metropolitan government A type of government that serves several different communities in the same region *(page 682)*

DRAWING FROM EXPERIENCE

Does your community have people living on the streets? Homelessness is one challenge urban areas face. This section focuses on challenges of urban growth.

READING STRATEGIES

Use the graphic organizer below to help you take notes and list the possible factors that contribute to social problems in urban areas.

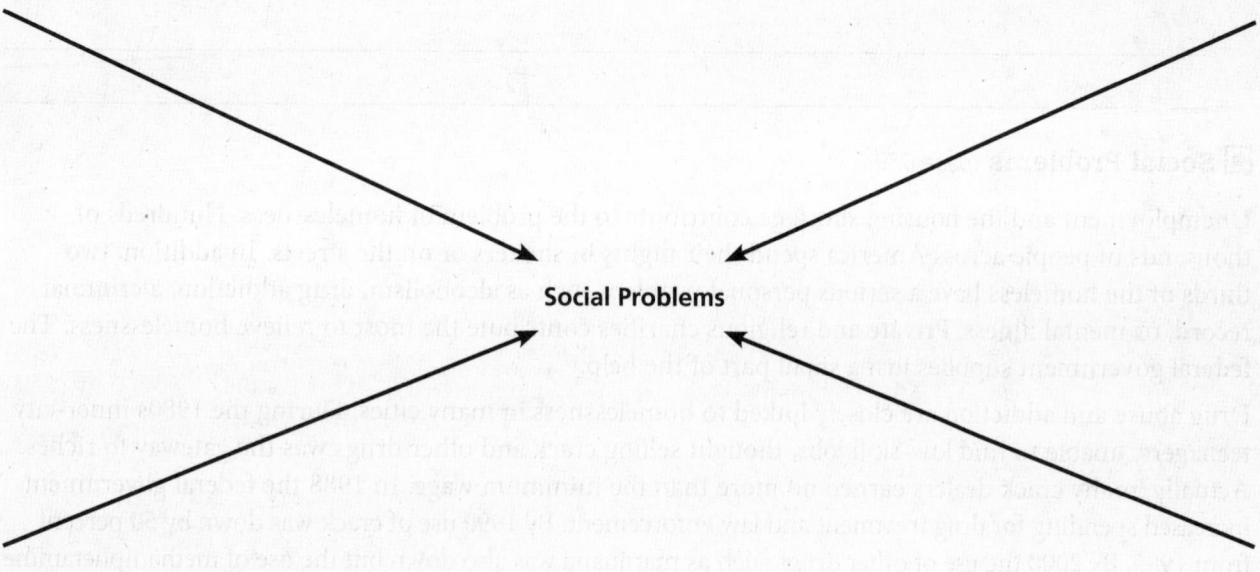

Social Problems

STUDY GUIDE (continued)   Chapter 24, Section 3

READ TO LEARN

⊙ Introduction (page 677)

Today many urban areas, suburbs, and small towns face housing shortages, inadequate transportation, pollution, poverty, and crime.

⊙ Population and Housing (page 677)

In recent years, cities in the Northeast and Midwest lost population, as those in the South and West grew rapidly. The populations of small towns and rural areas increased, and many people moved from cities to nearby suburbs.

Available land becomes scarce, and thus more costly, as the population in an area grows. Local government often has to decide whether available land should be used for new housing, industry, stores, or office buildings. Municipal governments try to manage land use to provide for orderly growth.

In the 1950s and 1960s, cities tried to address their housing problems by spending money from the federal government for ***urban renewal.*** Even after years of massive spending, fewer new housing units were built than were needed. Urban renewal added new low-rent public housing but slowed the production of other types of housing. Fewer total housing units meant higher rent costs overall.

In urban areas, minorities felt the effects of housing discrimination. Many smaller communities and suburbs excluded African Americans or the poor, elderly, and people with children. Then in 1968 Congress passed the Fair Housing Act, which bars discrimination in the sale and rental of housing.

Many cities responded to the shortage in housing by renovating, or redoing, older houses. These projects rewired houses, installed new plumbing, and rebuilt roofs, floors, and walls. Funds from local, state, and national governments contributed to renovation programs. The federal government also offered low-interest loans to build housing projects for low-income residents.

1. Why did urban renewal fail to solve the housing shortage?

_____

_____

⊙ Social Problems (page 679)

Unemployment and the housing shortage contribute to the problem of homelessness. Hundreds of thousands of people across America spend their nights in shelters or on the streets. In addition, two-thirds of the homeless have a serious personal problem such as alcoholism, drug addiction, a criminal record, or mental illness. Private and religious charities contribute the most to relieve homelessness. The federal government supplies just a small part of the help.

Drug abuse and addiction are closely linked to homelessness in many cities. During the 1980s inner-city teenagers, unable to find low-skill jobs, thought selling crack and other drugs was the gateway to riches. Actually, many crack dealers earned no more than the minimum wage. In 1988 the federal government increased spending for drug treatment and law enforcement. By 1990 use of crack was down by 50 percent from 1985. By 2000 the use of other drugs such as marijuana was also down but the use of methamphetamine was beginning to be viewed as a serious problem.

```
┌─────────────────────────────────────────────────────────────────────────┐
│  STUDY GUIDE (continued)            Chapter 24, Section 3                  │
└─────────────────────────────────────────────────────────────────────────┘
```

2. How did the federal government deal with drug abuse and addiction in the 1980s?

_____

_____

◉ Meeting Future Challenges *(page 679)*

One challenge that cities face is repairing or replacing their *infrastructure.* This is the paved streets and sidewalks, pipes that bring water to homes, sewers that dispose of liquid wastes, bridges, tunnels, and public buildings. Rebuilding the infrastructure will mean huge expenditures for cities well into the future. Fortunately, state and federal aid is available for road building, water and sewage systems, bridge construction, and many other public works.

Traffic and air pollution result from millions of Americans using their automobiles to commute to work. Many local leaders believe that more people would use mass transit if it were cleaner, faster, and more efficient. However, high costs discourage planners in many cities from building new mass transit systems.

Revitalization occurs when local governments make investments in new facilities in an effort to promote economic growth. A number of major cities have revitalized their downtowns. For example, Detroit invested $200 million in a regional shopping mall and two giant office buildings on its riverfront. A second way to develop a community's economy is by giving tax incentives to industries that relocate there. Local governments often try to attract new businesses by offering lower property tax rates. Some states offer tax reductions to businesses that relocate in areas of high unemployment. The federal government also offers tax reductions, or credits, to businesses that move into areas of poverty and unemployment.

Gentrification occurs when new people move into an old neighborhood, forcing out those who live there and changing the area's essential character. In the 1980s many middle-income suburbanites and new immigrants moved into the cities. They often chose areas where they could restore old buildings and take advantage of lower housing costs while enjoying the benefits of the city. Gentrification restores life to the city by reclaiming rundown property and bringing in new businesses. However, it also increases property taxes, and property often becomes too expensive for poorer residents.

The state and federal governments cut back their urban development aid in the 1980s. They argued that the move to suburbs might be a good thing. After the census of 1990, new district lines gave suburbs additional seats in Congress and state legislatures. The nation's focus shifted from city problems to suburban opportunities.

One way to address urban problems is by reorganizing a larger region under a *metropolitan government.* Supporters of metropolitan government feel that one government for an entire metropolitan area would be better equipped to handle regional problems such as pollution and paying for services everyone uses. They also feel metropolitan government would reduce waste and duplication of services. For example, water supply and transportation might be provided more economically on an area-wide basis.

3. Why might metropolitan government be a better idea than gentrification for reviving city life?

_____

_____

STUDY GUIDE  Chapter 25, Section 1

For use with textbook pages 689–694.

DEMOCRATIC GOVERNMENTS

CONTENT VOCABULARY

consolidated democracies Nations that have democratic elections, political parties, constitutional governments, independent judiciaries, and usually market economies *(page 689)*

parliamentary government Form of government in which executive and legislative functions both reside in an elected assembly, or parliament *(page 689)*

presidential government A form of democratic government in which a president heads the executive branch *(page 691)*

apartheid Segregation of races enforced by the government *(page 693)*

sanctions Imposing restrictions and withholding aid in order to influence another government *(page 693)*

DRAWING FROM EXPERIENCE

Do you have anything in common with the British, French, and Japanese? One thing you share with these people is democratic government.

This section focuses on democracies around the world.

READING STRATEGIES

Use the flowchart below to help you take notes and show how officials in a parliamentary government are chosen.

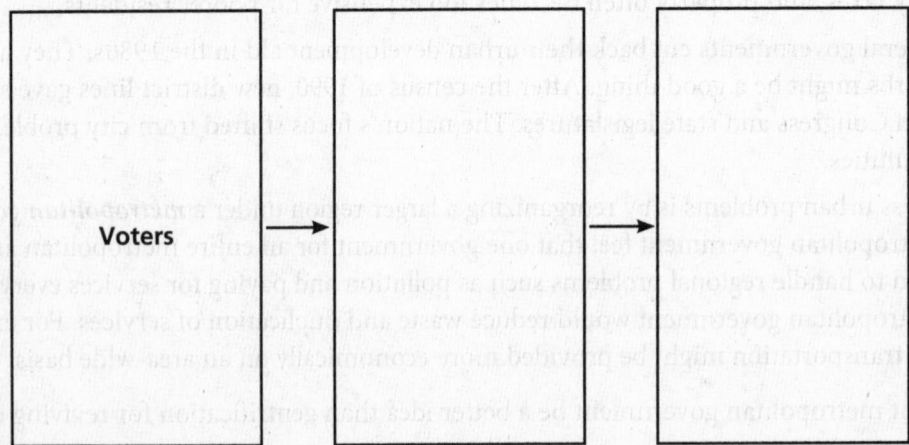

Voters

READ TO LEARN

◉ Introduction (page 689)

The three basic types of government are long-standing democracies, nations in transition to democracy, and authoritarian governments. Countries like the United States are called *consolidated democracies*. These are nations that have fair elections, competing political parties, constitutions that guarantee individual rights, an independent judiciary, and some form of a market economy.

◉ Parliamentary Systems (page 689)

One of the most widespread forms of democracy is *parliamentary government*. In this form, executive and legislative powers reside in the parliament, or elected assembly. Often the parliament selects the leaders of the executive branch, who are known as the cabinet.

In Great Britain, Parliament is a bicameral legislature. It includes the House of Lords and the House of Commons. The House of Commons has greater power than the House of Lords. The people elect members to the House of Commons, who are known as Members of Parliament (MPs), for five-year terms. The House of Commons determines Great Britain's legislative and financial policies. Most bills are introduced by the majority party. A majority vote is needed to pass a bill. The House of Lords is dominated by 540 life peers, people who have been awarded a title for outstanding service or achievement.

The leader of the majority party in the House of Commons becomes the prime minister. He or she chooses other ministers to head executive departments and serve as cabinet members. A prime minister who loses the support of his or her own party resigns from office. The party then chooses another prime minister. If the party should lose a vote on an important issue, Parliament is then dissolved. New general elections are held to determine what party will control the House of Commons.

In Japan, the bicameral legislature is called the National Diet. The upper house is the House of Councillors, and the lower house is the House of Representatives. The Japanese constitution states that the National Diet is the highest power in the state and the only lawmaker. The Diet also controls the nation's money policies.

The House of Representatives elects the prime minister and has the power to vote "no confidence" in the prime minister, or the chief executive, and the cabinet, just as in Great Britain. Both houses consider legislation. However, the House of Representatives may override a negative vote in the House of Councillors by a two-thirds majority. Members of the House of Councillors are chosen for six-year terms. Unlike the lower house, the House of Councillors cannot be dissolved.

In a parliamentary government, members of the cabinet preside over departments or ministries such as justice, foreign affairs, finance, education, health and welfare, agriculture, and labor. Japan's system also includes other cabinet members known as ministers of state. They include the deputy prime minister and heads of various agencies like the Economic Planning Agency.

In parliamentary systems, the prime minister and the cabinet together are called "the government." This is the equivalent of the American "administration." If the government should lose a vote on an important issue, it must resign. The legislature is then dissolved, and new general elections are held.

1. In what ways are the British and Japanese governments similar?

_____

_____

STUDY GUIDE (continued)   Chapter 25, Section 1

⦿ Presidential Government *(page 691)*

Another form of democracy is **presidential government**. The United States Constitution separates the executive branch from the legislative and judicial branches. The office of the president was created to carry out the laws. The president of France has even more official powers than the president of the United States.

The French president serves a seven-year term. He or she is the only member of the government directly elected by voters of the nation at large. The president of France has the power:

A. To negotiate treaties

B. To appoint high officials

C. To act as chair of the high councils of the armed forces

D. To appeal directly to the people by means of a referendum

E. To act as a dictator in times of national emergency

The president contacts the legislative branch of the French government through a premier, whom the president appoints. The premier appoints ministers, who form the cabinet. Together they conduct the day-to-day affairs of government. In theory, the premier and the cabinet are responsible to the deputies of the National Assembly—the lower house of the French Parliament. In practice, the premier and cabinet answer to the president. The president also has the power to dissolve the National Assembly and call for new elections.

2. Which two powers of the French president does the United States president not have?

_____

_____

⦿ Emerging Democracies *(page 692)*

With the collapse of communism, opportunities have emerged for nations to create democratic governments. Among the emerging democracies are Poland, South Africa, and Mexico.

Poland led the way in revolutions against communism in Eastern Europe when a trade union called Solidarity swept the first democratic elections since World War II. Solidarity's leader, Lech Walesa, was elected the nation's president. To ensure the development of democracy, Walesa's followers had to write a constitution. In 1992 President Walesa signed a temporary constitution. Over the next several years, coming up with a permanent constitution proved a difficult task. Finally in 1997, the National Assembly adopted the new Constitution of the Republic of Poland. The majority of Polish voters approved the new plan, which included an emphasis on strengthening local government. Despite challenges to Poland's democracy, such as a weakened economy and the rise of Communist political supporters, Poland joined the European Union in 2004.

Beginning in 1948 in *South Africa*, blacks (Africans), whites, coloreds (mixed European and African descent), and Asians were strictly segregated. Blacks suffered most under this legalized segregation called *apartheid*. In the last half of the century, black nationalist groups such as the African National Congress (ANC) pressed for reforms. By the 1960s, ANC leader Nelson Mandela had formed a military force. In 1962, South African officials charged Mandela with treason and jailed him for life. In the 1980s, the United States and the nations of the European Economic Community ordered economic *sanctions*, or imposing restrictions and withholding aid, against the South African government. By the late 1980s, pressure from the anti-apartheid movement brought an end to apartheid, and Mandela was released in 1990. In April 1994, South Africa held its first nonracial national elections. The ANC won 252 out of the 400 seats in the National Assembly, which chose Nelson Mandela as president. Minority parties criticized the new government, and in 1996 the Afrikaner Nationalist party withdrew from the government. In 1999 the ANC again dominated elections. Future challenges for South Africa include ensuring equal rights throughout the society, and raising the standard of living while maintaining economic growth.

In 1917, *Mexico* adopted a constitution that divided the national government into three branches: executive, legislative, and judicial. However, the power of the president and the control of the government for more than 60 years by one political party, the Institutional Revolutionary Party (PRI), made the Mexican government seem more authoritarian than democratic. For decades massive resources, political patronage, and the support of the media kept the PRI in power. But in 1994, the PRI candidate for president, Ernesto Zedillo Ponce de Leon, won the presidency and introduced reforms that helped other parties compete fairly in Mexico's political process. As a result, Vicente Fox, the candidate of the National Assembly Party (PAN), became president in 2000. Since PAN did not have an outright majority, Fox's government had to form coalitions with other parties to pass legislation. His government supported global trade and made some economic progress, but many of the poorer classes were discontented. Global trade did not benefit the poor as much as upper and middle-class Mexicans. In the 2006 election, the more conservative candidate won, but only by a very narrow margin. Supporters of the defeated candidate did not immediately accept the outcome of the election and the nation faced many political challenges.

3. What are some of the challenges faced by the newly formed democratic governments in Poland, South Africa, and Mexico?

_____

_____

STUDY GUIDE Chapter 25, Section 2

For use with textbook pages 696–701.

AUTHORITARIAN GOVERNMENTS

CONTENT VOCABULARY

Muslim A follower of Islam *(page 699)*

mullah Specially trained religious leaders who interpret and uphold traditional Islamic teachings *(page 700)*

shah Iranian king *(page 700)*

DRAWING FROM EXPERIENCE

Imagine you had to build a democratic government from scratch. Where would you begin? Emerging democracies have had to answer similar questions.

This section focuses on nations struggling to establish democracy.

READING STRATEGIES

Use the time line below to help you take notes and list the important events in the history of Communist China and Cuba.

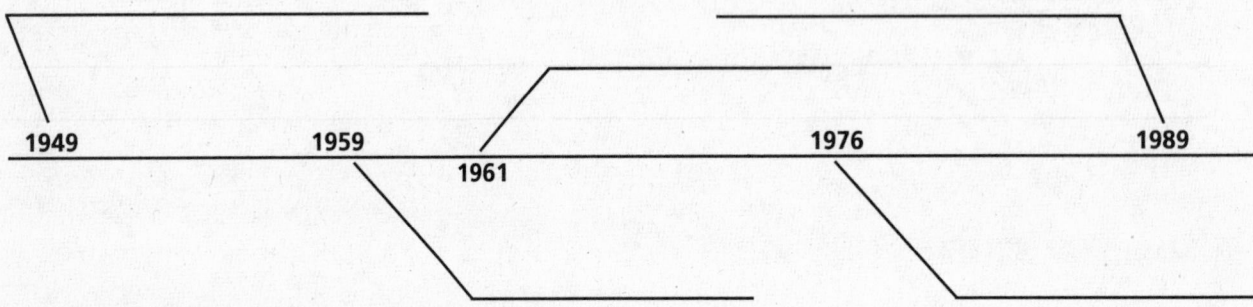

1949	1959	1976	1989
	1961		

READ TO LEARN

◉ Introduction *(page 696)*

The number of democratic nations is increasing. However, governments such as those in the People's Republic of China, Cuba, North Korea, Saudi Arabia, and Iran present a stark contrast to democracies.

◉ The People's Republic of China *(page 696)*

In 1949 Communist revolutionaries led by Mao Zedong seized power in China. Mao led China for the next 30 years and, like the Soviet Union, established a totalitarian government controlled by the Chinese Communist Party (CCP). Mao's government turned China into a socialist state by taking control of all industry, farmland, and workers.

Today China has two parallel systems of government. There is a ceremonial national government, which is actually controlled by the CCP. This is how the CCP is organized:

A. The Communist Party's highest governing body is the National Party Congress. It serves as a rubber stamp for the party's policies.

B. At the top of the CCP is the General Secretary, the most powerful party leader.

C. National policy is made by the party's Political Bureau, or Politburo. The Politburo's Standing Committee is made up of the top seven CCP leaders. This elite group makes all of China's key political, economic, and military decisions.

In 1989 Chinese forces massacred hundreds of unarmed, pro-democracy students demonstrating in Beijing's Tiananmen Square. Today the authoritarian government oppresses minorities, such as Muslims and Tibetans, and suppresses criticism and popular organizations. It also tries to control the flow of ideas and information. For example, China has developed the world's most extensive Internet censoring system. The United States ended official diplomatic relations with China when the Communists gained control of the mainland in 1949. Since then relations have improved, though the United States wants China to end its human rights abuses and act as a stabilizing force in Asia.

1. What are China's two parallel systems of government?

_____

_____

◉ Communism in Cuba *(page 698)*

In 1959 Fidel Castro led Cubans in a revolt that overthrew dictator Fulgencio Batista. Under Castro, Cuba became a Communist dictatorship. Twice, tensions between Cuba and the United States have boiled over. The first time was the 1961 failed invasion of Cuba, called the Bay of Pigs. A year later, the United States discovered Soviet missiles in Cuba. The Cuban Missile Crisis brought the world to the brink of nuclear war.

The end of the Cold War left Cuba isolated in the early 1990s. The loss of Soviet aid and low prices for sugar exports caused an economic crisis, but the United States kept up its trade embargo against Cuba. Americans pressured Castro to move toward a democratic system in return for better relations and economic aid. However, these efforts have failed to move Castro toward instituting democratic reforms. In 2008, Castro resigned as president. His brother Raúl Castro was elected president by Cuba's parliament.

2. Why did the United States impose a trade embargo against Cuba?

_____

_____

╔══╗
STUDY GUIDE (continued)   Chapter 25, Section 2
╚══╝

◉ North Korea *(page 698)*

After World War II, the Korean peninsula was divided into two parts. South Korea, aided by the United States, became a democracy. North Korea, supported by the Soviet Union, became a Communist nation. Today, the government of North Korea, led by dictator Kim Jong Il, controls all aspects of its peoples' lives. North Koreans are cut off from outside information and told to give Kim "absolute devotion," despite their economic suffering. Since the early 1990s, North Korea has begun to develop chemical, biological, and nuclear weapons. The United States has sought to limit this development.

3. What were the two parts of the Korean peninsula after World War II?

_____

_____

◉ Islamic Governments *(page 699)*

Islam is a religion spread by the prophet Muhammad, who claimed that he received the teachings of God (Allah) in a vision. These teachings were written in the Quran. A ***Muslim*** is a follower of Islam. Today there are over one billion Muslims spread throughout the Middle East and many other non-Arab countries, such as Iran. Islamic leaders believe that there is no need for a separation between religion and the government as there is in the United States. Thus, in Islamic governments, the Quran provides the guidance needed on issues such as the duties of citizens and rulers, and how the government should exercise power.

Some Muslims, called secularists, believe that religious doctrine and secular (nonreligious) law should be kept separate. Others, Muslim fundamentalists, believe Islamic countries should base their law solely on the Quran. They look to ***mullahs***, specially trained religious leaders who interpret traditional Islamic teachings, to unite Muslims around the world into one community. Many fundamentalist Muslims see Western culture and society as a threat to Islam. Their goal is to bring down moderate Islamic governments that accept foreign customs.

Iran During the 1960s and 1970s, the shah, or king of Iran, led a Western-oriented government. It developed a capitalist economy based on oil. Muslim religious leaders opposed the shah. In 1979, under the leadership of the Shiite Muslim leader, Ayatollah Ruhollah Khomeini, they revolted and set up an Islamic republic. In an Islamic republic, religious leaders can veto political decisions. In 2005, President Ahmadinejad was elected. A hardliner, he supports terrorists who want to destroy Israel. He has also begun building a nuclear weapons program, despite United Nations opposition.

The government of Saudi Arabia, a country that has provided oil and important military bases to the United States, is a monarchy based on a fundamentalist interpretation of Islam. There is no separation of church and state. Aside from the royal family, the most powerful political force in the country is the mullahs, who impose traditional Islamic ideas through government sponsored organizations. In the 1950s, the discovery of oil transformed Saudi Arabia into a wealthy, urban nation. More and more Saudis began demanding an elected government. Since the September 2001 terrorist attacks on the United States, many American critics have accused the Saudi government of indirectly supporting terrorism to appease fundamentalist Muslims within Saudi Arabia.

4. How do secularist Muslims differ from fundamentalist Muslims?

_____

_____

STUDY GUIDE  Chapter 25, Section 3

For use with textbook pages 702–706.

INTERNATIONAL ORGANIZATIONS

CONTENT VOCABULARY

nongovernmental organizations Made up of individuals and groups outside the scope of government, such as the International Red Cross *(page 702)*

intergovernmental organizations Made up of members of national governments, such as the United Nations *(page 702)*

supranational organizations Organizations whose authority overrides the sovereignty of its individual members *(page 704)*

DRAWING FROM EXPERIENCE

Do you read about world events? Then you may have seen items about the leaders of China, Cuba, Iran, and Iraq.

This section focuses on authoritarian states, which outnumber democracies.

READING STRATEGIES

Use the graphic organizer below to take notes and list the various aspects of the government of the European Union.

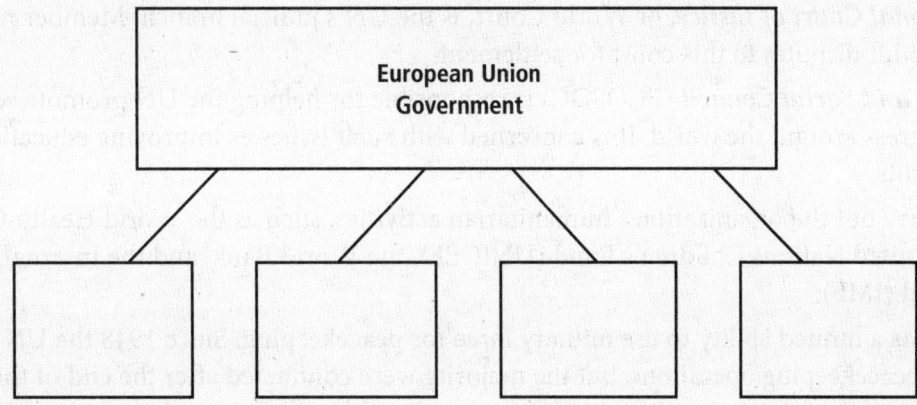

STUDY GUIDE (continued)   Chapter 25, Section 3

READ TO LEARN

◉ Introduction (page 702)

International organizations play a key role in world politics. There are two types of such organizations. *Nongovernmental organizations (NGOs)*, such as the International Red Cross, are made up of individuals and groups outside the scope of government. *Intergovernmental organizations (IGOs)*, such as the United Nations (UN), are composed of members of national governments. IGOs are created through agreements, usually treaties, negotiated by the member states. The powers of an IGO are established and limited by its members.

◉ The United Nations (page 702)

The United Nations was established in 1945 to provide a forum for nations to settle their disputes peacefully. Today, membership includes 192 nations. The organization has three main goals:

A. To preserve world peace and security;

B. To encourage nations to deal fairly with one another; and

C. To help nations cooperate in trying to solve their social and economic problems.

The main headquarters of the UN is located in New York City and is divided into a variety of units:

The General Assembly is at the heart of the UN. It discusses, debates, and recommends solutions for major international problems, and also controls the UN's budget.

The Security Council is a kind of executive board for the General Assembly. It has the authority to make peacekeeping decisions. For example, it may call for breaking off relations with a nation, ending trade with a nation, or using military force. However, the Security Council is unable to act if one of its members vetoes a measure.

The Secretariat does the UN's day-to-day business. The General Assembly appoints a Secretary General to carry out the instructions of the Security Council.

The International Court of Justice, or World Court, is the UN's judicial branch. Member nations may voluntarily submit disputes to this court for settlement.

The Economic and Social Council (ECOSOC) is responsible for helping the UN promote social and economic progress around the world. It is concerned with such issues as improving education, health, and human rights.

Other units carry out the organization's humanitarian activities, such as the World Health Organization (WHO), the United Nations Children's Fund (UNICEF), the World Bank, and the International Monetary Fund (IMF).

The UN also has a limited ability to use military force for peacekeeping. Since 1948 the UN has conducted 56 peacekeeping operations, but the majority were conducted after the end of the Cold War in 1990. UN peacekeeping involves inserting an international force of troops between combatants as a way to calm or monitor the situation. Lightly armed peacekeeping forces may also undertake other missions, such as overseeing elections or providing humanitarian aid. The 1990 Persian Gulf War was a UN peacekeeping operation. After Iraq invaded neighboring Kuwait on its way to Saudi Arabia, the UN Security Council voted to condemn Iraq and allowed U.S. forces to lead a coalition of seven nations to repel the invaders. The UN also imposed economic sanctions to force Iraq to agree to destroy its weapons of mass destruction and comply with UN weapons inspectors.

1. What are the three main goals of the United Nations?

_____

_____

◉ The European Union (page 704)

The European Union (EU) has evolved farther than any other intergovernmental organization towards becoming a *supranational organization*, or an organization whose authority overrides the sovereignty of its individual members. Since its founding, the EU has developed into a quasi-government with the authority to make and enforce decisions that apply to all of its members.

The EU was created in 1957 when six Western European nations decided to move toward a common trading market called the European Economic Community (EEC) to remove all economic restrictions between the member nations. In 1993 the EC was renamed the European Union, which today has 27 members. As more countries joined the EU, they began to press for more political, as well as economic, integration. With the 1993 Maastricht Treaty, member nations began to yield power to the EU, which allowed the EU to act more as a political unit able to enforce common rules for trade, crime fighting, immigration, citizenship, and more. In 2004, EU leaders drafted a constitution to clarify various EU treaties and EU powers. Voters in France and the Netherlands refused to ratify this constitution, however. People in some European nations may have felt that integration had gone far enough.

The EU government is complex in order to accommodate the distinct cultures, languages, and political traditions of its members:

The Council of the European Union is a group chosen by each member nation that decides the key directions for EU policy.

The European Parliament (EP) is the legislative branch of the EU. It works alongside the Council to form the annual budget and supervise smaller EU institutions.

The European Court of Justice, the judicial branch of the EU, has one judge per member state. It often uses EU treaties as a kind of constitution by which to judge cases, and can declare laws of member nations invalid if they conflict with EU treaty obligations.

The European Commission does much of the EU's daily work, such as drafting proposals for new laws. One commissioner is selected by the Council to be the President of the Commission. The president directs the large EU bureaucracy and oversees the annual budget.

Many Europeans complain that the "Eurocracy," as the EU bureaucracy is called, has grown too large and is no longer responsive to the public.

2. How did the 1993 Maastricht Treaty change the power of the European Union?

_____

_____

STUDY GUIDE  Chapter 25, Section 4

For use with textbook pages 707–712.

ⒼLOBAL ISSUES

CONTENT VOCABULARY

terrorism The use of violence by nongovernmental groups against civilians to achieve a political goal *(page 707)*

state-sponsored terrorism Terrorism that is secretly supported by a government *(page 708)*

nuclear proliferation The spread of nuclear weapons *(page 709)*

human rights The basic freedoms and rights that all people should enjoy, regardless of age, gender, nationality, or ethnicity *(page 710)*

DRAWING FROM EXPERIENCE

How would you feel if Canada and Mexico went to war? You might be afraid that the United States would go to war, too. Often national security depends on the peace and security of other nations.

This section focuses on how nations try to protect the safety of the world.

READING STRATEGIES

Use the diagram below to help you take notes and list the promises made by the major nuclear powers when they signed the nuclear Non-Proliferation Treaty.

Non-Proliferation Treaty

STUDY GUIDE (continued) Chapter 25, Section 4

READ TO LEARN

◉ Introduction (page 707)

Solving global issues may require cooperation among nations. Important global issues today include defeating terrorism, limiting the spread of nuclear weapons, promoting human rights, and protecting the environment.

◉ International Terrorism (page 708)

Terrorism is the use of violence by nongovernmental groups against civilians to achieve a political goal. Recently over 300 attacks of terrorism per year have occurred worldwide. Since World War II most terrorist attacks against America have been carried out by Middle Eastern groups. Some reasons for this include American support of Middle Eastern oil industries—which increases the disparity between rich and poor Middle Eastern families and increases Middle Eastern cultural contact with the West—and American support of Israel. In the 1970s several Middle Eastern nations realized they could fight the United States by supporting terrorist groups. When a government secretly supports terrorism, this is called *state-sponsored terrorism*. The governments of Libya, Syria, Iraq, and Iran have all sponsored terrorism.

Osama bin Laden, a wealthy Muslim terrorist, founded an organization in 1988 called al-Qaeda. Bin Laden believed that Western ideas had contaminated Muslim society, and that superpowers like America could be beaten. He dedicated himself and al-Qaeda to driving Westerners, especially Americans, out of the Middle East. Attacks throughout the 1990s culminated in al-Qaeda's devastating attacks on New York City and Washington, D.C., on September 11, 2001. The United States responded by going to war.

In October 2001 the United States began bombing targets in Afghanistan. President Bush emphasized that the targets of American attacks were al-Qaeda's camps and the Taliban's military forces, and that Islam and the Afghan people were not the enemy. However, he also vowed that the war on terrorism would not end "until every terrorist group of global reach has been found, stopped, and defeated." Defeating global terrorism will require many nations to work together towards this common goal.

1. Why are most terrorist attacks against the United States carried out by Middle Eastern groups?

_____

_____

◉ Nuclear Weapons Threat (page 709)

Another global problem is the spread of nuclear weapons, or *nuclear proliferation*. The United States, Russia, Great Britain, France, and China have had nuclear weapons for many years. Several other nations are believed to possess nuclear weapons, or have acquired the capability to produce them. In 1968 the major nuclear powers created the nuclear Non-Proliferation Treaty (NPT), in which they promised:

A. Not to provide nuclear weapons technology to other countries;

B. To ensure the safe use of nuclear power; and

C. To encourage general disarmament and destruction of existing nuclear weapons.

The United Nations has also imposed sanctions on nations seeking to build nuclear weapons. However, it is now possible to build small nuclear weapons using cheaper, more readily-available substances. This means that a wider range of nations, including terrorist groups, may have access to the materials needed to build a nuclear weapon. Two nations that the United States is particularly concerned about are North Korea and Iran. Both of these nations have developed, or are developing, the capacity to manufacture nuclear weapons. Because both nations have also been accused of sponsoring terrorism, many fear that these countries' weapons could be sold to international terrorist groups. The United States, Britain,

Canada, France, Germany, Italy, Japan, and Russia have pledged to spend a total of $20 billion over the next 10 years on non-proliferation efforts.

2. What are the three components of the nuclear Non-Proliferation Treaty?

_____

◉ Human Rights *(page 710)*

Human rights are the basic freedoms and rights that all people should enjoy, regardless of age, gender, nationality, or ethnicity. In 1948 the United Nations adopted the Universal Declaration of Human Rights, which included:

A. Political and civil rights, such as the right to seek asylum, the right to marry, and the right to own property. These articles list things a government *should not* do to limit a person's freedoms.

B. Economic, social, and cultural rights, such as the right to equal pay for equal work and the right to an education. These are "positive rights," or things governments *should* do for people.

The international community has developed numerous institutions and procedures for safeguarding human rights. The UN Security Commission on Human Rights monitors and reports on human rights violations. The UN's international criminal tribunals are temporary courts convened under UN authority to prosecute human rights violators. The countries of the European Union (EU) stand behind the European Convention of Human Rights, which sets forth a long list of civil liberties that apply to all EU countries. Finally, a permanent International Criminal Court (ICC) was established in 2002 to investigate and prosecute those accused of major human rights violations and war crimes. However, the United States, along with several other nations, refused to sign this treaty because they feared that American military troops and leaders could become the targets of frivolous complaints of war crimes by enemies of the United States.

3. What are "positive rights"?

_____

◉ Protecting the Environment *(page 711)*

Exploding population growth, increasing consumption of natural resources, and growing pollution all threaten the environment. Dealing with these issues requires international cooperation. The dilemma is how to attain sustainable development, or a balance between economic development and protection of the environment. Developed nations like the United States are able to find ways to make its industry more efficient and less damaging to the environment. Developing nations, however, feel they need to place their highest priority on economic growth.

Many international conferences and treaties have dealt with the issue of the environment. In 1992 the UN's "Earth Summit" produced the Biodiversity Treaty, which set forth procedures for conservation of ecosystems and natural habitats. In 1997, the Kyoto Protocol set down timetables for reducing greenhouse emissions. The United States signed the protocol, but it was never submitted to Congress for ratification. Presidents Clinton and George W. Bush disliked the fact that some nations were exempted or feared the impact its guidelines would have on the American economy.

4. What three issues threaten the well-being of the global environment?

_____

Name _____ Date _____ Class _____

For use with textbook pages 717–721.

CAPITALIST AND MIXED SYSTEMS

CONTENT VOCABULARY

scarcity A condition that exists when society does not have all the resources to produce all the goods and services that everyone wants *(page 717)*

traditional economy Economic system in which customs dictate the rules for economic activity *(page 717)*

command economy Economic system in which the government controls most of the economic activity *(page 717)*

market economy Economic system in which buyers and sellers acting in their individual interests make economic decisions *(page 718)*

factors of production Resources that an economy needs to produce goods and services *(page 718)*

entrepreneur A person who takes a risk to produce goods and services in search of profit *(page 718)*

monopoly A business that controls so much of an industry that little or no competition exists *(page 720)*

profit The difference between the amount of money used to operate a business and the amount of money the business takes in *(page 720)*

mixed economy A system in which the government regulates some private enterprise *(page 721)*

DRAWING FROM EXPERIENCE

Have you bought anything lately? Whenever you buy an item, you participate in the capitalist system. This section focuses on how capitalism works.

READING STRATEGIES

Use the outline below to help you take notes about global economic systems. Add points as needed.

> **Capitalist and Mixed Systems**
>
> I. Factors of Production
>   A.
>   B.
> II. Forms of Economic Organization
> III. Characteristics of Capitalism

STUDY GUIDE (continued)   Chapter 26, Section 1

READEST TO LEARN

◉ Introduction (page 717)

Scarcity exists when society does not have all the resources to produce all the goods and services that everyone wants. The following economic systems address this problem:

In a *traditional economy,* habit and custom set the rules for all economic activity, determining what, how, and for whom goods and services are produced.

A *command economy* has a central authority—usually the government—that makes most of these economic decisions.

A *market economy* allows buyers and sellers acting in their own interests to determine what, how, and for whom goods are produced.

◉ Factors of Production (page 717)

The resources of an economic system are called factors of production. Economies must have certain things to produce goods and services. They may be grouped in the following categories:

Land includes all natural resources, such as soil, water, and air. Minerals, such as copper and iron ore, are land resources.

Capital includes the means of production—money, factories, and machinery—used to produce other goods.

Labor includes human resources, or the people who produce goods and services. Examples are factory workers, sales clerks, and teachers.

Entrepreneurs are businesspersons who organize and direct the other factors of production to produce goods and services. Entrepreneurs take risks to make a profit.

1. What are the four factors of production?

_____

_____

_____

_____

◉ Forms of Economic Organization (page 718)

The three major forms of economic organization are:

Communism This is a command system in which the central government directs all major economic decisions.

Socialism This is a partial command system in which the government influences economic decisions.

Capitalism Under this system, buyers and sellers make the economic decisions in free markets.

Most countries in the world today have mixed economic systems.

2. How does communism work?

_____

_____

STUDY GUIDE (continued)   Chapter 26, Section 1

◉ Characteristics of Capitalism (page 718)

Capitalism is based on private ownership of the means of production, or capital, and on individual economic competition. Most capitalist economies today have the following characteristics:

Private Ownership Capitalist economies depend on the private ownership of property and resources. However, government provides some public services, such as road building and sewers. Capitalism also emphasizes respect for personal property not used in production.

Individual Initiative In a capitalist system, the law allows anyone to be an entrepreneur. For example, each year thousands of Americans go into business for themselves.

Competition When there are a number of sellers of a product or service, no seller can control the market price. The opposite of competition is a *monopoly.* It exists when an industry includes only one seller, resulting in no competition at all. A more common situation is oligopoly—when only a few large firms make up an industry.

Freedom of Choice Consumers can buy the products they can afford from whatever companies they choose. Businesses are free to provide whatever legal goods and services they think people want. Workers can decide where they will work and what they will do.

Profit or Loss Profit is the difference between the amount of money used to run a business and the amount the business takes in. Profits are part of the reward to an entrepreneur for assuming risk. They also pay for expanding businesses and provide for unexpected expenses. Of course, entrepreneurs can lose money as well as make it. That is the risk they take.

3. Why are profits important to capitalism?

_____

_____

◉ Changing Face of Capitalism (page 720)

For its first 100 years, the United States government left business largely unregulated. By the late 1800s, powerful industrialists dominated the economy and were squeezing out competitors. As a result, the state and federal governments passed laws to ensure competition and to promote public safety. In the 1930s, the federal government began to look after the well-being of individuals and the finances of the nation. As a result, the United States has what economists call a *mixed economy,* or modified capitalism.

In Japan government works closely with business to limit foreign competition at home. The governments of Singapore and Taiwan also have a close relationship with private business. Most Western European economies are more controlled and regulated than that of the United States. However, many Western European governments have moved toward freer markets in recent years.

4. Why is the United States economy called "modified capitalism"?

_____

_____

STUDY GUIDE  Chapter 26, Section 2

For use with textbook pages 722–726.

EMERGING ECONOMIES

DRAWING FROM EXPERIENCE

What does your family do to help the needy? Just as concerned individuals try to help the poor in their communities, many governments try to help the poor in their countries.

This section focuses on economies in developing and newly developed countries.

READING STRATEGIES

Use the graphic organizer below to help you take notes and list the practical problems of Socialism.

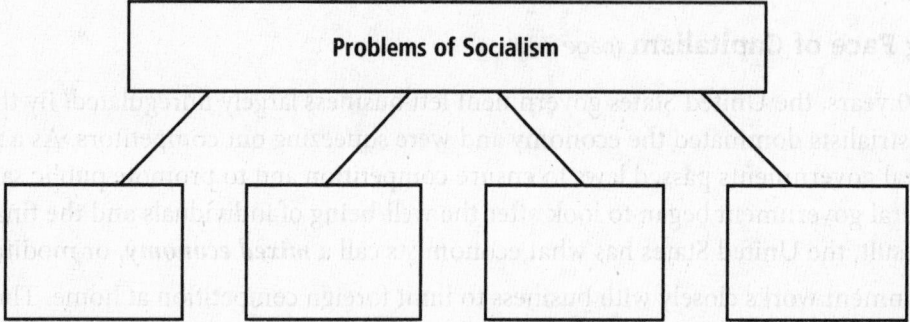

STUDY GUIDE (continued)   Chapter 26, Section 2

READ TO LEARN

⊙ **Introduction** (page 722)

The gap between rich nations and poor nations concerns world leaders, just as the gap between wealthy people and poor people troubles the leaders of many developing countries.

⊙ **Developing and Newly Developed Nations** (page 722)

Developing nations are states with little or no industry. Much of the world's population lives in developing nations. *Newly developed nations* are states that have had much or rapid industrial growth in recent years. These countries are mostly in Eastern Europe, Asia, and South America.

    1. How do developing nations differ from newly developed nations?

    _____

    _____

⊙ **The Economic Choices** (page 723)

Some developing and newly developed nations lean toward a capitalist economic system. Other developing and newly developed nations have chosen socialism as their model. Under socialism, the government owns some of the factors of production and distribution of products. Under communism, the government owns all the factors of production. Other differences that distinguish the command elements in democratic socialist economies and communist economies are:

A. Under democratic socialism, voters can replace the managers of the economy and the government.

B. Most socialist countries use the command system to control only certain key industries.

C. In practice, socialist states do not distribute wealth directly but make basic goods and social services equally available to everyone.

Critics of socialism claim that socialism leads to a welfare state. They believe having many welfare programs makes people overly dependent on the government. Socialists answer that every person should be able to receive such basic needs as food, housing, clothing, and medical care.

    2. What do socialist economies do instead of distributing the nation's wealth?

    _____

    _____

⊙ **Searching for Economic Answers** (page 724)

Many developing and newly developed nations have adopted socialist economic policies. These polices try to raise the standard of living for the large numbers of poor people. Socialist governments in these countries often use centralized planning. This involves government control of the economy to a larger extent than in developed socialist countries. These socialist governments often turn to:

A. Nationalization of industries

B. Redistribution of land

STUDY GUIDE (continued)   Chapter 26, Section 2

C. Establishment of agricultural communes

D. Welfare systems

Socialist governments often take control of industries through *nationalization*. Many developing countries have had foreign-owned industries. Nationalization of these industries has been both an economic policy and a gesture of anticolonialism.

In 1970 Chileans elected socialist Salvatore Allende to the presidency. He nationalized businesses, including American-owned copper mines. The CIA led a coup against the Chilean government, and Allende was killed. General August Pinochet took over the government. Pinochet dissolved the congress and abused civil liberties. He was forced to resign in 1988. Since then Chile's leaders have increased spending on education, health, and housing, and Chile's economy has improved.

In the early 1900s, Jewish immigrants brought European socialist ideas to what is now Israel. They built collective farms called kibbutzim. Since Israel's founding in 1948, communes have allowed some private property. Today kibbutzim still contribute to Israel's economy but make up a small part of the population.

After independence, many African nations developed economies based on one cash crop or resource for trade. Some governments in Africa followed a capitalist model and others organized socialist economies.

Beginning in the 1970s, droughts, growing populations, lack of capital, and falling world prices for their exports weakened most African economies. African nations south of the Sahara relied heavily on foreign help, accumulating $130 billion of debt by the 1980s.

By 1996, due to rising interest rates and economic stagnation, the total debt reached $227 billion. The World Bank identified 33 African countries as Heavily Indebted Poor Countries. A movement to cancel Africa's debt has gained momentum around the world. Without cancellation, Africa will continue to pay more toward debt service than toward such things as health care and economic development.

3. Why did the CIA lead a coup against President Allende of Chile?

_____

_____

◉ Socialism's Practical Problems (page 726)

Socialist ideology is losing ground in the developing world. Several practical problems with socialism are:

A. The threat of nationalization can prevent attracting the capital needed for developing economies.

B. The failure of large-scale state planning to meet consumers' needs in Eastern Europe raised concerns about socialism's ability to do so in other regions.

C. Western governments prefer to trade with countries that have free markets.

4. Why are socialist economies unattractive to investors?

_____

_____

STUDY GUIDE  Chapter 26, Section 3

For use with textbook pages 728–731.

AJOR ECONOMIES IN TRANSITION

CONTENT VOCABULARY

state farm Farm owned by the government and run like a factory, with farmworkers being paid wages *(page 729)*

collective farm Farm in which the land is owned by the government but rented to a family *(page 729)*

DRAWING FROM EXPERIENCE

Imagine having enough money to buy all the CDs you want. How would you feel if the stores had no CDs for sale? Under Communist rule, Russians experienced similar problems.

This section focuses on why Soviet communism collapsed.

READING STRATEGIES

Use the graphic organizer below to help you take notes and identify obstacles that slowed democratization in Russia.

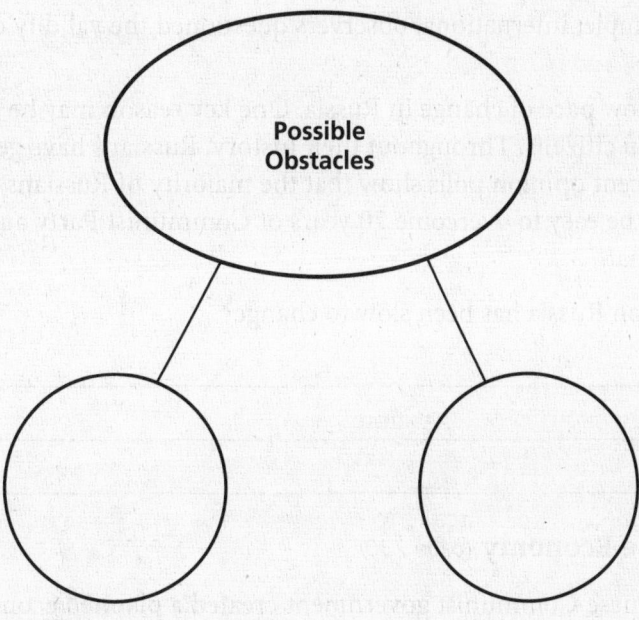

STUDY GUIDE (continued)   Chapter 26, Section 3

READ TO LEARN

⦿ Introduction (page 728)

Many nations today are attempting to make the transition from command to market economies. The two most significant nations doing so are Russia and China.

⦿ Transforming the Russian Economy (page 728)

The Soviet Union built the world's leading communist economic system. A major difference between democratic socialist systems and the Soviet economy was that the Soviet economy was closely controlled by the Communist Party. All enterprises were state-owned and state-operated. The Soviet government also controlled labor unions, wages, and prices. About 98 percent of all Soviet farmland was under government control. About two-thirds of the land consisted of *state farms* owned by the government and run like factories, with the farmworkers being paid wages. The remaining one-third of Soviet farmland consisted of *collective farms*. On these farms, the government owned the land but rented it to families. Farmworkers on state farms had little reason to work hard. Inefficiency was widespread.

The Soviet economy began to stagnate. Beginning in the 1980s the Soviet *gross national product* (GNP)—the annual sum of the nation's goods and services—grew by only 2 to 3 percent a year. When Mikhail Gorbachev resigned as Communist Party leader in 1991, several Soviet republics declared their independence, effectively ending the Soviet Union.

Since the collapse of communism in Russia, the country has tried to move toward capitalism and democracy. For example, some reforms include attempts to create stock markets, simplify tax laws, and end corruption in banking and finance. However, even with these reforms, the country is run much as it was during the communist years—and by many of the same people. Efforts at democratization have begun to slow. For example, international observers questioned the validity of Russia's 2003 parliamentary elections.

Several factors explain the slow pace of change in Russia. One key reason may be a lack of commitment to democracy among Russian citizens. Throughout their history, Russians have generally experienced order imposed by rulers. Recent opinion polls show that the majority of Russians regret the breakup of the Soviet Union. It will not be easy to overcome 70 years of Communist Party authority and centuries of czarist autocracy before that.

   1. What is one key reason Russia has been slow to change?

   _____

   _____

   _____

⦿ Changing the Chinese Economy (page 730)

After World War II, the Chinese Communist government created a planned economy modeled after the Soviet economy. However, China eventually found itself unable to compete economically with the market-based economies of its neighbors like Japan and South Korea. In the late 1970s, China's Communist leaders began dismantling the economy and encouraging private enterprise. Since then, the Chinese economy has started to grow between 5 and 8 percent per year.

STUDY GUIDE (continued)   Chapter 26, Section 3

China's economy has developed rapidly for several reasons:

A. A large labor pool of 1.3 billion citizens has made China the center for low-cost production for companies all over the world.

B. The Chinese government has promoted manufacturing by giving foreign companies tax breaks and cheap land.

C. The government has also assisted manufacturers by spending billions on highways, ports, and fiber-optic communications.

The Chinese government is attempting to move from a command to a market economy while maintaining an authoritarian political system controlled by the Communist Party. However, it is uncertain whether the current political system can keep up with the dramatic changes caused by the economic boom. Threats to communism in China include:

A. A growing middle class which will want to have more of a say in how China is governed;

B. A new class of urban poor, angry with the government; and

C. Increased corruption, as Communist Party members are able to use their positions to gain unfair advantages in the booming market economy while remaining unaccountable to the people.

Economic changes in China are having a huge effect on Americans. Trade with China opens new markets for American goods and new places for corporate expansion. Today, the United States is one of the largest foreign investors in the Chinese economy. Chinese products do have a negative effect on American jobs. But many experts argue China is less likely to become a military or political threat if the United States maintains strong trade relations with that nation.

2. What impact do Chinese economic changes have on Americans?

_____

_____

_____

STUDY GUIDE  Chapter 26, Section 4

For use with textbook pages 732–736.

THE GLOBAL ECONOMY

CONTENT VOCABULARY

comparative advantage Economic principle that each country should produce those goods it can make more efficiently and trade for other goods *(page 732)*

tariffs Taxes placed on imports to increase their price in the domestic market *(page 733)*

quotas Limits on the quantity of a product that may be imported *(page 733)*

trading blocs Groups of nations that trade without barriers such as tariffs *(page 734)*

DRAWING FROM EXPERIENCE

Do you look at labels to see where the things you buy come from? You probably own things that were made in countries around the world.

This section focuses on the global economy.

READING STRATEGIES

Use the graphic organizer below to help you take notes and list the ways in which governments may restrict international trade.

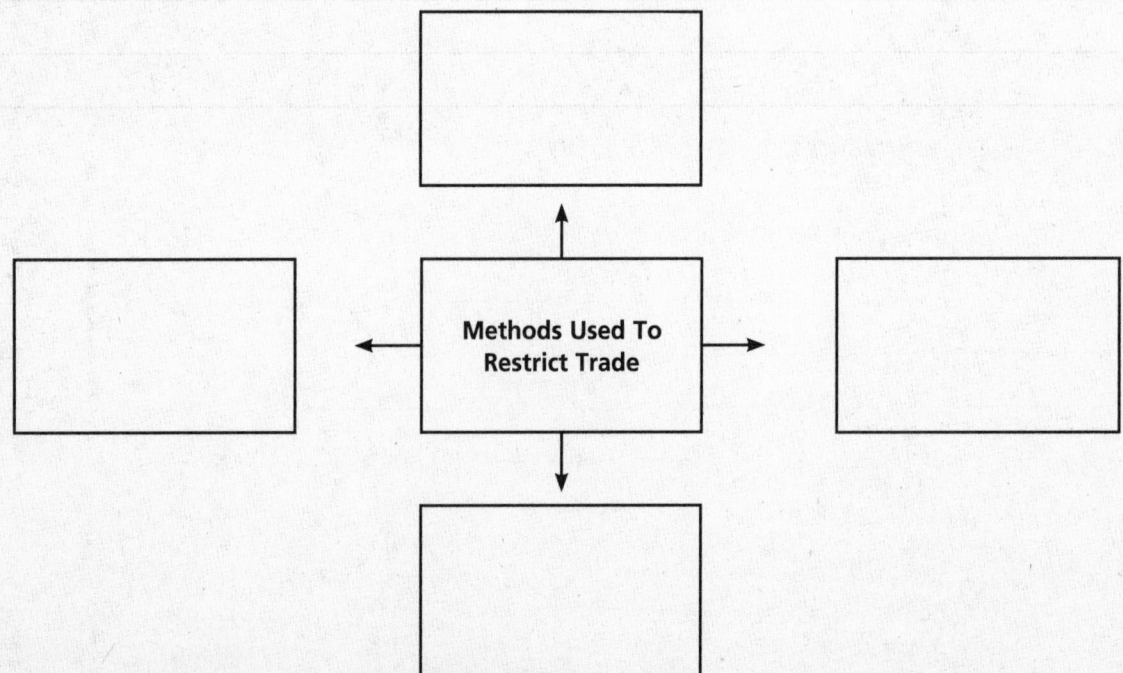

STUDY GUIDE (continued)   Chapter 26, Section 4

READ TO LEARN

◉ Introduction (page 732)

Global economic activities include investments, banking and financial services, and currency exchange. The major activity in the global economy is trade among nations.

◉ International Trade (page 732)

Nations engage in international trade for several reasons:

A. To obtain goods and services they cannot produce

B. Because of the principle of ***comparative advantage***, which states that each country should produce those goods it can make more efficiently and purchase those that other nations produce more efficiently. Thus the total cost of all products is less and the average cost of any product is less, benefiting all consumers.

C. To create jobs

Unrestricted international trade promotes efficient production. However, it can also threaten domestic industries and workers. As a result, national governments use several methods to restrict international trade:

A. ***Tariffs***, taxes placed on imports to increase their price in the domestic market

B. ***Quotas***, limits on the quantities of a foreign product that may be imported

C. Non-tariff barriers (NTBs), very strict health, safety, or other regulations that must be met before a foreign product can be offered for sale in a country

D. Embargoes, or a complete prohibition of trade by law

Nations may also engage in unfair trade practices. The most common is dumping, the practice of selling products in another country below their manufacturing or domestic cost in order to drive other producers out of a market.

The balance of trade, also called the balance of payments, is the difference between the value of a country's imports and exports. It is a measure of the entire flow of money in and out of a country. Economists and policymakers look at a nation's balance of trade to measure the nation's overall performance in the global market.

1. What are four methods that governments use to restrict international trade?

_____

_____

_____

_____

◉ Trade Agreements (page 734)

After World War II, the major nations of the world began creating organizations and agreements aimed at limiting unfair trade practices. These agreements have created ***trading blocs***, groups of nations that trade without barriers such as tariffs.

GATT and WTO To promote international trade, 90 countries signed the General Agreement on Tariffs and Trade (GATT). Under this agreement, member nations meet in trade "rounds" to reduce or remove barriers on trade, such as tariffs. In 1994 GATT was replaced by the World Trade Organization (WTO). The WTO hears complaints brought to it by member countries and has the authority to assess penalties against nations that violate the terms of the GATT treaty. Today 149 nations are members of the WTO.

The European Union The EU has allowed the various countries of Europe to achieve full economic integration. There are no trade barriers among the EU member nations; goods, services, and workers can move freely between the countries. In 2002 the EU achieved significant monetary integration when the euro replaced the different national currencies of 12 of the EU countries.

North American Free Trade Agreement Another large trading bloc is North America. In 1992 the leaders of the United States, Mexico, and Canada concluded negotiations for the North American Free Trade Agreement (NAFTA), which will eventually remove all trade barriers among the three countries. As a result, trade among the three countries has grown rapidly. However, NAFTA is also controversial. Critics in Canada and Mexico worry about being overwhelmed by American culture and dollars. American critics fear a loss of jobs to Mexico, where labor is cheaper and less regulated. Supporters argue that NAFTA will make goods cheaper for Americans.

2. Which trading bloc seems to have made the most sweeping changes? Explain your answer.

_____

_____

_____

_____

◉ Trade Alternatives for the United States *(page 735)*

Though the United States has generally wanted increased trade and fewer trade barriers, workers in a particular industry may be hurt by the free flow of trade. There are sometimes disagreements about what is the best approach to trade policy. Four major types of trade policy are:

Free Trade This would allow all nations to buy and sell goods without any limitations. All trading nations could gain as each uses its resources to produce those things that they produce more efficiently than other countries. The United States has never followed a pure free trade policy because of the government's desire to protect domestic workers and industries from foreign competition.

Fair Trade This is trade regulated by international agreements that outlaw unfair business practices or limit tariffs. Supporters of fair trade argue that it opens up new markets and jobs for American workers, as well as providing Americans with lower-cost products. Fair trade also promotes economic interdependence around the world.

Managed Trade In this policy category, the government intervenes in a trade arrangement in order to achieve a specific result. For example, the U.S. government negotiated trade agreements with Japan to allow American businesses to have a larger share of the Japanese auto parts market.

Protectionism This is the policy of using trade barriers to protect domestic industries from foreign competition and to prevent free trade. Protectionists argue that international trade should be used to

STUDY GUIDE (continued)   Chapter 26, Section 4

promote the United States national interests. They worry that foreign investors and companies will gain undue influence in the American economy or threaten American jobs.

3. What are some reasons to support fair trade?

_____

_____

_____

_____